FAMINE

FAMINE
A Short History
Cormac Ó Gráda

Princeton University Press   Princeton and Oxford

Published by Princeton University Press, 41 William Street,
Princeton, New Jersey 08540
In the United Kingdom: Princeton University Press, 6 Oxford Street,
Woodstock, Oxfordshire OX20 1TW
press.princeton.edu

Second printing, and first paperback printing, 2010
Paperback ISBN: 978-0-691-14797-0

The Library of Congress has cataloged the cloth
edition of this book as follows

Ó Gráda, Cormac.
Famine : a short history / Cormac Ó Gráda.
p.   cm.
Includes bibliographical references and index.
ISBN 978-0-691-12237-3 (hardcover : alk. paper) 1. Famines–
History. 2. Food supply–History. I. Title.
HC79.F3O57 2009   363.809–dc22   2008032488

British Library Cataloging-in-Publication Data is available

This book has been composed in Scala

Printed on acid-free paper. ∞
Printed in the United States of America
3 5 7 9 10 8 6 4 2

For David, Joel, Louis, and Peter

Contents

Figures and Tables

TABLES

Acknowledgments

This book began and ended in Princeton, New Jersey. Without the time off permitted by stays at the Shelby Cullom Davis Center in 2003–4 and the School of Historical Sciences of the Institute of Advanced Study during the fall semester of 2007, the book would simply not have been possible. My colleagues in the School of Economics, University College Dublin, were also supportive throughout.

I am grateful to the following friends for reading previous drafts, and their advice and support: Paddy Geary, Bill Jordan, Liam Kennedy, Joel Mokyr, Máire Ní Chiosáin, Pól Ó Duibhir, Fionn Ó Gráda, Peter Solar, David Stead, Brendan Walsh, and Stanley Waterman. Several others—including Tom Bernstein, Lance Brennan, Tim Dyson, Stanley Engerman, Morgan Kelly, Gerald Mills, Karl-Gunnar Persson, Carl Riskin, Eric Vanhaute, and Stephen Wheatcroft—helped with individual chapters or sections. I also owe thanks to Brigitta van Rheinberg of Princeton University Press, who first suggested the idea several years ago, and offered constructive suggestions along the way. At the Press, Peter Dougherty, Sara Lerner, and Clara Platter were also helpful. Cindy Milstein did a thorough job of copyediting. And a special thanks, *mar is gnáth*, to Sadhbh, Ruadhán, and Máire.

Cormac Ó Gráda

FAMINE

Chapter I

The Third Horseman

Famyn schal a-Ryse thorugh flodes and thorugh foule wedres.

—*William Langland*, Piers Ploughman

And lo a black horse . . . and he that sat on him had a pair of
scales in his hand . . . a quart of wheat for a day's wages.

—*Book of Revelation 6:5*

IN THE DEVELOPED WORLD, famines no longer capture the
headlines like they used to. Billboard images of African infants with distended bellies are less ubiquitous, and the
focus of international philanthropy has shifted from disaster relief to more structural issues, particularly those of
third world debt relief, economic development, and democratic accountability. Totalitarian famines of the kind associated with Joseph Stalin, Mao Tse-tung, and their latter-day
imitators are on the wane. Even in Africa, the most vulnerable of the seven continents, the famines of the past decade
or so have been, by historical standards, "small" famines.
In 2002, despite warnings from the United Nations World
Food Programme and nongovernmental relief agencies of a
disaster that could affect millions, the excess mortality during a much-publicized crisis in Malawi was probably in the
hundreds rather than the thousands. As for the 2005 famine in Niger, which also attracted global attention, experts
now argue that it does not qualify as a famine by standard

criteria. Mortality there was high in 2005, but apparently no higher than normal in that impoverished country.[1]

Writing about famine today is, one hopes, part of the process of making it less likely in future. The following chapters describe its symptoms, and how they have changed over time; more important, they explain why famines happened in the past, and why—since this is one of the themes of this book—they are less frequent today than in the past and, given the right conditions, less likely in the future. Research into the history of famine has borrowed from many disciplines and subdisciplines, including medical history, demography, meteorology, economic and social history, economics, anthropology, and plant pathology. This book is informed by all of them.

So is it almost time to declare famine "history"? No, if the continuing increase in the number of malnourished people is our guide; yes, perhaps, if we focus instead on malnourished people's declining share of the world population and the characteristics of famine in the recent past. And if yes, has this been due to economic progress in famine-prone countries? Or should the credit go to the globalization of relief and better governance where famines were once commonplace? How have the characteristics and incidences of famine changed over time? Are most or all modern famines "man-made"? Can the history of past famines help guard against future ones? This book is in part an answer to such questions.

Famines have always been one of the greatest catastrophes that could engulf a people. Although many observers in the past deemed them "inevitable" or "natural," throughout

---

[1] Howe and Devereux 2004; Menon 2007.

history the poor and the landless have protested and resisted at the approach of famines, which they considered to
be caused by humans. The conviction that a more caring
elite had the power and a less rapacious trading class had
the resources to mitigate—if not eradicate—disaster was
usually present. This, after all, is the message of Luke's par-
able about Dives and Lazarus.[2] It is hardly surprising, then,
that famines have attracted both the attention of academics
and policymakers as well as the indignation of critical observers and philanthropists. In today's developed world the
conviction that famines are an easily prevented anachro-
nism, and therefore a blot on global humanity, is widespread
and gaining ground. That makes them a continuing focus
for activism and an effective vehicle for raising conscious-
ness about world poverty.

Economist and demographer Robert Malthus was one of
those who regarded famine as natural. In 1798, he famously
referred to famine as "the last, the most dreadful resource
of nature,"[3] and indeed other natural disasters such as
earthquakes, floods, and even volcanic eruptions tend to be
more local and short-lived in their impact. The impact of
famines is also more difficult to measure. We measure the
energy expended in earthquakes on the Richter scale, volcanic eruptions by a Volcanic Explosivity Index, and weather
by rain precipitation, temperature, humidity, and wind
speed, but how can we measure famine? Excess mortality is
an obvious possibility, but besides being often difficult to
measure, it is as much a function of the policy response to
famine as of the conditions that caused the crisis. The Indian

[2] Luke 16:19–31.
[3] Malthus 1798, chapter 7.

Famine Codes, introduced in the wake of a series of major famines in the 1870s, defined famine by its early warning signals. These signals—rising grain prices, increased migration, and increased crime—dictated the introduction of measures to save life.

A recent study in this spirit defines the transition from food crisis to famine by rises in the daily death rate above one per ten thousand population, the proportion of "wasted" children (that is, children weighing two standard deviations or less below the average) above 20 percent, and the prevalence of kwashiorkor, an extreme form of malnutrition mainly affecting young children.[4] By the same token, "severe famine" means a daily death rate of above five per ten thousand, a proportion of wasted children above 40 percent, and again, the prevalence of kwashiorkor. The first two of these measures could not have been implemented in India a century ago, but the swollen bellies and reddened hair associated with kwashiorkor are age-old signs of crisis.[5] In what follows, famine refers to a shortage of food or purchasing power that leads directly to excess mortality from starvation or hunger-induced diseases.

The etymology and meaning of words signifying famine vary by language. The Roman orator Cicero (106–43 BC) distinguished between *praesens caritas* (present dearness or dearth) and *futura fames* (future famine) or *deinde inopia* (thereafter want of means), and Roman sources employed several synonyms for both (e.g., *difficultas annonae, frumenti*

---

[4] Kwashiorkor was originally a coastal West African term referring to illnesses affecting an infant "rejected" when the next sibling is born.

[5] Howe and Devereux 2004.

inopia, and *summa caritas*).[6] In Italian the word for famine, *carestia*, is derived from *caritas*, and signifies dearness. This suggests one measure of a famine's intensity since, usually, the greater the increase in the price of basic foodstuffs and the longer it lasts, the more serious the famine. In medieval and early modern England, *dearth* signified dearness, but meant famine. For economist Adam Smith, however, dearth and famine were distinct, whereas by John Stuart Mill's day "there is only dearth, where there formerly would have been famine."[7] Famine, in turn, is derived from the Latin *fames*. In German, *Hungersnot* connotes hunger associated with a general scarcity of food. The most common terms for famine in the Irish language are *gorta* (starvation) and, referring to the infamous 1840s, *an drochshaol* (the bad times). In pharaonic Egypt, the standard word for famine (*hkr*) derived from "being hungry," but that signifying plague (*i:dt*) also connoted famine, highlighting the symbiotic relationship between famine and disease.

Many individual famines are remembered by specific names that only sometimes hint at their horrors. Examples include *la famine de l'avenement* (the famine of the Accession of Louis XIV) in France in 1662, *bliain an áir* ("the year of the slaughter") in Ireland in 1740–41, the *Chalisa* (referring to a calendar date) and *Doji Bara* ("skulls famine") in India in 1783–84 and 1790–91, the *Tenmei* and *Tempo* (Japanese era names) in Japan in 1782–87 and 1833–37, the *Madhlatule* ("eat what you can, and say nothing") famine in southern Africa in the 1800s, *Black '47* in Ireland in 1847, the *Mtunya* ("the scramble") in Kenya in

---

[6] Virlouvet 1985, 25.

[7] Mill 1857, II. Iv. Ii. 270.

1917–20, *Holodomor* ("death by hunger") in the Ukraine in 1932–33, *Chhiyattarer Manvantar* (the Great Famine of the Bengal year 1176) and *Panchasher Manvantar* ("the famine of fifty," a reference to the Bengal year 1350) in Bengal in 1770 and 1943–44, *manori* (etymology unclear) in Burundi in 1943–44, and *nạn đói Ất Dậu* ("famine of the Ất Dậu Year") in Vietnam in 1945.

In any language, however, the term famine is an emotive one that needs to be used with caution. On the one hand, preemptive action requires agreement on famine's early warning signs; the very declaration of a famine acknowledges the need for public action, and may thus prevent a major mortality crisis. On the other hand, the overuse of the term by relief agencies and others may lead to cynicism and donor fatigue.

In the recent past, definitions of famine have included events and processes that would not qualify as famine in the catastrophic, historical sense. Some scholars have argued for a broader definition that would embrace a range extending from endemic malnutrition to excess mortality and its associated diseases. In support of this view, the term famine indeed represents the upper end of the continuum whose average is "hunger."[8] Malnutrition, which eight hundred to nine hundred million people still endure every day, might be seen as slow-burning famine. Moreover, in famine-prone economies malnutrition is usually endemic, and individual deaths from the lack of food are not uncommon. Yet classic famine means something more than endemic hunger. Common symptoms absent in normal times include

[8] On the range of alternative definitions proposed, see Howe and Devereux 2004. See also Devereux 2007.

rising prices, food riots, an increase in crimes against property, a significant number of actual or imminent deaths from starvation, a rise in temporary migration, and frequently the fear and emergence of famine-induced infectious diseases.

All of these symptoms are listed in one of the earliest graphic depictions of famine, which comes from Edessa in northern Mesopotamia (today's Ourfa in southeastern Turkey) in AD 499–501. It describes in mordant detail many of the features that have characterized famine through the ages: high food prices ("there was a dearth of everything edible . . . everything that was not edible was cheap"); spousal or child desertion ("others their mothers had left . . . because they had nothing to give them"); public action ("the emperor gave . . . no small sum of money to distribute among the poor"); unfamiliar substitute foods ("bitter-vetches, and others were frying the withered fallen grapes"); migration ("many villages and hamlets were left destitute of inhabitants . . . a countless multitude . . . entered the city"); and infectious diseases ("many of the rich died, who were not starved; and many of the grandees too").[9] Although the list of famine's horrors does not end there, what is striking is how little it has changed over the centuries—until the recent past, at least.

The outline of the rest of this introductory chapter is as follows. First, I briefly survey the link between living standards and geography or regionality, on the one hand, and vulnerability to famine, on the other. Next, I turn to the frequency of famines in the past. Finally, I describe in brief how famine is remembered in folklore and oral history.

[9] Wright 1882, 29b–34b.

THE ULTIMATE CHECK

The view that famine was the product of—though not necessarily a corrective for—overpopulation can be traced back nearly five millennia to the Babylonian legend of Gilgamesh. In this epic tale, the gods cut population back to size when their peace was destroyed by "the people bec[oming] numerous, the land bellow[ing] like wild oxen." Another early reference to the link between population pressure and famine may be found in the Old Testament's book of Nehemiah, dating probably from about 430 BC, in which overpopulation left the poor without food, and forced men with some property to mortgage it in order to buy food. It also made them sell their children into bondage or borrow at exorbitant rates from their fellow Jews.[10] The first economist to describe the link may have been Irish-born economist Richard Cantillon (who died in Paris in 1734), according to whom the human race had the capacity to multiply like "mice in a barn," although he did not discuss the checks needed to prevent the earth from becoming overpopulated.[11]

For Robert Malthus (1766–1834), there was no equivocation: when all other checks fail, "gigantic inevitable famine stalks in the rear and, with one mighty blow, levels the population with the food of the world.[12] The Malthusian interpretation, stark and simple, was highly influential. It led historians to describe famines in India as "a demonstration of the normal effect of the fertility of nature on the fertility of man,"

---

[10] Loveday 1914, 2; Book of Nehemiah 5:1–5.
[11] Cantillon [1755] 1931, 73.
[12] Malthus 1798, chapter 7.

seventeenth-century Languedoc as a "society . . . suffering from a surplus of people" eventually producing a "violent contraction" through famine, and prefamine Ireland as "a case study in Ricardian and Malthusian economics."[13]

Famines have nearly always been a hallmark of economic backwardness. Most documented famines have been the products of harvest failures—what were dubbed "natural causes" by the Victorian actuary Cornelius Walford—in low-income economies.[14] Both the extent of the harvest shortfall and the degree of economic backwardness mattered. To-day's developed world has been spared major "death-dealing" famine during peacetime since the mid-nineteenth century, and this applies to England since the mid-eighteenth century at the latest.[15] Japan, where famines had been common in the seventeenth century, suffered its last major famine in the 1830s.

At the other extreme is Niger, the focus of global media attention in 2005, and among the poorest economies in the world. The gross domestic product (GDP) per head in Ethiopia and Malawi, also still vulnerable to famine, is in real terms less than half that of the United States two centuries ago. And five of the six economies most prone to food emergencies since the mid-1980s—Angola, Ethiopia, Somalia, Mozambique, and Afghanistan—were ranked in the bottom 10 of 174 countries on the United Nations' Human Development Index in the mid-1990s; the sixth, war-torn Sudan, was ranked 146th.[16] There are exceptions to all historical

[13] Le Roy Ladurie 1974, 213–16; Solow 1971, 196.

[14] Walford 1879, 20.

[15] Campbell 2008. I am grateful to Professor Campbell for allowing me to cite this paper, to be published in a Festschrift in 2009.

[16] United Nations Development Programme, *Human Development Report 1996*. Available at http://hdr.undp.org/en/reports/global/hdr1995/.

generalizations, though. Ireland in the 1840s was a poor region of what was then the wealthiest economy in the world, while in 1932–33 the economy of the Soviet Union was backward, but by no means among the world's poorest.

Today, given goodwill on all sides, famine prevention should be straightforward, even in the poorest corners of the globe. Transport costs (which I will discuss later) have plummeted since the nineteenth century, and the global GDP per capita has quintupled since the beginning of the twentieth century; bad news travels fast; food storage is inexpensive; international disaster relief agencies are ubiquitous; and nutritional requirements and medical remedies in emergencies are better understood. In addition, penicillin and electrolyte drinks for dehydration are readily available, albeit at a cost; most recently, the discovery of cheap, storable, easily transportable, nutrient-dense ready-to-use foods has facilitated the task of relieving the severely malnourished.

A combination of these factors certainly reduced the incidence of famine in the twentieth century. Nowadays, where crop failures are the main threat, as in southern Africa in 2002 and Niger in 2005, a combination of public action, market forces, and food aid tends to mitigate mortality during subsistence crisis. Although noncrisis death rates in sub-Saharan Africa remain high, excess mortality from famine—unless linked to war—tends to be small.[17]

Why, then, did and does famine persist? In the past famines have usually been linked to poor harvests; a distinguishing feature of twentieth-century famines is that famine

---

[17] Seaman 1993; Sen 1995. On famine in Niger in 1931, compare Fugelstad 1974.

mortality was more often linked to wars and ideology than to poor harvests per se. Many of the major famines of the twentieth century were linked to either civil strife and warfare (as in the Soviet Union in 1918–22 or Biafra/Nigeria in 1970) or despotic autarky (as in China in 1959–61 or North Korea after 1996). Human action had a greater impact than, or greatly exacerbated, acts of nature. The relative importance of political factors—"artificial causes or those within human control"—and food availability *tout court* was reversed.[18] Mars in his various guises accounted for more famines than Malthus.

Several of the past century's major famines would have been less deadly—or might not have occurred at all—under more peaceful or stable political circumstances.[19] Toward the end of World War I, the *Mtunya* ("Scramble") in central Tanzania was mainly the product of excessive food procurements by the imperial powers, first by the Germans, and then by the British; similar pressures also led to famine in Uganda and French Africa. World War II brought famine to places as different as India, the western Netherlands, and Leningrad (today's Saint Petersburg). In Bengal, fears of a Japanese invasion in 1942–43 determined the priorities of those in authority, and the so-called Denial Policy, which removed stored holdings of rice, cargo boats, and even bicycles from coastal regions lest they fall into the hands of

[18] Walford 1879, 21. Walford's distinction simplifies, of course, since human actions today (through the overutilization of the soil, deforestation, and so on) can increase the likelihood of famine from "natural causes" in the future.

[19] Compare de Waal 1991, 1997 (on Ethiopia); Moskoff 1990 (on the Soviet Union). The Bengal famine is discussed in more detail in chapters 6 and 7.

the invaders, undoubtedly compounded the crisis. Most fundamentally, the poor of Bengal were left unprovided for due to military considerations. The main responsibility for the Ethiopian famine of 1984–85 rested with a regime waging a ruthless campaign against secessionists in the country's northern provinces.[20]

In the book of Jeremiah, which describes a tempestuous period in Jewish history (ca. 580 BC), the sword and famine are mentioned simultaneously several times. In ancient Rome famines were few in peacetime, but crises flared during the Punic Wars and the civil wars of 49–31 BC. Classical Greece was also relatively free of famine before the Macedonian conquest in 338 BC. There are countless examples of the threat or reality of military activity leading to famine, even in the absence of a poor harvest. Warfare was also likely to increase the damage inflicted by any given shortfall. This was the case—to list some notorious examples—throughout Europe in the 1310s, Ireland in the 1580s and 1650s, the Indian Deccan in 1630, France in the 1690s, southern Africa in the 1810s and 1820s, Matabeleland in the 1890s, Finnish Ostrobothnia in 1808–9, Spain (as depicted by Francisco Goya in the "Horrors of War") in 1811–12, and the Soviet Union in the wake of the October Revolution.

Still, another distinguishing feature of the past century was the rise of the totalitarian, all-embracing state. Totalitarianism greatly increased the human cost of policy mistakes and the havoc wrought by government, even in peacetime. The damage caused by poor harvests in the Soviet Union in 1932–33 and China in 1959–61 was greatly exacerbated

[20] Maddox 1990; de Waal 1991, 1997.

by political action. What Adam Smith claimed, incorrectly, for famines in early modern Europe—that they never arose "from any other cause but the violence of government attempting, by improper means, to remedy the inconveniences of a dearth"—applies far more to the twentieth century than to the seventeenth or eighteenth.[21]

Clearly, then, politics, culture, and institutions also matter. Even Malthus did not entirely exclude cultural factors; in the 1800s he argued—atypically perhaps—that granting Irish Catholics the same civil rights as other UK citizens would check population growth, by making them look forward "to other comforts beside the mere support of their families upon potatoes."[22] Of course, these factors are not independent of the degree of economic development, but they are worth considering separately. Effective and compassionate governance might lead to competitive markets, sanctions against corruption, and well-directed relief. Healthy endowments of social capital might mean less crime, and a greater willingness to help one's neighbor or community. Evidence that famines are very much the exception in democracies (see chapter 8) corroborates this view.

TIME AND PLACE

What does history tell us about the spatial spread of famines? The earliest recorded famines, all associated with prolonged droughts, are mentioned on Egyptian stelae (inscribed stone pillars) dating from the third millennium BC.

[21] Smith [1776] 1976, 526.
[22] Malthus 1963, 50.

From earliest times, Egyptian farmers relied on the Nile, swollen by annual monsoon rains in Ethiopia, to burst its banks and "water" the soil. The flooding deposited layers of highly fertile silt on the flat lands nearby, but it was a risky business: one flood in five was either too high or too low. The stelae commemorated members of the ruling class who engaged in philanthropy during one of the many ensuing crises.

Geography must have influenced the intensity and frequency of famines in the past, if only because some famine-related diseases were more likely in particular climates than in others. History indeed suggests that while no part of the globe has been always free from famine, some regions have escaped more lightly than others. Malthus believed that although untold millions of Europeans had their lives blighted by malnutrition in the past, "perhaps in some of these states an absolute famine may never have been known."[23] Even though in this instance Malthus was being atypically complacent, the historical demography of early modern Europe supports the case for a "low pressure demographic regime" in which the preventive check of a lower birthrate was more important than elsewhere.[24]

Most of the worst famines on record have been linked to either too much or too little rain. In Dionysios Stathakopoulos's catalog of documented famines in the late Roman period, drought was the main factor in three cases out of four; some in the Near East were blamed on locust invasions, but none on excessive rainfall alone. In prerevolutionary China, drought was twice as likely to cause famine

[23] Malthus 1798, VII.19.
[24] Wrigley and Schofield 1981, 450–53.

as floods. This was particularly so in wheat-growing regions; in Sichuan, a rice-growing province and the most famine prone of all, drought was responsible for three out of every four famines. Drought was also responsible for the massive Bengal famine of 1770, which may have resulted in millions of deaths—though probably not "at least one-third of the inhabitants," as claimed by Indian governor general Warren Hastings.[25] Zimbabwe's earliest recorded subsistence crisis in the late fifteenth century was caused by a severe drought.[26] The catastrophe in northern China in the late 1870s came in the wake of exceptional droughts in 1876 and 1877, while much of western and central India in the late 1890s saw virtually no rain for three years. At the height of the Great Leap Forward famine during summer 1960, "eight of Shantung's twelve rivers had no water in them, and for forty days in March and June, it was possible to wade across the lower reaches of the Yellow River."[27]

In temperate zones, cold or rain, or a combination of both, were more likely to be the problem. The Great European Famine of 1315–17 was the product of torrential downpours and low temperatures during summer 1315. The *grand hiver* of 1708–9 was the proximate cause of severe famine in France during that period, and the Great Frost of 1740 led to *bliain an áir* (the year of carnage) in Ireland in 1740–41. In France, ice-covered rivers were the most spectacular aspect of the "big winter" of 1708–9, while in mid-January 1740 one could walk across Ireland's biggest lake for miles—an unprecedented feat. Liquids froze indoors

---

[25] Cited in Sainath 2005.
[26] Iliffe 1990.
[27] MacFarquhar 1983, 322.

and ice floes appeared at river mouths, while in Holland it was recorded that "the drip from the nose, and the spittle from the mouth, both are frozen before they fall to the ground."[28] In Kashmir, the great flood of 1640–42 wiped out 438 villages "and even their names did not survive."[29]

Long-term climatic trends also probably mattered. In harsher, more marginal areas such as Scandinavia the colder weather made coping more difficult, and the abandonment of Norse settlements on Greenland during the fifteenth century along with the end of corn cultivation in Iceland during the sixteenth have been linked to climatic shift and famine. The 1690s (the nadir of the so-called little ice age) brought disaster to Scotland, Finland, and France.[30]

The extreme weather produced by the El Niño–Southern Oscillation (ENSO) of 1876–77 gave rise to the most deadly famines of the nineteenth century. As with all ENSOs, winds driving warm water westward across the southern Pacific Ocean provided the spur, and the resultant low air pressure led to extensive rainfall over the surrounding countries in Southeast Asia and Australasia. In due course, the area of low pressure shifted back east, causing drought in Southeast Asia and heavy rainfalls in the tropical parts of the Americas. The shift almost simultaneously produced droughts farther east, in Brazil and southern Africa. The combination of extreme droughts and monsoons led to millions of deaths under hellish conditions. Another El Niño followed in 1898, wreaking further havoc in India and Brazil's *Nordeste*.

---

[28] Dickson 1997; Post 1985.
[29] Kaw 1996.
[30] Appleby 1980; Juttikala 1955; Cullen, Whatley, and Young 2006.

The impact of the late nineteenth-century ENSOs is well-known, but recent research has uncovered several more such synchronized climatic assaults. Examples include the great drought-famine of 1743–44, which devastated agricultural production across northern China, and the 1982–83 ENSO that sparked off the Ethiopian famine of 1984–85. El Niño struck again as recently as 1997. Yet the impact of these strikes was mild compared to those of the late 1870s and late 1890s.[31]

Major historical famines linked to extraordinary "natural events" seem to have been more common than ones associated with ecological shocks. Several famines have been connected to volcanic eruptions. The well-documented impact of the volcanic dust emanating from Laki in 1783 and Mount Tambora near Bali in 1815 on two of northern Europe's last peacetime famines has prompted searches for links between other volcanic explosions and famines elsewhere. In Europe, the beginning of the Dark Ages has been linked to an undefined disastrous event ca. AD 530 that affected vegetable growth for over a decade. Qualitative accounts imply a massive famine around this time. Tree-ring evidence corroborates the severity of AD 536 as one of the coldest summers ever, and a "dust veil" from a huge volcanic aerosol cloud is a plausible explanation for it. In Japan, the Kangi famine of 1229–32 and the Shōga famines of 1257–60 have been tied to likely volcanic eruptions.[32] Similarly the One Rabbit famine, which struck the Mexican Highlands a few decades before the arrival of the conquistadores, has been

---

[31] Davis 2001.

[32] Hassig 1981; Farris 2006, 38–39, 53. The pioneering work is Lamb 1970.

linked to the eruption of Kuwae, in Vanuatu, circa AD 1452. A volcanic eruption in Iceland in AD 934, one of the largest on record, is also held to have led to cold spells and poor crops in Europe. The freezing winter of 1740–41, which led to widespread famine in northern Europe, may also owe its origins to a volcanic eruption: a volcano on the Kamchatka Peninsula in Russia is one suspect, although Kamchatka is absent from the latest eruption lists derived from ice cores. Examples of ecological shocks associated with famines include *phytophthora infestans* (potato blight, in Ireland and elsewhere in northern Europe in the 1840s), rinderpest (cattle plague, in Africa in 1888–92), and *helminthosporium oryzae* (rice brown spot, in Bengal in 1943).[33]

Today, Africa is the continent most at risk from famine. Its premodern famines are poorly documented, notwithstanding accounts of individual famines in medieval Egypt, precolonial Zimbabwe, Nigeria, Mali, and elsewhere. Yet in the second (and later) editions of his *Essay on the Principle of Population*, Malthus claimed, mainly on the basis of reading explorer Mungo Park's *Travels in the Interior Districts of Africa* (1799), that famines were common in Africa. Park interpreted the sale of humans into slavery as evidence of "the not unfrequent recurrence of severe want," and referred in particular to a recent three-year famine in Senegambia, which had resulted in widespread resort to voluntary enslavement.[34] Even more devastating was the mid-eighteenth-century famine that forced the ruling Hausa clans to cede

---

[33] Compare Carefoot and Sprott 1969; Solar 1996; Ó Gráda, Paping, and Vanhaute 2007; Bourke and Lamb 1993; Bourke 1993; Tauger 2003; Phoofolo 2003.

[34] Malthus 1872, 72.

much of the southern Sahel to the more drought-resilient Tuareg. Recent specialist accounts claim, however, that famines were rare in precolonial Zimbabwe, and that between the 1750s and 1913, the Hausa lands straddling northern Nigeria and Niger did not experience any "massive subsistence calamity that embraced the entire savannas and desert-edge community"—although regional crises were becoming "increasingly common."[35]

The link between colonialism and famine, in Africa and elsewhere, is a controversial and ambivalent one. Rudyard Kipling's facile depiction of colonialism as white men "filling full the mouth of Famine" across the British Empire has little basis in reality. On balance, the initial impact of colonial conquest and "pacification" was almost certainly to increase famine mortality (as in Mexico in the 1520s, Ireland in the 1580s and 1650s, Namibia/Angola before 1920, the Xhosa lands in South Africa in the 1850s, and northern Nigeria in the early 1910s), although where it replaced a dysfunctional indigenous ruler (as in Madagascar in the 1890s) it may well have reduced it.[36] Its subsequent impact is less clear; it depended in part on whether it generated economic growth and whether the fiscal exactions of the colonists exceeded those of indigenous rulers. In the longer run, although colonial rule may have eliminated or weakened traditional coping mechanisms, it meant better communications, integrated markets, and more effective public action, which together probably reduced famine mortality.

Colonialism did not prevent massive famines in nineteenth-century Ireland and India, but those famines were less the

[35] Iliffe 1990, 111–12; Watts 1983, 104.
[36] Campbell 2005, 149–56; Kreike 2004, 57–80.

product of empire per se than the failure of the authorities of the day to act appropriately. The colonial regime that presided over several major famines in eighteenth- and nineteenth-century India also helped to keep the subcontinent free of famine between the 1900s and the Bengal famine of 1943–44. The change was partly due to improved communications, notably through the railway, although the shift in ideology away from hard-line Malthusianism toward a focus on saving lives also mattered. Colonial exactions during World War I produced famine in several parts of Africa, but famines were almost certainly much fewer between the 1920s and the end of the colonial era than they had been before the post-1880 "scramble for Africa."

The greater capacity of Africa to sustain population change during the colonial era—the average annual rate of population growth rose from about 0.2 percent in 1700–1870 to 1.3 percent in 1870–1960—is striking, but the extent to which this was due to the decreasing incidence and severity of famines remains moot. Yet the improved communications resulting from empire certainly helped, and the medical knowledge brought by the colonizers must also have attenuated famine mortality because it weakened or sundered the link between epidemics such as smallpox and cholera, on the one hand, and famine, on the other.

Tragically, across much of Africa the departure of European colonizers in the mid-twentieth century saw not an end to famine but what John Iliffe terms a "return of mass famine mortality." Iliffe attributes this to a combination of postcolonial wars and the collapse of famine-prevention mechanisms created in the later colonial period. The spatial incidence of famine across the continent since the 1960s is instructive in this respect. Civil war alone was enough to trigger a major famine in Nigeria in 1968–70; elsewhere poor harvests were usually a factor, but they were rarely the main cause of mass mortality—the major exceptions being the Sahel in the early 1970s and Darfur in the mid-1980s.[37]

The incidence of famine in the New World remains an enigma. The Brazilian *Grande Seca* of 1877–79—which took the lives of a half million or so—has been characterized as "the most costly natural disaster in the history of the western hemisphere."[38] This may well be so in absolute terms, since the population of the pre-Columbian New World was small. Pre-Columbian America was not famine free, however. The Famine of One Rabbit in 1454 was a major catastrophe in Mexico.[39] Again, in 1520, "there was death from hunger; there was no one to take care of one another; there was no one to attend to one another."[40] Conditions worsened after the *conquista*. Using price and production data to distinguish epidemics from famines, David A. Brading and Celia Liu have uncovered serious famines in Mexico in 1695–96, 1713, 1749–50, and 1785–86. The last of these, perhaps the greatest catastrophe to strike Mexico since the conquest, is well documented. A study of the parish registers of León (which had a population of about twenty thousand at the time) suggests a sixfold rise in burials and a drop of two-thirds in the number of marriages in 1786, while baptisms fell by half in both 1786 and 1787. The gigantic rise in the price of maize, from a precrisis average of four reals to forty-eight reals per fanega in 1786, hints at

[37] Iliffe 1987, 250; 1995, 268.
[38] Cited in Davis 2001, 114.
[39] Loveday 1914, 2. One Rabbit is a year in the Aztec calendar cycle.
[40] Brooks 1993, 28.

the horrors endured.[41] Still, famine in the Americas seems to have been less common in the past than in Europe, Africa, or Asia. Despite undoubted disasters such as those just mentioned, population pressure does not appear to have been as great in the New World as in parts of the Old.

At the other extreme, one of the globe's most famine-prone places for nearly half a millennium has been Cape Verde, a volcanic archipelago of forty thousand square kilometers located about six hundred kilometers off the coast of Senegal. Uninhabited when discovered by the Portuguese ca. 1460, Cape Verde's destiny in the following centuries was linked to slavery and the slave trade. Despite its name, Cape Verde is an arid landmass with minimal agricultural potential. The excess mortality associated with its major famines is unparalleled in relative terms. A famine in 1773–76 is said to have removed 44 percent of the population; a second in 1830–33 is claimed to have killed 42 percent of the population of seventy thousand or so; and a third in 1854–56 to have killed 25 percent. In 1860 the population was ninety thousand; 40 percent of Cape Verdeans were reported to have died of famine in 1863–67. Despite a population loss of thirty thousand, the population was put at eighty thousand in 1870. Twentieth-century famines in Cape Verde were less deadly, but still extreme relative to most contemporaneous ones elsewhere: 15 percent of the population (or twenty thousand) in 1900–1903; 16 percent (twenty-five thousand) in 1920–22; 15 percent (twenty thousand) in 1940–43; and 18 percent (thirty thousand) in 1946–48.[42] The pivotal role of drought-related famine in the

---

[41] Brading and Liu 1973.
[42] Patterson 1988; Drèze and Sen 1989, 34.

TABLE I.I
Estimated death tolls from selected famines

Year	Country	Excess mortality (million)	% Death rate	Observations
1693–94	France	1.5	7	Poor harvests
1740–41	Ireland	0.3	13	Cold weather
1846–52	Ireland	1	12	Potato blight, policy failure
1868	Finland	0.1	7	Poor harvests
1877–79	China	9.5 to 13	3	Drought, floods
1876–79	India	7	3	Drought, policy failure
1921–22	USSR	9	6	Drought, civil war
1927	China	3 to 6	1	Natural disasters
1932–33	USSR	5 to 6	4	Stalinism, harvest shortfall
1942–44	Bengal	2	3	War, policy failure, supply shortfall
1946–47	Soviet Union	1.2	0.7	Poor harvest, policy failure
1959–61	China	15 to 25	2 to 4	Drought, floods, Great Leap Forward
1972–73	India	0.1	0.03	Drought

(Continued)

TABLE 1.1
Continued

Year	Country	Excess mortality (million)	% Death rate	Observations
1974–75	Bangladesh	0.5	0.5	War, floods, harvest shortfall
1972–73	Ethiopia	0.06	0.2	Drought, poor governance
1975–79	Cambodia	0.5 to 0.8	7 to 11	Human agency
1980–81	Uganda	0.03	0.3	Drought, conflict
1984–85	Sudan	0.1	0.5	Drought
1985–86	Ethiopia	0.5	1	War, human agency, drought
1991–92	Somalia	0.3	4	Drought, civil war
1998	Sudan (Bahr el Ghazal)	0.07	0.2	Drought
1995–2000	North Korea	0.6 to 1	3 to 4	Poor harvests, policy failure
2002	Malawi	Negligible	0	Drought
2005	Niger	Negligible	0	Drought

Sources: Lachiver 1991, 480; de Waal 1997, 106; de Waal 2007; Devereux 2000, 6; Devereux 2002, 70; Davis 2001, 7; Ó Gráda 2007.

demography of Cape Verde need not be labored. Nevertheless, such death tolls imply extraordinary noncrisis population growth. For instance, if the population estimates for 1830 and 1860 are credited, making good the damage inflicted by the famine of 1830–33 would have required an annual population growth rate of about 4 percent between 1833 and 1860—despite the loss of a quarter or so of the population in 1854–56.

HOW COMMON WERE FAMINES IN THE PAST?

Some have been forgotten altogether, because the object of Indian historians was generally to record the fortunes of a dynasty rather than the condition of a people.

—Report of the India Famine Commission, *1880*

An important unresolved puzzle about famines is, How often did they strike in the past? In general, the more backward an economy is, the less likely it is to yield documentary traces of famine. Yet again and again, historians have been unable to resist the temptation to infer the incidence and frequency of famines from the documentary record. That more than three-quarters of the famines listed in Walford's idiosyncratic chronology of *The Famines of the World Past and Present*, published in 1879, are European and over half of the remainder are Indian is hardly surprising. Moreover, Walford's Indian famines struck with increasing intensity over time: eleven before 1700, eleven more during the eighteenth century, and twenty-three during the nineteenth. The illustrious *Cambridge History of India*, published a century or so later, is equally guilty of discounting the

more distant past; the volume covering the 1750–1970 period contains a four-page chronology of famine, while the
sole mention in the volume covering the previous 550 years
relates to the Deccan famine of 1630–32, the first about
which there is significant documentary evidence. Less subject to chronological bias than Walford's is Paul Greenough's
checklist of Indian famines between 298 BC and 1943–44:
it identifies four famines before AD 1000, twenty-four between AD 1000 and AD 1499, eighteen in the sixteenth
century, twenty-seven in the seventeenth, eighteen in the
eighteenth, and thirty in the nineteenth.[43]

Long before Walford, Thomas Short produced a list of
254 famines in *A General Chronological History of the Air . . .
in Sundry Places and at Different Times* (1749), extending
back to that "which occurred in Palestine in the time of
Abraham." In an attempt to infer famine's past demographic impact, Malthus invoked Short's research, subtract-
ing the fifteen famines that occurred "before the Christian
era." Malthus reckoned Short's chronology to imply an average interval of only 7.5 years between famines.[44] In 1846, the
eminent statistician William Farr (1807–83) believed that he
had discovered "the law regulating scarcities in England"—
ten years of famine per century between AD 1000 and AD
1600—in references to them in ancient chronicles, but
again, the fallibility of such sources is clear.[45] A few years
later, William Wilde produced a similar chronology in the
1851 Irish census, based on accounts in Gaelic and Anglo-
Norman annals. Excluding reports of storms, cattle murrain,

[43] Greenough (1982, appendix A) also offers a useful guide to the subcontinent's most famine-prone regions over the ages.

[44] Malthus 187, 256.

[45] Farr 1846.

and the like, Wilde's data imply a famine every fifteen years
or so, and a famine straddling two or more years about every
half century. In Wilde's data, the frequency was greater
before the Black Death (1348) than after it, but again this
may be a reflection of the shifting quality of the evidence.

Following the same tradition, the chronology of famine
in the area around Timbuktu in the Malian Sahel has been
inferred from surviving *tarikhs* (historical annals). They
imply a sixteenth century that was relatively free of famine,
followed by two centuries of recurrent disaster. The list be-
gins with a famine in 1617 that led (allegedly) to the consumption of human flesh, and another in 1639, when the
dead were buried on the spot "without washing the body or
saying a prayer." By the end of the eighteenth century, Timbuktu and its neighbors had become "small backward cities
in an extensive backward region."[46] The distinction between
famine proper and epidemic outbreaks in the tarikhs is
usually clear enough. In the case of Ethiopia, however, not
only do references to crises in Amharic hagiographic writings and Arabic sources make it difficult to distinguish between the two, but they also vary in quality over time. The
documentation improves in the fifteenth and sixteenth centuries, and in 1543–44 according to an imperial chronicle,
there was "a great famine, a punishment sent on the country by the glorious God," but the emperor "fed the entire
people as a father feeds his son."[47] A recent tally of famines
in Ethiopia reckons there were four between AD 100 and
AD 1400, four between AD 1400 and AD 1600, eight between
AD 1800 and AD 1900, and twenty-three between 1900

[46] Cissoko 1968.
[47] Pankhurst 1986.

and the present.[48] Here, too, the apparent increasing incidence of famine is surely a product of the available documentation.

Geographer William Dando's account in *The Geography of Famine* is in the same tradition, and equally problematic. On the basis of an unpublished data bank containing eight thousand famines over six millennia, Dando divided the secular chronology of famine by "major world famine region." But the correspondence between region and "famine type" is purely a function of surviving documentation. Dando's earliest region, northeast Africa and the Middle East, is where the first documented famines occurred; his latest region, which refers to the post-1700 period, is Asia, and this is also a function of when the sources date from. By the same token, Africa plays a marginal role throughout in Dando's schema.[49]

A recent invaluable analysis of the surviving documentary evidence on famines in Rome and Byzantium circa AD 300–750 is quick to point out that the most urbanized regions of Italy and the Balkans are most often represented.[50] These areas are followed by Syria, where the presence of Islamic scholars from the seventh century on led to increased recording of such phenomena. Least mentioned are Egypt, North Africa, and Palestine, but as noted by the author, this again is surely more a reflection of the lack of source material than the relative absence of famines.

The demographic evidence on famine in Japan before about 1800 is also thin. An ingenious analysis of earlier

---

[48] Available at http://www.crdaethiopia.org/Emergency/Conference/Dr.%20Berhanu.pdf (accessed June 2005).

[49] Dando 1980, chapter 5.

[50] Stathakopoulos 2004.

crises by Osamu Saito, based on sourcebooks published in 1894 and 1936, can only offer a crude chronology. It yields a weighted total (0.5 for regional famines, and 1.0 for national famines) of 185 years of famine between AD 600 and AD 1885, or one year in every seven. Still, nearly half the total records refer to the eighth and ninth centuries, when there were several multiyear famines. Focusing on the second millennium only suggests a rising incidence of famine between AD 100 and AD 1500, and a decline thereafter. By this reckoning the eighteenth century endured 10.5 years of famine, while the nineteenth endured 6 years.[51] The analyses of Stathakopoulos on the late Roman Empire and Osamu Saito on Japan show that sources like those utilized by Walford and Wilde have their uses when handled with care. Their fallibility is also clear. As a student of Indian famines noted in 1914, "The frequency of the mention of famine in the later history . . . increases in exact proportion with the precision and accuracy in detail of her historians."[52]

Support for the Malthusian view that famines were a common occurrence in the past may be found in the work of historian Fernand Braudel, whose listing of famines in "a privileged country like France" mentions "ten general famines during the tenth century; twenty-six in the eleventh; two in the twelfth; four in the fourteenth; seven in the fifteenth; thirteen in the sixteenth; eleven in the seventeenth and sixteen in the eighteenth." And this, Braudel believes, "omits the hundreds and hundreds of local famines."[53] On the basis of a listing of Indian famines over nearly two

---

[51] Saito 2002, 222–23.

[52] Loveday 1914, 10.

[53] Braudel 1992, 74.

millennia, Alexander Loveday argued for a frequency of one per five years, with one really serious famine per half century, while W. H. Mallory reckoned that over two millennia of recorded history, from 108 BC to AD 1911, China experienced 1,828 famines, or one per year, somewhere in the empire. In Tanzania, according to Iliffe, "men measured out their lives in famines . . . not even the most favoured regions were spared."[54] Such sentiments have been echoed more recently by the likes of Stanford University biologist Paul Ehrlich.

Others have maintained that famines were not so frequent. As noted, Malthus believed that Europe and America were largely immune from famine. Some historians use European exceptionalism to highlight the risk of famine elsewhere. For one eminent scholar, "at the minimum the effective demographic shock in Asia was double that in Europe, and the best of the estimates suggest that it was an order of magnitude greater," while another claims that normal mortality in Asia "may be said to contain a constant famine factor."[55] Malthus's assertion that famines were "perhaps the most powerful of all the positive checks to the Chinese population" is questioned by recent research, however, which finds that the preventive check was more common in Qing China than previously thought, and that the short-run mortality response to rises in food prices (at least in Liadong in the northeast) was much weaker than in Europe.[56] The rapid growth of Chinese population during

[54] Loveday 1914, 25; Mallory 1926; Iliffe 1979, 13.

[55] Eric Jones and William Petersen, as cited in http://www.alanmacfarlane.com/savage/A-FAM.PDF (accessed October 2007).

[56] Malthus 1872, 109.

the eighteenth century—at about 1 percent per annum, or twice as fast as in Europe—makes endemic famine unlikely then, but in the following century it was a different story.

By definition, nothing is known of the severity or relative frequency of famines in the prehistoric era—between ca. 30,000 BC and ca. 3000 BC. Pre-Mughal India, pre–AD 1800 Africa, and the pre–AD 1500 New World are also virtually "prehistory" in this sense. Yet there are several indirect routes to the past. First, the vulnerability and health status of hunter-gatherer and semisettled populations in the present or more recent past may tell us something about the frequency of famines in past times. On the basis of a study of such populations, anthropologist Mark Nathan Cohen sees no reason why prehistoric hunter-gatherers would have been undernourished, or "suffered inordinately high rates of hunger or starvation."[57] Paleopathological evidence from skeletal remains suggests that life became harder with the shift from hunter-gatherer to settled farming communities.

Second, while the historical record implies that seven-year famines as described in the book of Genesis are rare, it also indicates that many of the deadliest famines on record have been due to back-to-back harvest failures. Famine scholar and human rights activist Alex de Waal has noted that "a visitor can only see a single year of drought, and that is not enough to cause famine."[58] In most cases, famines developed into major catastrophes only in the event of successive harvest failures; even the poorest societies could muster the resources to guard against occasional failures,

[57] Cohen 1990.
[58] De Waal 1997, 115.

which were much more frequent. At the same time, low yield-to-seed ratios and the high cost of storage imply that one bad year might have a secondary effect on food supplies in the following year.

Let us consider some "bang-bang" famines—that is, ones due to successive harvest failures. One of the first famines on record, in the reign of Djeser (ca. 2770–2730 BC), was attributed to the failure of the Nile to break its banks for seven years in a row. A key feature of the Great European Famine of the 1310s was its long-drawn-out character. People coped with the initial harvest failure of 1315, when rain caused much of the seed grain to rot before it could germinate. Few perished, it seems, in 1315, but the 1316 growing season was also cold and wet. Poor harvests in 1316 and 1317 converted privation into disaster. Contemporaries described the severe Scottish famine of the 1690s as "the seven ill years" or "King William's dear years" (the price of oatmeal more than tripled).[59] Other examples of famines following in the wake of a succession of bad harvests include the Bengal famine of 1770, which came after two bad years, "with complete failure of the rains in a third year," the European famine of 1816–18, and the Great Finnish Famine of 1867–68.[60] Again, Japan's worst famines in the Tokugawa era—the Tenmei (1782–87) and Tempo (1833–37)—stretched over several "famine years," and put a brake on population growth, while the calamitous death rate in part of the Indian state of Maharashtra in 1900 was the culmination of a disastrous decade of monsoon failures, poor harvests, and epidemics. Had the potato failed in Ireland

[59] Tyson 1986; Cullen, Whatley, and Young 2006.
[60] Post 1977; Pitkänen 1993.

only in 1845 there would have been no "Great Famine".[61] Finally, the Russian famine of 1921–22 is another famous example of crisis in the wake of two dismal harvests and several years of warfare.

Meteorological data offer some insight into the probability of back-to-back crop failures. For instance, monthly mean temperature data are available for an area in central England since 1659. The data are characterized by positive serial correlation—that is, better-than-average years tend to be followed by better-than-average years. Extreme temperatures matter more for harvests than annual averages, though. If "bad" years are defined as ones with deviations 10 percent or more from expected values, then the likelihood of such bad years occurring back-to-back is miniscule. The entire period yields only two cases of back-to-back cold years in 1694–95 and 1697–98.[62] There were no pairs of years where the temperatures were more than 10 percent above trend in both. In tropical zones, drought and floods matter more than temperature. The frequencies of drought and flood years between 1871 and 2002 in both India as a whole and the state of Rajasthan are described in table 1.2, along with the number of back-to-back extreme events. At both the national and state levels, the probabilities of occasional, extreme events were relatively high, but those of back-to-back events were low.

Agricultural output data also provide some insight into the frequency of famines in the past, although such data are

---

[61] Solar 1989.

[62] These two episodes might well be considered part of a single prolonged crisis. The 1690s were years of hardship and famine in much of northwestern Europe.

TABLE 1.2
Extreme droughts and floods in India, 1871–2002

Area	Drought		Flood	
India	Frequency	Back-to-back	Frequency	Back-to-back
India	20	1	18	2
East Rajasthan	21	0	20	5
West Rajasthan	14	1	17	4

Source: Http://ipcc-wg1.ucar.edu/meeting/Drght/restricted/present/Pant.pdf.

also scarce before the nineteenth century. The renowned accounts of the medieval bishopric of Winchester in southern England offer one straw in the wind: on the assumption that harvests 15 percent or more below average were extremely poor, the accounts for the 1283–1350 period returned only two back-to-back harvest deficits, in 1315–16 and 1349–50.[63] Both were due to excessive rains and flooding.[64] Crop output data are preferable to yield data, since the latter fail to take account of the impact of low yields on the acreage sown in the following year. Fitting a range of nineteenth- and twentieth-century agricultural output data to an appropriate polynomial, and then identifying bad years as those with short-

[63] In 1349–50, in the wake of the Black Death, corn seems to have been plentiful despite the low yields (Farr 1846, 164).

[64] Titow 1960.

falls of over 10 or 20 percent, implies that such back-to-back events were "rare," although they were more likely than might be expected on a random basis.[65] To the extent that the underlying patterns were unlikely to change much over time and space, the results may be interpreted as tentative evidence that famines were less common in the past than claimed by Malthus or Braudel. On reflection, this is not implausible: given that life expectancy was low even in non-crisis years, frequent famines would have made it impossible to sustain population.

Although some historic famines really stand out, trends in the relative severity of famines in western Europe can only be guessed at before the seventeenth century. A reduction in their frequency in the wake of the European discoveries of the fifteenth and sixteenth centuries may be assumed, if not proven. Other things being equal, the "Columbian exchange" of foodstuffs and farming methods—potatoes, maize, and tomatoes to Europe; wheat, horses, livestock, and capitalist agriculture to the Americas; maize, cassava, and groundnuts to Africa; and tomatoes and sweet potatoes to Asia—can only have reduced global vulnerability to famine. The reduction was gradual, as the European discovery of crops such as the potato and maize gave way to adoption. In western Europe at least, there is also evidence that the integration of food markets attenuated year-to-year price fluctuations from the middle of the second millennium on. The big increases in population between the sixteenth and nineteenth centuries—before industrialization or medical technology could have had much impact—corroborate this.

[65] Ó Gráda 2007.

Proportionately, moreover, the damage wrought by famine was much greater in the nineteenth century and earlier
than in the twentieth century (see table 1.1 above). While
peacetime famines had disappeared from Europe by the
early nineteenth century, with the awkward exceptions of
Ireland in the 1840s, Finland in the 1860s, and Russia in
1891–92, thirty million is a conservative estimate of famine
mortality in India and China alone between 1870 and about
1900. Data are lacking for major famines such as those in
China before and during the Taiping Rebellion (1851–1864),
and India in 1802–4, 1812, 1832–33, and during the 1860s,
but one hundred million would be a conservative guess at
global famine mortality during the nineteenth century as a
whole. Given that the world population was much higher in
the twentieth century than in the nineteenth, the relative
damage wrought by nineteenth-century famines was much
more severe. The late nineteenth century, however, saw a
reduction in famine intensity in India, due to a combination
of better communications and improvements in relief policy; in Russia too famine became more localized. In Japan,
famine was common in the seventeenth century, less so in
the eighteenth, and disappeared in the nineteenth.

Finally, elementary demographic arithmetic argues against
famines being as severe a demographic corrective as Malthus and others have suggested. A series of famines that
carried off, say, 5 percent of the population every decade,
would require a population growth of 0.5 percent in noncrisis years to prevent population from declining in the long
run. That would require living standards well above subsistence in noncrisis years. A more likely scenario is slower
noncrisis growth, coupled with fewer or less severe famines. That would not rule out what Adam Smith called

dearths (*disettes*), or the endemic malnutrition that, according to economic historian Robert Fogel, characterized pre-industrial economies.[66]

The relative power of famine and epidemics as positive checks also bears noting. Nonfamine-related checks such as the epidemics responsible for the enormous declines in the populations of pre-Columbian America and precolonial Australia as well as the Black Death probably wreaked more demographic havoc than most famines in recorded history. Likewise, the influenza pandemic of 1919 killed more people than any twentieth-century famine, with the possible exception of the Great Chinese Famine of 1959–61, while today the demographic cost of HIV/AIDS exceeds that of famine in Africa's recent population history.

Where famine has been conquered, did the era of famines end with a bang or a whimper? A neo-Malthusian perspective might posit a scenario whereby famines decline gradually in intensity and frequency before permanently disappearing from a region or country: a slow improvement in living standards would have entailed an ever-smaller proportion of the population at risk. The historical record on this is mixed. India experienced "a declining trend in the overall number of excess deaths" between the 1870s and the 1900s, followed by four famine-free decades. The Bengal famine of 1943–44, which killed over two million, was very much an "outlier." Since that time India has been spared major famines. Colonial Africa, which saw few "famines that kill" between 1927 and the end of the colonial era (apart from Ethiopia), also fits such a scenario. Iliffe attributes the gradual improvement to a combination of bet-

---

[66] Fogel 2004.

ter governance, improved communications, higher living standards, and more rainfall.[67]

Demographic historians of England have noted how the history of famine's demise in England also fits such a neo-Malthusian scenario. The late Andrew Appleby has linked the virtual elimination of famine after the 1620s to the reduction in the number of tenant farmers and the growth of towns, and signs of a diversifying agriculture as population ceased to bite at the margin. Anthony Wrigley and Roger Schofield's analysis of years of crisis mortality—which they define as years when the crude death rate was at least 10 percent above a twenty-five-year moving average—in England between the 1540s and the 1860s also suggests that both the size and duration of crises declined gradually over time, although it indicates further subsistence crises associated with significant excess mortality as late as 1728–30 and 1740–42. Meanwhile, a recent analysis of famine in Japan indicates that "in the seventeenth century famines occurred more or less regularly, and they gradually become less frequent in the eighteenth century."[68]

Malthus highlighted the prevalence of years of "very great suffering from want" in Scotland, singling out 1680 "when so many families perished from this cause, that for six miles, in a well-inhabited extent there was not a smoke remaining."[69] But the experience is not all one-way. Ireland between the 1740s and the 1840s also broadly conforms to such a pattern of gradual decline, but then the Great Potato Famine brought the era of famines to a cataclysmic end.

[67] Maharatna 1996, 175; Iliffe 1987, 157–58.
[68] Appleby 1978; Wrigley and Schofield 1981; Saito 2002, 227.
[69] Malthus 1872, 227.

Finland's last famine in 1867–68 was also a major one. In prerevolutionary Russia there is evidence of a gradual decline in famine intensity; then the famines of 1918–22 and 1932–33 were massive crises, the siege-famine of 1942–43 in Leningrad and the postwar crisis of 1946–47 less so. Thus the evidence is mixed, both because of the role of contingency in human behavior and the strong element of randomness in natural and ecological occurrences.

REMEMBERING FAMINE

Oral history and folk memory of famines may plug some of the gaps left by the lack of standard documentary sources. Ordinarily these sources are invoked only for the light they can shed on the recent past, as in the case of oral poetry describing the Ethiopian famine of 1984–85. This example is a reminder of the porosity of memory; a mere decade or so after the event, "most peasants regretted the fact that they had forgotten" the poems composed during the famine. Even those who composed verses at the time had forgotten most of them—or perhaps did not want to remember them.[70]

Nevertheless, much of what we know about famine in precolonial Africa comes from oral accounts, perhaps transmitted across several generations. The chaos caused by the South African "Madhlatule" famine of the early 1800s, therefore, was described over a century later as "far greater than the Mbete famine in Mpande's time (in the early 1860s)." People had to guard their crops, "for starving people would

---

[70] Azeze 1998, 28–29; compare Watts 1983, 515–20.

eat the green mealies growing there."[71] The claim of a Sudanese herdsman at the time of the rinderpest outbreak of
1889–97 that "a similar calamity had occurred long ago: the
Fulanis had suffered," highlights the singularity of the later
outbreak.[72] The evidence for cannibalism—bandits waylay-
ing victims on the way to the city, and mothers eating their
children—in Ethiopia in the 1890s is all based on (possibly
embellished) folkloric evidence. Mashonaland suffered a
catastrophic famine about 1860, "when so many people died
that they had to be left unburied to be devoured by carrion."
Curiously, local missionaries did not record any human casualties from famine, but given that famine was widespread
elsewhere in southern Africa at this time, the oral evidence
from indigenous narrators is telling. Folk memories of
famine in precolonial Burundi point to a "cumulative combination of climatic accidents, microbial shocks, and internal
and international political instability, all occurring in a context of undue pressure on an agro-pastoral system and socio-political gridlock."[73] The tendency for particular famines
to pass into folklore may imply that major famines were not
so common or that those that were remembered dwarfed
all the others.

Folklore offers a more intimate medium than the
"colder" accounts of officialdom, and arguably gets closer to
the way ordinary people felt and were affected, as the following few examples show:

Ireland, 1848–49: Michael Garvey got the cholera, and he
and the entire household succumbed. They perished

---

[71] Ballard 1986, 370–71; Kreike 2004, chapter 4 passim.
[72] Weiss 1998, 181.
[73] Iliffe 1990, 18; Thibon 2002.

together. I think he died before his wife. . . . Somebody went to their cottage door and could see that they were all dead. All they did then was to set fire to the cottage, burn it, and knock in the walls. I remember myself in autumn-time how we used to pick blackberries near that spot—because there were lots of bushes where the house used to be—my mother warning us to keep away from the place. "Stay away from there," she used to say, "or you will be harmed."[74]

Bengal, 1943: "I was a widow. I stayed for several months longer in my in-law's house, but I received no rice." Sindhubala [the widow] began to sell off her brass and bell-metal utensils—plates, cups, etc.—and then purchased *mug-dāl*, salt, millet, and so forth, to eat. After selling all the utensils, she sold the cow. Then she began to eat wild vegetables, waterlily stalks, wild arum.

Late in 1943 her father came to take her back to Tanguria. "He said it was not right for a woman to live alone in the household of her in-laws." She agreed to leave but first sold her husband's property—about 1½ *bighas* of land—to her brother-in-law for Rs. 136. [The price was low.] Her father took the money from her, giving her in return about ½ *bigha* and building on to his house a separate room for her. Some years later she managed to marry off her daughter, and her son-in-law now lives with her.[75]

Greece, 1942–43: When the Germans came [to Syros] no one would say anything [to you], the Italians [in contrast]

---

[74] Ó Gráda 1999, 211.
[75] Greenough 1982, 155.

would take [everything]. When you were going somewhere, whether you had cauliflowers or eggshells or
lemon rind they would take them from you ...
whereas the Germans had this. They would say to you
do anything you want but don't mess about with me.
That was all.[76]

Leningrad, 1941–44: But I wanted to say that even though
it was so deadly cold, and almost everyone's windows
were broken, even then not one Leningrader cut down a
living tree. No one ever did that. Because we loved our
city, and we could not deprive it of its greenery.... They
could tear down a fence, break up some kiosk, tear off
an outer door. But they couldn't saw down a tree. They
burned furniture, various rags, letters (it was painful to
burn letters). They burned many books (also a pity).[77]

Folklore is prone to forget the more distant past, however,
and suffer from chronological confusion. It is also subject
to hidden biases and evasions. Thus, although about one-
fifth of those who perished during the Great Irish Famine
of the 1840s breathed their last in a workhouse, hardly any
of the famine narratives collected mainly in the 1930s and
1940s refer to an ancestor in the workhouse. Given the enduring stigma attached to workhouse relief in Ireland, the
silence could be due to selective memory; it may also be
that the more articulate members of a community, those
who transmit the memory, are atypical descendants of more
resilient families, and so recall events witnessed rather than
those experienced by their forebears. Accounts of participa-

[76] Hionidou 2006, 63.
[77] Simmons and Perlina 2002, 111.

tion in the public works, which employed seven hundred thousand people at their peak in 1847, are also doubly vicarious in this sense.[78]

A recent account of famine conditions on the Micronesian atoll of Chuuk in 1944–45 during Japanese occupation is based largely on the memories of elderly resident survivors, whose stories of substitute foods, intrafamily tensions, theft, and ingenuity in adversity highlight the power of oral history to retrieve anecdotes and impressions of famine often undocumented in conventional sources. At their best, not only do such stories offer new perspectives on the past but they also enrich our reading of the written record. The pitfalls of oral history, though, also need to be kept in mind: autobiographical memory tends to be self-serving, and rarely free of contamination by extraneous data. It can be subject to chronological confusion. Yet even silences can be revealing. For example, the resilience of Chuuk's rural economy is implicit in these stories; excess mortality was light, even though the island had to sustain a population four times the norm in the face of blockade and nightly bombardments. Clearly it had the capacity to increase and diversify food output considerably at short notice. And the impression gained of the Japanese presence on Chuuk is relatively benign: there is evidence of the requisitioning of food and land on the part of the Japanese military, but it is telling that the hearsay reports of cannibalism refer to the Japanese troops, not to the indigenous population. Again, the oral record is silent on infectious diseases, which might have been expected to accompany any significant excess mortality.[79]

[78] Ó Gráda 1999, chapter 6; 2006, chapter 10.
[79] Poyer 2004.

In Tanzanian folklore, the word famine is often used as a metaphor, and genuine famines were perhaps less frequent in the colonial era than usually claimed. Folklore "remembers" the well-documented famine of the 1890s, other serious famines in the 1830s and 1860s, and more frequent "localized food shortages."[80] In his classic study of Chinese agriculture, John Lossing Buck also relied on the memory of his informants for insight into the frequency of famines in the past. The informants recollected an average of three famines each. These famines, which lasted on average a year, reduced one in four of the population to "eating grass and bark," forced one in eight to emigrate, and led one in twenty to starve.[81] Such subjective accounts, though evocative and indispensable on other grounds, are rather fallible guides to the frequency of famines in the past.

[80] Koponen 1988; see also Vaughan 1989; Thibon 2002.
[81] Buck 1937.

Chapter II

The Horrors of Famine

Each sate sullenly apart
Gorging himself in gloom: no love was left;
All earth was but one thought—and that was death,
Immediate and inglorious, and the pang
Of famine fed upon all entrails. Men
Died, and their bones were tombless as their flesh.

—*Lord Byron, "Darkness"*

A bundle of bones that had once been a baby . . . was being
given water by a woman who was too emaciated to feed it.
They were seated near a tram stop and were practically
trampled under foot by the prosperous people of Calcutta.

—*Michael Brown,* India Need Not Starve!

Nobody can prepare you. No television pictures or written reports
of starvation can possibly prepare you for its reality.

—*Deirdre Purcell, Ethiopia 1984*

AN INCREASING SQUEAMISHNESS TOWARD VIOLENT, graphic images of wars and famines is part of what is sometimes called the civilizing process. Perhaps this explains the preference today for more sanitized, "feminized" images of passive suffering during famines than a reality that is as likely to prompt revulsion as compassion. It may also explain why in European art gruesome pictorial images of famine, such as Goya's disturbing etchings of famine in Spain in 1812, are very much the exception. None of the many illustrations

FIG. 2.1.   Sketch by Zainul Abedin, taken from http://banglapedia
.org/HT/F_0016.HTM (accessed on March 24, 2008).

of the Great Irish Famine of the 1840s, contemporary or
historical, has quite the same horrific resonance as, say, the
depictions of the Great Bengali Famine of 1943–44 by campaigning artists and photojournalists such as Zainul Abedin and Sunil Janah, or those of the drought-stricken Sahel
in the 1980s by Sebastião Delgado and of Ethiopia in 1984
by Pat Langan.[1] Figure 2.1 reproduces one of Abedin's famine
sketches. Figures 2.2, 2.3, 2.4, and 2.5, obtained from the
Getty Archive, are in the same tradition; they describe famine
conditions in Leningrad (1942), India (1943), China (1946),
and Sudan (undated, but probably mid-1980s). Too graphic

[1] Salgado 2004; Purcell and Langan 1985.

FIG. 2.2.   Leningrad corpse, 1942. Photo by D. Trakhtenberg.
Courtesy Getty Images.

to grace the cover of this book, they are effective representations of the horrors of famine.

Famines have always brought out the best and the worst
in human nature. Most famines have yielded examples of
brave, selfless behavior by members of the clergy, relief and
medical workers, and disinterested donors.[2] As an apho-
rism referring to the Leningrad blockade-famine states: "Everyone who survived the blockade/Had a kind guardian
angel."[3] At the same time, famines challenge the instinct
for self-preservation in large numbers of people. Primeval
impulses, such as the biological urge for sex, the need to
socialize and cooperate, the desire to help others, and the

[2] See, for example, Kerr 1994, 42–45; Wright 1882, 32b.
[3] Cited in Kirschenbaum 2006, 243.

Fig. 2.3.   An old starving woman lying on the road, Calcutta, 1943.
Photo by William Vandivert. Courtesy Getty Images.

sense of pride and self-respect, give way to drastic efforts to
preserve one's own being. Famines therefore invariably entail much antisocial behavior, as the bonds of family and
neighborhood break down. Famine victims become desperate and self-absorbed, and lack shame, their baser instincts
prompting actions that would be unthinkable in normal
times. Famines erode hospitality, solidarity, and community,
and examples abound of appalling inhumanity and heart-
lessness among victims.

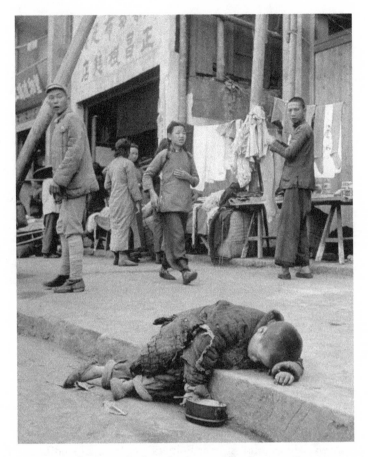

FIG. 2.4. China, 1946. Photo by George Silk. Courtesy Getty
Images.

The following brief cameos make the point:

- A chronicler wrote of a famine in the Russian city of
  Novgorod in 1230: "There was no kindness among us,
  but misery and unhappiness; in the streets unkindness

Fig. 2.5. A well-nourished Sudanese man steals maize from a starving child during a food distribution at a Médecins sans frontières feeding center at Ajiep, southern Sudan, 1998. Photo by Tom Stoddart. Courtesy Getty Images.

to one another, at home anguish, seeing children crying for bread and others dying."

- At the height of the French famine of 1693–94, Louis Jacquelin, a haberdasher on his way to a fair, was waylaid in a forest near Poitiers by a gang of soldiers, "who stole his trunk and his money and beat him to death."
- A survivor of the Great Finnish Famine of 1868 reminisced how "the flow of beggars was so great that the farmers became quite tired of them" and how the farmers had "only scraps of food" themselves.
- On a cold night in January 1848, a farmer in the Irish county of Tipperary bludgeoned to death one Mary

FIG. 2.6. A man suffering from famine, causing his bones to seep through his skin, India, 1942. Photo by William Vandivert. Courtesy Getty Images.

Ryan, a destitute woman, for stealing "a few sheaves of wheat" from his farmyard.

- In the Warsaw Ghetto in 1942, a rabbi complained of seeing victims in the street, "without anyone showing compassion to them."
- In Dinki in Ethiopia, in the wake of the 1984 famine, one survivor exclaimed, "There was no way of helping

each other. It was a time of hating—even your own mother."[4]

Famines often imposed stark choices on households as to who should die. Usually, the survival of the very young and the elderly was in effect deemed less important than that of others. In China, Malthus noted in later editions of the *Essay on the Principle of Population,* "mothers thought it a duty to destroy their infant children, and the young to give the stroke of fate to the aged, to save them from the agonies of such a dilatory death."[5] Such sacrifices were sometimes inevitable on the lifeboat ethics principle. A U.S. medical doctor working in Africa in the mid-1980s lamented that "we are spending too much time trying to save people nearing death, instead of preventing illness."[6] During the Leningrad blockade, some critics accused the political and military leadership of living better than the citizenry; but the deaths of figures so central to the relief efforts would have helped nobody. Equality must yield if somebody has to starve. In some societies, status might determine who died first; in others, the survival of the fittest condemned the old and the young.

CRIME

The Indian Famine Codes (which will be discussed in chapter 7) considered an increase in the crime rate as one of the early warning signals of famine. Crime is indeed a

---

[4] Ó Gráda 2006, 223; Webb and von Braun 1994, 75.

[5] Malthus 1872, 109.

[6] Heiden 1992, 41.

marker of famine: hunger increases the pressure to steal, and the risk of getting caught is likely to fall. But the character of famine criminality is distinctive. Food riots and the looting of shops, warehouses, and bakeries are typical features. In Ireland in the late 1840s, the incidences of burglary and robbery quintupled, while the number of reported rapes plummeted. Many of those arrested, already weak from hunger, perished in jail. For some, the prospect of prison or the convict ship to New South Wales was preferable to the workhouse or death on the road, so that there were cases of recently released defendants being recommitted for attempting to break *into* jail and people eagerly pleading guilty in hopes of being kept inside. Reports from Australia in the wake of the Irish famine noted that many famine-era convicts were "wholly unfit for ordinary convict association and treatment, owing partly to their youth and partly to their general good conduct." A curious by-product of the famine in Dublin was an increase in the mean heights of prisoners, presumably indicating a shift in the socioeconomic background of offenders.[7]

In Belgian Flanders, where the potato blight also produced famine in the mid-1840s, criminality increased sharply as well. The greatest increases concerned begging and vagrancy, petty theft, and trespassing, while the number of violent crimes fell. The profile of the accused also shifted, with disproportionately more women and young offenders as well as more crimes against property. The number of children consigned to prisons and *dépôts de mendicité* in Belgium as a whole trebled between 1845 and 1847. The lower police courts were also kept busy, with huge increases in

[7] Ó Gráda 1999, 187–91.

the number of charges against *filles publiques* (prostitutes), cattle owners using the pastureland of others, and people blocking roads.[8]

According to sociologist Pitirim Sorokin, in Russia in 1922 the whole population, "regardless of sex, age, status, or profession," became "criminal." Petty crime was also rife in Saint Petersburg (then Leningrad) during the blockade of 1941–43. Harvest workers pocketed what potatoes and other vegetables they could; canteen staff, railway workers, and warehouse managers were also well positioned to pilfer food. During the winter, bread delivery vans required police protection. Crimes connected to the rationing system were widespread too. Corpses were hidden so that survivors could collect rations for their own use. The sick were robbed of their meager rations in hospitals. Maintaining order was not easy, and hundreds of police officers succumbed to overwork. Gradually, through better policing and more drastic penalties "necessary under the prevailing conditions," the situation improved. Most crime was unorganized, but groups of armed bandits also operated during winter 1941–42. In the first half of 1942, before the police got the upper hand, 1,216 people were arrested for murder or incitement to murder.[9]

The law usually dealt harshly with those convicted of famine crimes. In 1322, the rioters who took over the town of Douai in northern France faced fearsome retribution when order was restored, while in Lyon in 1709 the value of fines levied on criminals tripled. Repression during famines reached its limit with Stalin's infamous decree of

[8] Vanhaute 2007.
[9] Sorokin [1922] 1975, 230; Krypton 1954.

August 7, 1932, which stipulated sentences of either death or ten years' prison for those found guilty of "stealing or damaging socialist property." This law led to 0.2 million prison sentences of 5 to 10 years and over ten thousand executions.[10] A decade or so later, during the siege-famine in Leningrad, over two thousand people were shot for crimes of various kinds, mostly famine related.[11] During famines, property owners also frequently took the law into their own hands.

Although crimes against property were a marker of famine, the relationship between crime and famine intensity was not linear. Food riots—as distinct from individual acts of thieving and cheating—are more likely to have been the product of threatened famine or the early stages of famine than of out-and-out starvation. When starvation set in, anger and frustration against the authorities gave way to apathy and indifference. Physical deterioration was also a factor. According to Sorokin, "We must expect the strongest reactions from the starving masses at the time when hunger is great but not excessive."[12] This was certainly the case in Ireland in the 1840s, where collaborative protest and resistance gave way to despair as the crisis became a catastrophe. At the outset, there was widespread unrest about the export of foodstuffs, conditions on the public works, and mass evictions; by late 1847, when the dreaded workhouse was the only avenue of relief, resistance foundered, and the mass land clearances of 1848 and 1849 proceeded almost without a whimper. Almost a century later, at the height of the Bengal famine, the attitude of the starving destitute in Calcutta

[10] Ellman 2007.
[11] Jordan 1996, 166; Monahan 1993, 90; Belozerov 2005.
[12] Sorokin [1922] 1975, 236.

was "complete resignation: they attributed their misery to fate or *karma* alone."[13]

The intimidation, rioting, and thieving just described were usually the product of relatively mild subsistence crises, or else the early phases of grave crises. "*Mauvais pain, mauvais gouvernement* (bad bread, bad government)", yet famines have rarely sparked off out-and-out revolution.[14] In Ireland, which suffered more than anywhere else in Europe in the 1840s, the "revolution" of 1848 was confined to the one-day siege of a farmhouse in Tipperary. The Ethiopian famines of 1972–73 and 1985–86 are exceptions. In the former case, Haile Selassie's failure to relieve the famine led to the 1974 revolution. Yet the revolutionaries were not the starving masses of Wollo and Tigray provinces but army officers along with urban and student radicals. The responsibility for the famine of 1985–86 also proved the ultimate undoing of Colonel Mengistu Haile Mariam's brutal administration in 1991. In sum, the relationship between popular unrest and crisis is by no means straightforward.[15]

SLAVERY

> In general the prohibition against buying and selling one's kin is extremely strong. During the years of the famine only . . . shall we permit it?
>
> —*Edict issued in Japan, 1231*

The link between famine and slavery is not straightforward either. On the one hand, during severe famines, slave owners

[13] Eiríksson 1997; Das 1949, 10.
[14] Kaplan 2008.
[15] A point stressed in Dirks 1980, 27; Virlouvet 1985, 24.

may have been tempted to "emancipate" weaker slaves whom they no longer found profitable. In such circumstances, for some unfortunates the abolition of slavery or the slave trade may have been a mixed blessing. In Angola, the suppression of the trade in humans in the nineteenth century was linked to the slaughter during famines of people formerly sold as slaves. "They were simply taken out and knocked on the head to save them from starvation."[16] In the wake of famine in early twentieth-century northern Nigeria, former slaves "set free" by masters who could no longer maintain them were particularly vulnerable.

On the other hand, although enslavement is synonymous with brute force and exploitation, it was not unusual during famines for desperately poor people to sell themselves or their children into slavery, concubinage, or some other form of servitude as a survival strategy, or a means of escaping some worse fate such as abandonment or death by starvation. Again there is a biblical precedent; in Genesis (47:19) destitute Egyptians pleaded with Joseph, the pharaoh's agent: "Why should we die before your eyes, both we and our land? Buy us and our land for bread, and we and our land will be servants unto Pharaoh."

Documented examples of voluntary enslavement during famines are common. In AD 421–22, inhabitants of the provinces of Pontos and Paphlagonia on the Black Sea (in modern Turkey) reportedly had their children castrated and sold as eunuch slaves. During another famine in late AD 450, the emperor decreed that Italians who sold their children into slavery would be entitled to buy the children back at a premium of 20 percent. Another severe famine in Italy in AD 776 increased the supply of Lombard slaves sold by

[16] Dias 1981, 360.

Greeks to Arabs, and "some free men boarded the slave ships willingly, simply to survive."[17] Christianity, however, opposed the enslavement of the faithful at least from the Middle Ages on, and evidence of voluntary enslavement during later European famines is elusive.

Not so elsewhere. During the Famine of One Rabbit (ca. 1454), the Aztec king Moteuczomah ordered his people to quit the capital city in search of food. Many sold their children in the province of Totonacapan, where grain was abundant; girls fetched four hundred ears of maize and boys five hundred ears. In the Indian Deccan in AD 1630, "life was offered for a loaf, but none would buy." On the Indian subcontinent in the seventeenth century, famines led to short-lived booms in the slave trade, and Dutch colonial traders exported thousands of slaves to Ceylon, Indonesia, and elsewhere. Famines in the 1820s and 1884–85 in northeastern Tanzania also prompted the considerable export of slaves. Peaks in slave sales at Saint Louis (Senegal) in 1754 and on the Angolan coast in the 1780s have been linked to serious droughts in their respective hinterlands.[18]

During the "famine of the female servants" of 1800–1803 in Lesotho, husbands freed their wives because they could not feed them.[19] In the late 1850s, famished men and women "inundated local markets on the north bank of the Kwanza, exchanging their own or their relatives' freedom for small bags containing a mixture of manioc flour, beans, maize and groundnuts." A large proportion of the victims

[17] McCormick 2001, 626.

[18] Hassig 1981, 172–73; Vink 2003; Giblin 1986; see also Biswas 2000, 201.

[19] Eldredge 1987, 70–71.

were children, sold for less than half of what they would
have fetched in normal times. In Dodoma in central Tanzania, the pawning of children was widespread in 1918–20. In
Bengal in 1943 the sale of children was illegal, but it still
went on to a limited extent. In July, for example, in Midnapur a girl fetched one and a half maunds of paddy rice,
while in the 24-Parganas district a policeman bought a boy
and a girl for only five rupees.[20]

Sales varied according to the gravity of the crisis. An account of famine in China's Henan Province in the early
1920s reported unprecedented sales of children, some as
servants, some as concubines or prostitutes, and some as
second wives. Occasionally, a rich man might adopt a young
boy. Some of those forced to sell their children were "self-
respecting industrious farmer folks, who think highly of
their children and would only part with them in case of the
greatest suffering." A measure of the severity of famine in a
region was the number of children sold. It was said that in
Shang Kwong, a hamlet of 250 people in Henan Province,
some forty or fifty children were sold as servants, child
brides, or prostitutes. Parents parted with their children
with the greatest reluctance.[21]

PROSTITUTION, INFANTICIDE, AND
CHILD ABANDONMENT

References to destitute women driven to prostitution during famines are commonplace: "when famine is very severe,

[20] Dias 1981, 360; Maddox 1990; Greenough 1982, 222.
[21] Peking United International Relief Committee 1922, 11–15.

inhibiting factors are weak and buyers of women's flesh are always present."[22] In the late 1870s, for example, famine in northern China led to a marked increase in the traffic in women, and compelled "a large number of famine-stricken women" to become prostitutes in the Indian city of Bangalore, though they returned to their villages when the crisis was over. In eastern Bengal in 1943–44, poor women were selling themselves "literally in hordes, and young boys act[ed] as pimps for the military." At the height of the North Korean famine of the mid-1990s, an unknown number of famished North Korean women—possibly thousands—crossed the Chinese border and sold themselves to local men. In some cases, this shameful traffic may have been the price paid for the better survival chances of women during crises.[23]

Whether famines have always induced an increase in the number of prostitutes is a moot point, however, since presumably the demand fell as the supply rose. During the Great Irish Famine of the late 1840s, the "quality" in Dublin rose in the sense of a reduction in the mean age and a rise in the proportion of very young women. There was also an increase in the proportion of women born in counties distant from Dublin. Whether famine resulted in an increase in births outside wedlock is also a moot point. Nor is it clear a priori that an increase is to be expected, since (as discussed in more detail in chapter 4) sexual activity tends to decline during famines. The evidence from nineteenth-century Ireland and Finland is, at best, only weakly supportive

[22] Sorokin [1922] 1975, 128.
[23] Edgerton-Tarpley 2004, 140; Hodges 2005; Greenough 1982, 178.

of the case for famines producing an increase in the proportion of illegitimate births.[24]

Another feature of major famines is an increasing resort
to child abandonment and infanticide. Only when a famine
was particularly murderous did the market for children collapse; in such cases child abandonment—often amounting
to infanticide by another name—might be the final resort.
While in northern India in the 1830s families parted with
their children for a few rupees "and many begged at people
to take them for nothing," in China's Henan Province in
1942 Christian missionaries resorted to rescuing wandering
waifs by night, for fear of increasing the numbers abandoned on mission doorsteps. While such examples reflect
the pressure on the family as a redistributive unit, child
abandonment was also a kind of brutal group survival strategy aimed at keeping the maximum number alive.[25]

Several stories survive of maternal resilience in the face
of famine. During the Leningrad blockade of 1941–43, an
emaciated mother whose breast milk had run out opened a
vein in her arm and put her baby's mouth to the wound,
which it sucked eagerly. Both mother and baby survived.
Another Leningrad mother almost throttled a starving
youngster who had tried to steal some bread from her;
bursting into tears, she explained that she had a little boy
like him who was dying at home.[26] Yet severe famines often
induced mothers—like Hansel and Gretel's stepmother in

[24] Ó Gráda 1999, 178–82; Kennedy 1999.
[25] "Chinese Famine Sufferers Abandon Children," *New York Times*,
November 29, 1928; "The Desperate Urgency of Flight," *Time Magazine*,
October 26, 1942; Dirks 1980, 30; Li 1991.
[26] Barber and Dzeniskevich 2005, 142; Krypton 1954, 262.

the famous German folktale—to abandon their infants or young children. A mother in Lyons in 1709 attached a note to her abandoned infant reading, "This girl is called Claudine, aged three years. Necessity obliges me to expose her. I hope when the times change to get her back." In some cultures, girls were more likely to be abandoned than boys; in others, such as in central Tanzania during World War I, "a boy could be had for . . . one cow while a girl close to marriageable age would go for two."[27] Sometimes the selling or pawning of children was an open and accepted practice, while in others it may have been practiced privately, with the passive acceptance of society. In the cities of the Ukraine in 1933, an English businessman was struck by the numbers of "wild children." On inquiry he found that peasants forced back to their villages by official regulations left their children behind to fend for themselves in the belief that they were more likely to survive that way.

Almost certainly, famines also led to an increase in the number of suicides. The statistical evidence on suicides is both thin and problematic, but during famines in nineteenth-century India and Finland in 1867–68 the number of reported suicides rose.[28] Qualitative references to famine suicides are plentiful. Just as (according to Livy) the Roman famine of 440–439 BC caused many of the poor to despair, whereupon they "covered up their heads and threw themselves into the Tiber," so people reportedly threw themselves off the walls of Constantinople in AD 742–43 in order to avoid death by starvation.[29] In India in AD 1291, whole

[27] Monahan 1993, 90; Greenough 1982, 221–22; Maddox 1990, 191.
[28] Dyson 1991, 19.
[29] Livy 1912: Vol. 4, Book 4.12; Stathakopoulos 2004, 377.

families drowned themselves. Again in Bundelkhand in India in 1833, shame led some to suicide: "respected families . . . took poison and died all together, rather than expose their misery." There are reports of famine-induced suicides from Ethiopia in 1888–92 and China in 1878, whereas in China in 1931 one saw the poor "everywhere . . . hopelessly, apathetically killing themselves."[30]

CANNIBALISM

A young healthy child well nursed, is, at a year old, a most delicious nourishing and wholesome food.

—*Jonathan Swift*, A Modest Proposal

Malthus believed that cannibalism "must have had its origin in extreme want, though the custom might afterwards be continued from other motives.[31] Yet the issue of how widespread cannibalism was during famines remains unresolved and controversial among historians, archaeologists, and anthropologists. Like much else about famine, it is mentioned in the Old Testament. The context was the Syrian siege of Samaria in the ninth century BC, so severe that it lasted "until a donkey's head was sold for eighty pieces of silver, and the fourth part of a *kab* (or pint) of wild onions for five pieces of silver" (2 Kings 6:25–28). Deuteronomy 28:57 describes a mother who "shall eat [her children] for want of all things secretly in the siege and straitness."

---

[30] "After Deluge, Famine," *Time Magazine*, August 31, 1931; Sharma 2001, 112.

[31] Malthus 1872, 25.

Although hard evidence of survivor cannibalism during famines remains extremely scarce, there can be little doubt of its existence.[32] Sometimes it is evoked as a powerful metaphor for horror and disaster, so that distinguishing fact from fiction is difficult. In his study of the Great European Famine of the 1310s, William Jordan sides with those who deem accounts of cannibalism mainly a "literary trope" employed to make narrative accounts of famine "real."[33] Others deem famine cannibalism to have been more widespread than modern Western cultural sensibilities can readily grasp. Stathakopoulos's invaluable survey of the late Roman Empire produced thirteen cases of cannibalism between the early fifth century and mid-eighth century, mostly associated with sieges. They include examples of both necrophagy (eating the flesh of the dead) and killing for food.[34] The latter category is associated with women killing, cooking, and eating their children, or doing the same with adult men. Nevertheless, the evidence is never firsthand and is thus hard to evaluate.

At the height of a major famine in AD 1065, Egyptians "kept careful watch on themselves, for there were men in hiding on house-terraces with ropes furnished with hooks, who latched onto passers-by, hoisted them up in a flash, carved up their flesh and ate them." Another graphic account of famine cannibalism refers to a later Egyptian famine in AD 1201. At first the practice "formed the topic of every conversation," but as the crisis deepened it was met

---

[32] Compare Diamond 2000; Marlar et al. 2002; Lucas 1930, 376. Read (1974) is a popular account of a recent example.

[33] Jordan 1996, 149–50.

[34] Stathakopoulos 2004, 85–87.

with indifference. The claims, however, that "this mania for eating other people became so common among the poor that the majority of them perished that way" and there was not "a single inhabited spot where eating people was not extremely common" must be rhetorical exaggeration.[35]

Famine in the early 1820s, in the wake of King Shaka's conquests, led to cannibalism among refugees in Natal: "there was no famine in Bungane's day; nor Mtimkulu's, but when Mtimkulu was murdered and the tribe became dispersed, and as a drought set in, people, having nothing to eat, began to live on one another."[36] During the catastrophic Ethiopian famine of 1888–92, the product of both cattle disease and harvest failure, there were occasional claims of cannibalism. One report told of a group of migrants headed for Harar being waylaid by famished bandits; another spoke of a man from Shawa who killed and ate his wife, thereby, according to a once-popular Shawan song, giving "him indigestion." Stories of mothers eating their children also circulated.[37]

A poem appended to a graphic woodblock published at the height of the "Incredible Famine" of 1876–78 in north China contained the following couplet:

The old man cannot bear to take his child and boil her
So, he sends her to the market, to exchange her for one
 or two sheng of grain.

Half a century later, a U.S. missionary organization in China reported "several" authenticated cases of cannibalism

[35] Cited in Tannahill 1975.
[36] Ballard 1986, 374.
[37] Pankhurst 1986, 84–85.

in its pleas for donations. Theodore White's graphic account of the Henan famine of 1942–43 refers to a Mrs. Ma who was charged with eating her little girl; she, he reported, merely denied that she had killed it.[38]

The Soviet famines of the early 1920s and 1930s also yielded hard evidence of cannibalism, both in the more restricted sense of survivors eating the flesh of unfortunates who had succumbed and in the sense of victims being murdered for consumption. In 1932–33 the authorities punished cannibalism, "but not nearly as severely as say the theft of a horse or a cow from a collective farm."[39] In Leningrad, nearly nine hundred people were charged with crimes related to cannibalism between December 1941 and mid-February 1942. The number of cases declined thereafter, and none was reported in 1943 or 1944. At the height of the blockade, "not a few" soldiers "not infrequently" fell victim to cannibals. Meat patties sold in the city's Haymarket may have contained human flesh, but no questions were asked.[40]

Three other highly publicized events lend credence to claims of cannibalism in extremis. The first relates to the whaling ship *Essex*, which sank in the South Pacific in November 1820 after striking a sperm whale. Its crew survived the shipwreck, but malnutrition soon exacted a heavy toll. As their plight became more desperate, sailors resorted to eating those who had predeceased them. The second relates to the Donner Party, a group of California-bound migrants attempting to travel west during winter 1846–47. Some

[38] "Mission Board Asserts Some Chinese Have Resorted to Cannibalism," *New York Times*, July 7, 1929; "Until the Harvest Is Reaped," *Time Magazine*, March 22, 1943.

[39] Cited in Dalrymple 1964, 269.

[40] Salisbury [1969] 2000, 474–79.

members of this group, stranded and without food in the Sierra Nevada, were almost certainly reduced to cannibalizing the remains of their co-travelers who had already succumbed to hunger. The third relates to survivors of an air crash high in the Andes in October 1972; in order to live, they made a conscious decision to consume flesh from the corpses of their dead friends.

For all the anecdotal evidence, how common cannibalism was remains a moot point. There was surely a cultural aspect to it. In the east, according to Ancel Keys and his colleagues, "where vast numbers are so often reduced to the extremity of want . . . cases of cannibalism are so few as to excite wonder." Keys surmised that the power of religion was responsible: "In the Orient, the concept of the complete dissociation of body and soul [was] less fixed than in the Western world."[41] In India, the widespread famines of the nineteenth century do not seem to have been accompanied by cannibalism. The one instance described by a journalist traveling through the famine-stricken countryside in 1896–97 referred to a woman belonging to an obscure flesh-eating caste who had been surviving on corpses left floating in a river, and the news caused tremendous publicity in the region in which it happened.[42] At the height of the Bengali famine of 1943–44, the destitute and starving refused even the bully beef proffered by soldiers.

Famine victims in Biafra in the late 1960s and the Sahel in the early 1970s did not resort to cannibalism either.[43] Tuareg tribesmen refused to eat animal cadavers or leather

[41] "Hungry Men," *Time Magazine*, June 2, 1950.

[42] Merewether 1898, 213–24.

[43] Paque 1980.

objects; they also did not use violence "against the weakest members of the group," as happened elsewhere.[44] Perhaps fears that the corpses of famine victims were infected constrained the incidence of cannibalism, even allowing for the risks taken by those on the verge of starvation. The Great Irish Famine of the 1840s yielded little evidence for cannibalism either, although in Mayo a starving man was reported to have "extracted the heart and liver . . . [of] a shipwrecked human body . . . cast on shore." In Ireland in the early 1580s there were reports, credible although again unsubstantiated, of "ghosts crying out of their graves . . . eat[ing] of the dead carrions, happy were they who could find them, yea and one another soon after in so much as the very carcasses they spared not to scrape out of their graves."[45] Such accounts, like those of famished North Koreans "eating children" in the 1990s, cannot simply be taken at face value. Culture matters, even in extreme situations.

In surviving folklore about the Great Irish Famine, versions of an age-old motif resurface repeatedly. They set a compassionate wife against her tough-minded, grudging husband. Typically the husband berates his wife for feeding the destitute who come begging, but husband and wife are rewarded in due course by a miraculously bountiful harvest or some other token of good fortune. The currency of such moral stories in times of crisis implies that generosity was far from the norm.[46] Famine lays bare sentiments and instincts that are, fortunately, hidden and even unimaginable to most of us today.

[44] Brun 1980, 34–35.
[45] *Times* [London], May 23, 1849; Spencer 1970 [1596], 104.
[46] Compare Ó Gráda 1999, 213–15; Biswas 2000, 198–99.

CHAPTER III

Prevention and Coping

MOST OF OUR ANCESTORS lived close to the margin of subsistence. Still, history suggests that the communities they lived in were usually resilient enough to cope with once-off harvest failures. Such failures were too frequent to ignore and usually did not result in outright famine. The poor suffered, and some may have died, but on the whole they did not starve en masse. Instead, they employed a wide range of precautionary strategies in order to reduce the year-to-year variation in the availability of food. This entailed working hard in order to ensure their food supply and employing various forms of insurance against the elements. When disaster threatened, households almost always conserved resources through reductions in births and the postponement of marriages (see chapter 4). Sometimes their leaders made temporary trade and exchange arrangements with less-affected neighboring communities in order to relieve famine (chapter 7). And when famine threatened utter devastation, as a last resort individuals and communities utilized the gruesome coping strategies of enslavement and infanticide (chapter 2).

The list of preventive mechanisms adopted in a context where formal credit and insurance facilities were often lacking is long and varied. Extended family networks, more common in subsistence than in developed economies, probably offered some protection against harvest failure. We know that in classical Greece the poor coped through crop diversification, the deliberate overproduction of foodstuffs, and borrowing from kin. Experience taught them which crops offered the best insurance against the failure of the staple crop; in some areas it might be lentils, and in another beans or chickpeas. Stored knowledge about "famine foods" and precautionary stockpiles of storable foods (mainly grain) also helped. In medieval Europe, peasants diversified their crop portfolios through the open-field system. In precolonial Tanzania different crop species or varieties were planted on the same plot, and the local chieftain was expected to act as a kind of "tribal banker."[1] Fear of drought in precolonial Lesotho meant that sorghum was preferred to maize, and that wheat was resisted, except in the highland areas to which it was better suited. In northern China, too, the relative capacities of wheat, sorghum, and millet to resist flooding, drought, and pests were well understood, and affected cropping choices. Multiple crop plantings also helped. In northern Uganda in the 1910s, official insistence on early planting and shorter fallows removed—with disastrous effects—the insurance against climatic conditions offered by the traditional cultivation practices.[2]

A recent study of the response of BaSotho farmers to the rinderpest pandemic of the late 1890s, which threatened to be catastrophic, is revealing in this context.[3] The rinderpest probably entered Africa through the Red Sea port of Massawa in 1887 or 1888, reaching Sudan in that year and

[1] Koponen 1988.
[2] Vincent 1982, 184–85.
[3] Phoofolo 2003.

wreaking havoc in Ethiopia in 1889–92. It struck the area
north of the Zambezi several years before reaching Basuto-
land. There, as elsewhere, the loss of cattle constrained
plowing and transport, and the price of food rose significantly. Still, the BaSotho coped, in part by switching to
more labor-intensive agriculture. The hoe substituted for
the plow, and sorghum (more drought resistant) and maize
(more bird resistant) for wheat. The BaSotho also substituted horses and mules for cattle, sold their labor to white
farmers and the authorities, and most important, injected
healthy cattle with the bile of infected animals. In this last
respect they were lucky: the delayed arrival of the rinderpest
enabled them to profit from the discovery of an appropriate
prophylactic. Similarly, the pastoralists of Madagascar's An-
droy region reacted to the "end of cactus times" in the late
1920s—an ecological shock caused by the introduction of a
nonnative insect species—by temporary migration and the
reliance on alternative foodstuffs for their livestock. Less
fortunate were the Xhosa pastoralists in South Africa's Eastern Cape who lost most of their cattle to a mysterious lung
disease in the mid-1850s. At first they responded as might
be expected, by selling or eating cattle threatened with disease; then increasing panic and the millenarian prophecies
of a fifteen-year-old girl led many of them to join in "the
great Xhosa cattle-killing movement of 1856–57." The famine of 1856–57, however, which cost tens of thousands of
lives, seems to have been due more to repeated crop failure
than to the destruction of cattle herds per se.[4]

Certain tribal or ethnic groups developed their own "niche"
preventive strategies against famine. For the nomadic Fulbe

[4] Cobbing 1994.

people of the Sahel the niche was a form of transhumant pastoralism; for speakers of the Shari-Nile languages (who include the Luo and the Masai), it was a variety of sorghum that was particularly resistant to conditions of both extreme drought and extreme flooding. Culture mattered too. In Bengal in 1943–44, the increase in mortality among Muslims may have been limited to some extent by their greater readiness to eat meat. The relatively low numbers of Presbyterians resorting to workhouses during the Great Irish Famine was partly income related, but probably also related to culture. In the same vein, a recent comparison of demographic regimes in Europe and East Asia circa AD 1700–1900 argues that whereas in the West the nuclear family fended for itself in hard times, in the East those at risk had the extended family network to fall back on.[5] An alternative interpretation of Asiatic "superiority" in this respect, though, is that the need for insurance was much greater in Eastern households, given the much higher risk of famine there.

Some coping strategies amounted to "learning" from bitter experience. Thus, it was the constant threat of famine that prompted the pharaohs to build and maintain the system of irrigation canals for which ancient Egypt was justly famous. Moreover, that ambitious project required a sophisticated bureaucracy, which had broader ramifications for Egyptian grandeur.[6] After the famine of 1764 in southern Italy, "the habit of planting corn spread among farmers," and farming extended farther and farther up the mountain slopes. *Bliain an áir* (the year of the slaughter, 1740–41)

---

[5] Bengtsson, Campbell, and Lee 2004, 93.
[6] Vandier 1936, 57.

taught Irish potato cultivators never again to leave the potato crop exposed to ruin by frost.[7]

The remainder of this chapter focuses on three common means of resisting famine: recourse to famine foods, borrowing money, and migration.

FAMINE FOODS

When famine threatened, those at risk sought out ways of maximizing their survival chances. Resources normally allocated to other uses were diverted to obtaining food: personal saving came to a halt, and discretionary spending on household items, clothes, and hygiene was cut back or ceased. When the harvest was poor, people resorted to foods that would have been rejected in normal times. Cheaper, less palatable foods—barley bread in Lyons in 1709, and maize in Ireland in 1847—substituted for standard fare. When trading down to such inferior substitutes was not possible, people were left with no choice but famine foods— that is, leaves, shoots, pods, seeds, fruits, meats, or vegetables not usually consumed but acknowledged to be edible in times of severe food stress.

Again history is replete with examples. In Syria in AD 745, people resorted to making bread from ground kernels and the skins of grapes. Women and children on an herb-gathering trip during the famine of AD 808 in the Jazira were—so it is reported—devoured by wild animals. In Khurasan in AD 833 people made bread of dried palm nuts, which they cut up and ground; they also crushed and ate

[7] Dickson 1997, 70.

date stones. Famine in northern India in 1860 led to the consumption of mango stones, which were sold at "the high rate of one and a half maund (or about 50 kgs.) per rupee."[8] In Malawi's Shire Valley in 2005, near famine forced locals to supplement their rations of maize with water lily tubers called *nyika*.

The sheer spread of famine foods is amazing: they range from locusts and "tiny grains of *moseeka* grass threshed and ground" in Africa to lichens and tree bark in Scandinavia (and elsewhere); from farina (a flourlike compound made of unsound potatoes) and turnips in Ireland to domestic pets in Leningrad in 1941–42. A son of the Chinese Hongwu emperor prepared a manual in 1406 describing such foods. The manual listed over four hundred alternative plants, seeds, fruits, and vegetables, and was probably the first of its kind. Later editions added to the list. In the same vein is the memorandum published in 1877 at the instigation of the Madras government, which listed 118 wild plants and vegetables to be used as food by the poor "during seasons of distress, to appease the cravings of hunger," adding their Tamil and Telegu names. One of the plants needed to be eaten only "after careful boilings," and another "when freely eaten causes diarrhea."[9] The extraordinary database of substitute or famine foods compiled by Robert Freedman of Purdue University lists nearly fourteen hundred species, and how they are eaten.[10]

[8] Stathakopoulos 2004, 81–85; BPP 1862, vol. 39 [1670], "Statement Exhibiting the Moral and Material Progress and Condition of India during the Year 1860–61. Part II," 122.

[9] Digby 1878, vol. 2, appendix G, 474–82; Downs 1995, 178–81.

[10] Freedman 2008. Freedman's list is intended to provide "insight to potential new food sources that ordinarily would not be considered."

Such stored knowledge of which plants were edible is consistent with recurrent food shortages, if not out-and-out famine. A "house-to-house canvas" of famine foods in China during a famine in 1920–21 revealed "leaves, fuller's earth, flower seed, poplar buds, corncobs, *hung ching tsai* (steamed balls of some wild herb), sawdust, thistles, leaf dust, poisonous tree bean, kaoliang husks, cotton seed, elm bark, bean cakes (very unpalatable), peanut hulls, sweet potato vines ground (considered a great delicacy), roots, stone ground up into flour to piece out the ground leaves." During the Great Leap Forward famine of 1959–61, the central government shipped various substitute foods from province to province; "one was shaped like a small dog with golden hairs, which Jimo people called *jinmao gou* (golden-haired dogs); another was shaped like pig livers with a dark red color which Jimo people called *yezhu gan* (wild hog liver)." More horrifyingly, it is said that in Sichuan during the same famine, starving children gathered at Yunjing bus station in hopes of eating "the vomit off the long-distance buses."[11]

The nutritional content of such substitute foods is an important issue, both historically and today. Not only were these foods often unpalatable and inferior in the nutritional sense but their consumption also certainly increased the risks of gastric-related diseases. The "bread" produced with birch and lime leaves, acorns, dirt, and water in Russia in 1921–22 "looked and smelled like baked manure"; children could not digest it and died of stomach ailments. The famine gruels common in Ireland in 1846–47 and India in 1943–44 were also poor in dietary terms, and relied heavily on unfamiliar, coarse grains that the poor, already weakened

[11] Mallory 1926, 2; Han 2003; Leonard 1994.

by malnutrition, found difficult to digest. An added difficulty with maize-based relief rations was that they risked
the spread of diet-related diseases such as scurvy, pellagra,
and xerophthalmia. Some substitute foods were known to
be toxic if incorrectly prepared or consumed raw. In the
early fourteenth century it was said that eating diseased
plants led to illness and "irrationality," and modern research
suggests that toxins found in mold-infested food—more
likely to be consumed during crises—may lead to the suppression of the immune system and mental disturbances.[12]

Sometimes the puzzle is why people failed to substitute
even more. A recurrent question is why the Irish, an island
people, did not resort to eating more fish during the Great
Famine of the 1840s. Part of the answer is that fish alone
would not have saved them. The other part is that they did
try, but that the undeveloped state of the industry ruled out
storage and transport, and limited even inshore fishing to
part of the year. Inland, despite the risk of bailiffs, the rivers of county Cork were lit up at night by the torches carried by salmon poachers. In Xiakou in China's Sichuan
Province in 1959–61, the situation was not so different: "the
fish were not so big and so easy to catch as some would say,"
and in any case the tools were lacking and not everyone knew
how to fish. Yet some improvised. A telephone linesman in
Xiakou reversed the charge on the telephone wire leading
out of his commune and electrocuted fish in the river, and
he even traded surplus fish with commune officials for rice.
An elderly man processed a traditional fish poison from
tree bark, and placed a small quantity of it "at the bottom of
a deep and isolated pool where the big fish lived."[13]

[12] Matossian 1989.
[13] Ó Gráda 1999, 240; Leonard 1994.

In northwestern Europe the potato, a late sixteenth-century arrival from the New World, probably ensured the poor against malnutrition and famine at first. That was the intention of one of its great publicists, Antoine Parmentier, whose *Mémoire sur les plantes alimentaires* appeared at a time of near famine in France in 1772. When an English translation appeared a decade later, its translator pointed to its relevance in the grim conditions facing the English poor in the wake of the bad harvest of 1782. In Ireland, the potato for a time certainly shielded the poor against famine. Not only did it complement a traditional diet based on oats and milk but different potato varieties also could be used as insurance against one other. During the decades of the potato's diffusion across the island in the eighteenth century, Ireland's population grew faster than that of any other country in western Europe. Yet a monocultural dependence on one inexpensive crop, and an overreliance on a single, inferior variety (the notorious *lumper*) risked disaster. In Ireland, unfortunately, the potato filled this role: the Gaelic rhyme "potatoes in the morning, potatoes at noon, and if I arose in the night, it would still be potatoes" hardly exaggerated. On the eve of the famine, about one-third of the population was dependent on the potato for the bulk of its food, and the average consumption per male equivalent reached four to five kilos daily. Even so, had *phytophthora infestans*, the fungus responsible for the destruction of the potato crop, struck in 1845 only, there would have been serious privation, but no "great" Irish famine.[14]

In much of seventeenth- and early eighteenth-century France, the dependence on wheat was comparable to that on the potato in Ireland in the following century, and the

[14] Bourke 1993; Ó Gráda 1999, chapter 1.

margin over subsistence was narrow. The daily average consumption of bread was a mere 750 grams. When the wheat crop failed, as in the early 1660s, the early 1690s, and 1708–9, millions died. Only regions such as Brittany, with its twice-yearly harvests of buckwheat (*sarrasin*), were relatively safe. During the following decades rye and the potato made inroads in France, offering insurance during failures of the wheat harvest in the late eighteenth and nineteenth centuries.[15]

COUNTRY MISERS AND CALCULATING MERCHANTS

In a novel prompted by the Great Irish Famine, but inspired by the impact of an earlier famine on his native region of south Ulster, William Carleton described rural moneylenders as follows:

> There is to be found in Ireland, and, we presume, in all other countries, a class of hardened wretches, who look forward to a period of dearth as to one of great gain and advantage, and who contrive, by exercising the most heartless and diabolical principles, to make the sickness, famine, and general desolation which scourge their fellow-creatures, so many sources of successful extortion and rapacity, and consequently of gain to themselves. These are Country Misers or Moneylenders, who are remarkable for keeping meal until the arrival of what is termed a hard year, or a dear summer, when they sell it out at an enormous or usurious

[15] Lachiver 1991.

prices, and who . . . dispose of it only at terms dictated by their own griping spirit and the crying necessity of the unhappy purchasers.[16]

Dealers in small loans in cash and kind have been a feature of most economies in the past, however backward. Carleton dwelled on the hardships associated with trying to borrow from and repay the unloved "miser" or loan shark, who preyed on the ignorance of their customers and probably enjoyed significant local monopoly power. Yet credit markets, informal or formal, offered another partial, however unedifying, defense against famine. One of the tragedies of famine is the indispensability of people described more flatteringly by economist David Ricardo (with Ireland in mind) as "those patient, plodding, calculating merchants who would be contented to enter into a speculation on a prospect of its success in four, five, or ten years."[17]

Given the high risks and transaction costs involved, access to credit has always been problematic for the extremely poor, though. Endemic indebtedness in normal times—as in India in 1943–44 and earlier—reduced the scope for borrowing during famines.[18] An added problem is that the value of remaining assets, such as domestic utensils, ornaments, farm animals, and small plots of land, tended to fall during crises. Moreover, informal lending between neighbors, however useful in the case of individual-level shocks, may have been impossible in cases of harvest failure at the local level. Nonetheless, although credit markets did little to help the most destitute, and almost certainly accentuated

[16] Carleton [1847] 1972, 56–57.
[17] Ricardo 1951–72, 9:238.
[18] Bhatia 1967, 131–33, 150–55.

the inequalities left in famine's wake, they are also likely to
have mitigated the immediate damage inflicted by famine.

Unequal access to credit during famines usually fueled
suspicions that the rich and the powerful capitalized on the
plight of the poor, leading to asymmetrical relationships of
landgrabbing, dependency, and bondage. As Jordan notes
in the context of the northern European famine of 1315–17,
the surviving evidence, inevitably focused on bad debt and
extortionate charges, is "not pretty."[19] Sometimes rulers in-
tervened to protect borrowers: Solon's *seisachtheia* or "shak-
ing off" (ca. 594 BC) rescinded famine debts that had reduced a considerable proportion of Athens' population to
slavery, and banned all future contracts allowing debt servitude. In Kashmir, the sultan canceled debts incurred by
the poor during the famine of 1460.[20] In Germany, the
rival cooperative credit organizations founded by Hermann
Schulze-Delitzsch and Friedrich Wilhelm Raiffeisen owe
their origin to a belief that loan sharks exploited the poor
during the potato famine of 1846. Raiffeisen sought an alternative to both the village moneylender and the commercial banks, which at that time spurned the business of small
farmers.

Measures to control moneylending also followed the Indian famine of the late 1870s. Nevertheless, controls imposed
in Bengal in the 1930s "proved to be a curse in disguise at
the time of the famine" of 1943–44.[21] The legislation limited the extent to which people could borrow on the security
of land, with the result that during the famine the moneyed

[19] Jordan 1996, 111.
[20] Kaw 1996, 63.
[21] Das 1949, 122.

were more inclined to buy the property of the poor at reduced prices than to lend them money. The controls had led to a more limited supply of credit during the crisis. While the moneylenders charged high annual rates—50 to 100 percent was the norm in Bengal before the famine—they supplied the seasonal loans and working capital that were essential to small farms. The legislation constrained moneylenders without solving the problems that created the demand for them.[22]

In Ireland in the late 1840s, pawnbrokers, a well-documented subgroup, benefited during the early stages of the crisis as the demand for their services rose. As the famine intensified, however, the number of unredeemed pledges rose, and the sale value of unclaimed items such as clothing, household goods, farming utensils, and fishing nets dropped. Pawnbrokers reacted by reducing the average monetary value of pledges and cutting back the number of pawns. The volume of pawnbroking transactions fell during the crisis, and some were forced to quit the business altogether.[23] Their fate is a reminder of the risks associated with petty credit in times of extreme crisis.

MIGRATION

The official inquiry into the 1943–44 Bengali famine claimed that during recent Indian famines, "disorganized" mass migration was uncommon, and "its appearance during a famine shows that the famine is out of control."[24] Yet the free

[22] Chakraborty 1997, 150–55.
[23] Ó Gráda 1999, 149–56.
[24] Famine Inquiry Commission 1945, 2.

movement of labor arguably limits the damage wrought by poor harvests, since emigration to less-affected areas reduces the pressure on scarce food and medical resources in those areas in which the crisis is deepest. In other words, famine migration can be a crude form of disaster relief. It seems safe to assume that if the poor of nineteenth-century Asia or twentieth-century Africa had the same freedom to migrate long distances in times of crisis (in the sense of the legal ability to migrate to famine-free areas) as did the Irish in the 1840s, fewer of them would have perished.

Famines have always prompted people to migrate temporarily for assistance and work. A famine in the land of Canaan caused Jacob to go "down into Egypt to sojourn there," although there is no historical consensus as to when this might have been. Starving rural dwellers flocked to Constantinople in AD 370, Antioch in AD 362–63 and AD 384–85, Edessa in AD 500–502, and Alexandria in AD 619. In AD 1528–29, Venice was the focus of mass immigration from the famine-threatened countryside. In the same city in April and May 1570, "one could do nothing but answer the door to these peasants who hammered on the doors in the town." The large numbers of poor people arriving in the city of Madras in 1782–83 were given rice "on condition only of their departure from hence to seek subsistence elsewhere." In eighteenth-century China, the authorities sought to limit vagrancy by offering relief on the spot and blocking escape routes from stricken areas. In Bengal in 1896–97, the size of temporary migration by males out of remote areas meant that women were in the majority on the public works. Trickles of migrants into feeding centers in Ethiopia's Tigray Province in early 1983 were the first signs of what would become a major famine; later, militias and roadblocks prevented the poor from migrating within the country, but over a million made it to the relative safety of Sudanese refugee camps.[25]

From the late nineteenth century on, railways facilitated more distant migration. In northern China in 1920–21, people "journeyed up and down the railroads, going as far as Mongolia . . . and . . . Manchuria [and] into Shansi and Shensi." Younger men from famine-affected districts migrated in numbers in search of work or in order to beg. In some districts whole families left and plastered up their homes. Railway stations, where grain was unloaded and transshipped, were favorite resorts, in case some grain spilled. In 1929, the Chinese government provided free rail transport to emigrants willing to leave the worst-affected famine districts for more sparsely populated Manchuria. The 1921–22 Soviet famine prompted massive migrations, much of it by rail, from the worst-affected areas to western Russia, the Ukraine, and Turkistan. Those relying on horse transport were less likely to escape: "the exhausted horses were slaughtered and consumed as food, leaving the population no means of fleeing hunger."[26]

As the above examples suggest, in times of famine migration tended to be age and gender selective. Since young males were more likely to find work and less likely to be molested on their travels, and since women were expected to care for any children, migrants seeking relief through employment were disproportionately male. Sometimes, as

[25] Will 1990; Dunstan 2006, 414–28; Chakrabarti 2004, 386; http://www.isop.ucla.edu/eas/restricted/famine.htm; Webb and von Braun 1994, 80.

[26] Cited in Adamets 2003, 308.

in the case of Edessa in AD 500–502, males might venture in one direction to seek work, while women and children would head for the nearest city or town in search of food and refuge.[27] In Bengal in 1943 too, relief-seeking migrants to Calcutta were more likely to be females or children. In societies with extensive urban infrastructures, migration tended to be from the countryside to the city, as in France in 1709, Ireland in the 1840s, and Bengal in 1943. Since relief was usually better organized in the bigger cities, the poor were more likely to head for them. Between 1841 and 1851, Ireland's rural population fell by nearly a quarter while the population of its towns rose by 7 percent.

Sometimes, towns tried to keep out the rural poor by enacting laws against mendicancy and vagrancy as well as by posting guards and closing gates. In urban centers, the migrant poor were seen as the purveyors of unrest and disease. But the movement was not always from rural to urban; between 1917 and 1920, for instance, the populations of Moscow and Leningrad fell by half and two-thirds, respectively, mainly due to out-migration.

During the Russian famine of 1921–22 the migration occurred in two waves: first, with the realization that the harvest was a complete failure, and second, with the melting of the winter snows in late spring 1922. These migrations also highlighted migration's downside as a means of famine relief. Impoverished, desperate migrants traveled long distances from their own areas where epidemics were rife, "falling ill en route, and leaving lousy or infected every train, every station where they slept, each town in which they sought food or work, and thus infecting the whole countryside

[27] Stathakopoulos 2004, 79.

through which they passed with typhus and relapsing fever."
Large-scale migration was also a feature of the 1932–33 famine. In 1932 the movement was uncontrolled, but between
late January and mid-March 1933 over two hundred thousand migrants were arrested by the secret police, and most
were sent back to their place of origin.[28]

As conditions worsened in rural Bengal in mid-1943 the
destitute also headed for the towns and cities. In Calcutta,
the migrants were mainly from the nearby provinces of Midnapur and 24-Parganas. The luckier ones found shelter under
trees in the public parks and air raid shelters, and it was "not
unusual to find groups of twenty or thirty persons lying on
the pavement, side by side, sleeping under the open sky."[29]
Although the migrants usually traveled on foot, improvements in transport and communication must have increased
mobility. Mortality began to rise within a few months, but
there was no question of returning home. Scenes of corpses
being thrown into urban dustbins attracted wide publicity,
prompting the authorities to introduce a system of publicly
subsidized but privately run gruel kitchens (see chapter 6).

Even in centrally planned China in 1959–61, migration
may have played a significant role in alleviating the hardships caused by famine. If official demographic data are to
be believed, they imply that out-migration was highest from
the worst hit provinces; in Anhui, an extreme case, a death
rate of sixty-nine per thousand in 1960 was almost matched
by an out-migration rate of fifty-five per thousand (figure 3.1a).
On the other hand, several less-affected provinces (e.g., Jilin)
absorbed large numbers of immigrants during the crisis

---

[28] Davies and Wheatcroft 2004, 426–29.
[29] Das 1949, 3.

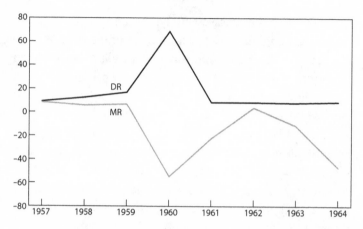

FIG. 3.1a. Migration and mortality in Anhui.

(figure 3.1b).[30] The extent to which these movements were encouraged or assisted by the state is hard to judge. Whether planned or spontaneous, without the safety valve of migration, the crisis would almost certainly have been worse.

In general, migration reduces the pressure on resources where the crisis is most severe, and offers the prospect of some relief from hunger to those who leave. Twentieth-century famines would almost certainly have been less lethal if the safety valve of emigration had existed, as it did for the impoverished Irish in the nineteenth century. But migration can also have its downside: as noted above, it tends to spread disease, and elites seek to prevent or control it for that reason. In Finland in the 1860s the connection between migration and mortality was complex, but temporary migration in a context of social disorder contributed significantly to excess mortality.[31]

[30] For more detail, see Ó Gráda 2008.
[31] Pitkänen 1992.

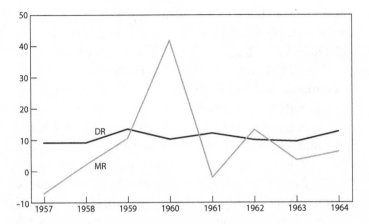

FIG. 3.1b.   Migration and mortality in Jilin.

By the same token, although migration saved lives in Ireland, it led to increased mortality across the Irish Sea. In
England and Wales, mortality was one hundred thousand
more than expected in the 1846–48 period; however, how
this is divided between arrivals from Ireland and natives
succumbing to famine diseases is not known. The birthrate
in England and Wales also fell in the late 1840s, indicating
that the crisis was not solely an import from "John Bull's
Other Island." The greater impact of the crisis on deaths
than on births probably means that most of the excess deaths
recorded were of Irish immigrants, who were heavily concentrated in the slums of the larger cities. These were also
years of high mortality in Scotland. Although this is remembered as the period of the "Great Highland Famine,"
excess mortality in the Highlands was light, and urban areas
suffered more than rural ones. Mortality was particularly
high in the western lowlands and border areas, where
Irish famine immigration was concentrated. In Glasgow

the number of burials doubled in 1847. This might be seen as the result of the influx of destitute Highlanders, but immigration into Glasgow from Ireland easily exceeded that from the Highlands. So the Irish famine may also have been mainly responsible for most of the typhus that led to excess mortality in Scotland.[32]

A century ago, British physician and author Charles Creighton claimed that the three worst outbreaks of "epidemic fever" in eighteenth-century Britain—in 1718–19, 1727–29, and 1740–42—were prompted by the migration of destitute famine refugees from Ireland. This has prompted the hypothesis that one-half of the modest increase in life expectancy in England between the 1710s and the 1750s can be attributed to the absence of serious famines in Ireland after 1740–41. Direct evidence on such migration and the causes of excess mortality in England in these years is lacking, though.[33]

Famine migrants often returned home when the worst of the crisis was over. The famine Irish of the 1840s are a well-known exception in this respect. Their exodus in loosely regulated or unregulated shipping produced its own carnage on the Atlantic crossing and in its wake, most infamously in Quebec's Grosse-Isle quarantine station. Yet most of those who fled reached their destinations safely. Not only did their leaving raise their own survival chances; they also improved those of the majority who remained in Ireland. In this sense migration reduced the overall mortality, and more public spending on subsidized emigration would have reduced the aggregate famine death toll. Most emigrants

[32] Neal 1998; Ó Gráda 1999, 111–13.
[33] Schellekens 1996.

relied on their own resources, although several landed proprietors helped through direct subsidies or by relieving
those who left of their unpaid rent bills. For the very poorest who were also the landless, emigration—like credit—
was less likely to have been an option.[34]

[34] Ó Gráda and O'Rourke 1997.

Chapter IV

Famine Demography

The decrease in the normal growth of population after
a period of deficient harvests is not so much a measure of
mortality as a demonstration of the normal effect of the fertility
of nature on the fertility of man.

—*Alexander Loveday*, History of Indian Famines

HIERARCHIES OF SUFFERING

WHO DIES DURING FAMINES? Karl Marx's quip in *Das Kapital*
that the Great Irish Famine killed "poor devils only"[1] holds
for all famines: mortality has always varied inversely with
socioeconomic status, but especially so during famines. In
Ireland, the first to die were destitute vagrants who lacked
family support to fall back on, and who were at the greatest
risk from the elements and disease. Laborers were more
likely to succumb than farmers, and substantial farmers were
more likely to survive than small farmers. In China in
1959–61, it was said that those who died were "the old people, infants, some young people, the honest, and the stu-
pid." Those with "with bad class backgrounds" were also
more at risk. It was said, too, that the honest and the gullible died because one had to "be tricky" and "to steal" in
order to survive. In Bangladesh in the mid-1970s there was

---

[1] Marx 1967, 704.

a strong class gradient to mortality. Excess mortality among the poor in one rural area of that country more than doubled, while among the rich it rose by a quarter.[2]

In environments with high loads of infectious diseases, even the wealthier classes were at increased risk from disease during famines. Maxim Gorky worried constantly about the impact of the Russian famine of 1918–22 on the "intellectual forces." In Ireland in the 1840s and Finland in the 1860s, mortality was higher among the medical profession than in the population as a whole. Paramedics and relief workers also faced serious risks; nearly half the staff of the North Dublin Union workhouse, for example, contracted famine fever during the Irish famine, and half of those died of it. One implication is that the rich had more reason to care for the poor in the past. The preamble to a Venetian decree in 1528 noted that a failure to relieve the poor would "import disease of the kind . . . which no human remedy has been able to extinguish." The fear was bubonic plague, carried by the rats that were likely to follow in the wake of rural migrants, and typhus, then a relatively recent import from Cyprus. Because nowadays the better-off in famine-prone environments are better equipped to shield themselves against infection, famines may be *even more* class specific than in the past.[3]

Malthus held that overpopulation caused famine. This chapter is about the reverse causation, from famine to population. It focuses in turn on measuring aggregate mortality, and its incidence by age and gender, the impact of famine

[2] Leonard 1994; Razzaque 1989.

[3] Wolfe 1968, 71–73; Ó Gráda 1999, 94–95; Pullan 1963–64, 159; Iliffe 1987, 257.

on the birthrate, the causes of famine deaths, and possible long-term health effects.

HOW MANY DIED?

Excess mortality, or at least the threat of excess mortality, is a defining feature of famine. The death toll, or the excess death rate relative to some noncrisis norm, is the single most popular measure of a famine's gravity. For most historical famines, however, establishing excess mortality is impossible. In the absence of any hard evidence, it is not possible to take literally claims such as that during the Ch'in-Han transition in China (ca. 209–203 BC) famine killed 80 to 90 percent of the population in some areas; in AD 967 a flood in Egypt caused a protracted famine that left six hundred thousand dead; the great Bengali famine of 1770 killed one-third of the population; East Prussia "lost forty-one per cent of its population to starvation and disease in 1708–11"; or Persia lost two-fifths of its people to a genocidal famine in 1917–19.[4] Such claims are usually rhetorical, and sure signs of a major disaster, but poor guides to actual mortality.

In the absence of civil registers and periodic censuses, the tolls of the vast majority of historical famines can only be guessed at. In the case of the well-known great European famine of the 1310s, for example, "an urban collapse of 5–10 per cent in 1316, the worst year of the famine in terms of harvest shortfalls," with lower mortality in rural areas, is the best that can be made of the limited quantitative evidence. Similarly, only the crudest guesses are possible for the Irish

---

[4] Yates 1990, 168; Jones 1981, 51; Majd 2003, 1.

famine of 1740–41, which may have matched or exceeded the famine of the 1840s in relative mortality terms; the paucity of direct evidence has prompted inferences based on hearth-tax data. Estimates of the toll exacted by a famine in south-western Madagascar in 1931 range from the five hundred to eight hundred deaths suggested by one colonial administrator to the thirty-two thousand lost from a combination of migration and mortality proposed by another.[5]

Sometimes, inferences derived from incomplete data are politically controversial. At the height of the Great Irish Famine of the 1840s, opposition leader Lord George Bentinck accused the authorities of "holding the truth down" about the human cost of the famine, and predicted a time "when we shall know what the amount of mortality has been" and people could judge "at its proper value [the government's] management of affairs in Ireland." The government of the day refused to regard the number of deaths as a measure of policy failure and deemed it impossible to estimate excess mortality. In the House of Commons, Prime Minister Lord John Russell fended off demands for a body count with the remark that "a man found dead in the fields would probably be mentioned in the police returns as having died of starvation." There have been many estimates since of excess mortality in the 1840s, with "revisionist" scholars casting doubt on its likely toll of about one million dead, and hard-line nationalists deeming that number too low. The estimates necessarily hinge on assumptions about noncrisis birthrates and death rates, the decline in births during the famine, and net emigration.[6]

[5] Lucas 1930, 369; Jordan 1996, 148; Dickson 1997; Kaufman 2000.
[6] Mokyr 1980, 241–51; Boyle and Ó Gráda 1986.

At the height of the Great Bengali Famine it was a similar story. Leopold Amery, secretary of state for India, claimed in the British House of Commons that the weekly death toll was about one thousand, though "it might be higher." This amounted to a virtual denial of a catastrophe whose real weekly toll was closer to forty thousand at the time. Later, Amery mentioned an estimate of eight thousand as the number of famine-related deaths in Calcutta between mid-August and mid-October. Subsequent estimates of the total mortality in Bengal range from 0.8 to 3.8 million; the true figure was over two million.[7]

In the absence of hard data, mortality gets talked up or down. In Vietnam, those who questioned the original figure of two million as the toll of the famine of 1945 were classed with those who ignored "the crimes of French colonialism and Japanese fascism." North Korea in the 1990s offers another example. An appalling toll of three million in the wake of a famine beginning in 1995, or 10 percent of the entire population, was regularly cited in the foreign press. Such a figure would make the North Korean famine a devastating one in relative terms—in Ireland in the 1840s, one-eighth of the population perished. Yet it seems to be a politically charged extrapolation based on refugee reports from North Korea's atypical northeastern provinces. The most plausible guess at excess mortality is closer to a half million—serious, to be sure, but less likely to make the headlines. This does not prevent journalist Jasper Becker from continuing to link the figure of three million deaths to Kim

---

[7] *Hansard*, Commons, ser. 5, vol. 392, col. 1078, October 14, 1943; *Hansard*, Commons, ser. 5, vol. 393, col. 352, October 28, 1943; Sen 1981, 195–96; Maharatna 1996, table 4.1.

Jong-Il's "lavish lifestyle" and "long-range missiles which landed in the Sea of Japan in 1998."[8]

The estimates of excess famine mortality in the Soviet Union in the early 1930s and China in 1959–61 are even more controversial. The Soviet famine of 1931–33 is nowadays reckoned to have cost up to six million lives, while the demographic impact of the Chinese famine remains uncertain. The Chinese authorities at first concealed and then denied the crisis, but forty million deaths is the figure given in *The Guinness Book of Records*, and one hostile source lends credence to "even larger figures of fifty and sixty million deaths . . . cited at internal meetings of senior Party officials."[9] The evidential basis for such claims is flimsy.

Two much-cited estimates published in the 1980s suggested a toll of thirty million, while more recent estimates range from eighteen to twenty-three million; the outcome depends on assumptions made about noncrisis vital rates. Thus, the trend in the aggregate death rate for 1950–69, as reported in official Chinese data released in the early 1980s, implies an estimated cumulative excess death rate of twenty-three per thousand in 1959–61. Assuming a population of 650 million on the eve of the famine, that would mean a toll of fifteen million lives lost to famine.[10] Such a figure would still make the Great Leap famine, which is discussed in greater detail in chapter 8 below, the biggest in history in absolute terms.

Yet that total is almost certainly too low, since the only way to reconcile the pre-1959 death rates behind this calculation

[8] Smith 2005, 73–74; Lee 2005; Noland 2007; Becker 2006.
[9] Becker 1996, 293.
[10] Ó Gráda 2007.

and United Nations' estimates of life expectancy in 1950–55 is to assume considerable underregistration of vital rates in the official data during and before the famine. Even allowing for a major decline in mortality after 1949, an official death rate of 11.4 per thousand in 1956–58 is not easily squared with a life expectancy at birth of about forty years in 1950–55. Attempts to estimate excess mortality with data that allow for underregistration produce considerably higher mortality tolls. Figure 4.1 compares the official data for 1953–70 with the reconstructions of demographer Sheng Luo. Note that both the official data and Luo's reconstruction imply net population loss only in one year—1960.

Though perhaps closer to the truth, none of these estimates should be taken as final. As sinologist Carl Riskin has pointed out, the baseline child mortality assumed in one well-known reestimate by Ashton and his colleagues inflates the number of excess child deaths; it also yields an age pattern of excess mortality atypical of famines generally. Demographer Judith Banister candidly points to the "arbitrary estimation process" involved in her adjustments for underregistration, while Luo's analysis (see figure 4.1) implies more excess deaths in 1961–62 than in 1960, which is hard to square with other evidence, and a trough in births in 1960 rather than 1961. Still, a toll of twenty-five million is as plausible as fifteen million. Either way, the Great Leap famine still remains ahead of its nearest competitors.[11]

Nonetheless, a toll of even twenty-five million bears comparison with a much-cited estimate of excess mortality—a range from 9.5 to thirteen million—during the Great North

[11] Banister 1987, 114–15; Ashton et al. 1984; Luo 1988, 136–40; Riskin 1998, 113–14.

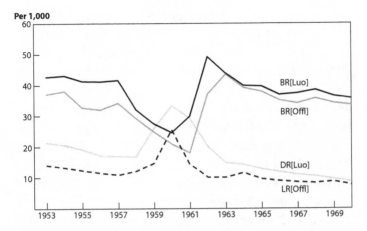

Per 1,000

FIG. 4.1.   Birthrates and death rates in China, 1953–70.

China Famine of 1987–78.[12] That estimate refers to a time
when the population of China was little more than one-half
of its 1958 level, and when the real GDP per head was
higher than in the mid-1950s.[13] Note, too, that major famines were commonplace in China before 1949: the aggregate estimated mortality from Chinese famines between
1900 and 1949 was 10.5 to 13.5 million.[14]

There can be little doubt that modern famines are, relatively speaking, far less murderous than earlier ones. Although noncrisis death rates in Africa remain high, the excess mortality from famine in recent decades has been low.
In Stephen Devereux's recent listing of major twentieth-
century famines, only two—the war famines of 1968–70 in
Nigeria and 1983–85 in Ethiopia—are accorded tolls nearing

[12] Compare Li 2007, 272; Edgerton-Tarpley 2008, 1.

[13] For more on these famines, see Davis 2001; Edgerton-Tarpley 2008.

[14] Devereux 2000.

one million. Both estimates probably exaggerate. In other well-known famines—in the Sahel in the early 1970s, Darfur in the mid-1980s, and Sudan (Bahr el Ghazal) in 1998— victims were far fewer. Other estimates in Devereux's list are also probably on the high side. That of 1.5 to two million deaths in Cambodia in 1979 bears comparison with estimates by the Central Intelligence Agency implying that 0.35 million, or 6 percent of a population of less than six million, perished from famine. The figure of 1.5 million given for Bangladesh in 1974–75 also exaggerates the likely toll: if the excess mortality rate of seven per thousand in Matlab thana is at all representative, then aggregate famine mortality in Bangladesh as a whole was about 0.5 million. The 2.8 to 3.5 million estimate for famine in North Korea in 1995–99, as noted above, is also much too high.[15]

GENDER AND AGE

The husband has deserted the wife;
The maternal uncle has sold his niece in order to eat;
The mother-in-law bakes bread, the father-in-law eats it,
While the daughter-in-law counts minutely each mouthful swallowed

—*Indian famine song, ca. 1900*

The sense that the horrors of famine fall disproportionately on women, highlighted in the above verse, is often reflected today in the publicity campaigns of development aid agencies and the writings of campaigning journalists. According to Agence France-Presse in 2003, "Despite international

[15] Http://www.mekong.net/cambodia/demcat.htm; Dyson 1991; Lee 2005; Noland 2007.

efforts to avert more suffering caused by food shortages in Ethiopia, women and children are still dying of malnutrition and diseases." In Lietuhom in southern Sudan in 1999 victims of famine were "children, women, men at an average of six per day." The "principal victims" of famine in North Korea in the 1990s were deemed to be "children, women, and the elderly." David Arnold's classic *Famine: Social Crisis and Historical Change* also "feminizes" famine, arguing that its burden fell, and falls, "with exceptional severity upon women."[16]

Today the feminization of famine, by highlighting women as its main victims, is commonplace. Yet most of the evidence suggests that males are more likely to perish during famines than females. As a sympathetic and close observer of the Irish famine noted in 1849:

> No one has yet . . . been able to explain why it is that men and boys sink sooner under famine than the other sex; still, so it is; go where you will, every officer will tell you, it is so. In the same workhouse, in which you will find the girls and women looking well, you will find the men and boys in a state of the lowest physical depression; equal care in every way being bestowed on both sexes.[17]

Demographic evidence corroborates this claim, finding that although the life expectancy of men in noncrisis times exceeded that of women, males were more likely to succumb during famines than females. For example, in the

---

[16] Http://act-intl.org/news/dt_1997–99/dtsud499.html (Sudan); Agence France-Presse, 2003; Arnold 1989, 86.

[17] Osborne 1850, 19.

wake of the disastrous famine that followed the eruption of Laki in 1784–85, the sex ratio of Iceland's population fell to 784 from a norm of about 850. In the six west Cork parishes surveyed in detail by a public official in late 1847, men were one-third more likely to succumb than women. During the Madras famine of 1876–78, when the ratio of male to female deaths was over 1.2 to 1, one Captain D. G. Pitcher noted that in the Rohilkand Division, "the excess of deaths in men over women is a singular fact well known to the people themselves."[18]

During the Leningrad blockade, it was a similar story. Males were much more likely to be admitted to a hospital in a state of semistarvation than females, and males were also much more likely to die than females. On the Greek island of Syros in 1941–42, the male death rate rose eightfold, while the female death rate rose only fivefold. The male disadvantage was widely noted at the time. Males aged fifteen to thirty-five years were at particular risk.[19] The patterns on Syros were replicated on Mykonos and in Athens/ Piraeus. Finally, Chinese demographic data imply that in the seven Chinese provinces that lost population between 1957 and 1961, there were 725,000 fewer males and 366,000 fewer females by 1961, while in the rest of China both male and female populations rose by 1.5 million.

The evidence that females survive famine better than males is by now overwhelming. Indian anthropologist Tarakchandra Das offered his own explanation for an analogous outcome in Bengal in 1943–44: women, he believed, had easier access to public relief, while greater physical

[18] Tomasson 1977, 420; Hickey 2002, 215–17; Das 1949, 93–95; Sami 2002; Macintyre 2002.

[19] Hionidou 2006, 168 (fig. 9.3b).

exertion, often in bad weather, told against the males. Das did not believe that women's control of the domestic food supply and their store of ornaments offered them a cushion against starvation; they were less at risk because their husbands "will very generally rather starve than see their wives starve before them."[20] Be that as it may, males accounted for over three-fifths of those who died after leaving home in Bengal in 1943–44.

The most plausible explanation for this female mortality advantage—which is usually the reverse of nonfamine patterns—is physiological. Females store a much higher proportion of body fat and a lower proportion of muscles—an encumbrance in famine conditions—than males. The gender advantage is not confined to humans: there is a good deal of research showing that other male mammals also suffer disproportionately in times of food shortage. Among Siberian deer, for example, the harsh winter of 1976–77 "produced a particularly high mortality differential between stags and hinds." In this instance, dimorphism works to the female's relative advantage. The evidence is still too thin to say how the female advantage has changed over time. Still, there is some presumption that the more important is literal starvation rather than infectious disease as the cause of death, the greater the female advantage. This would imply that during World War II, women were at proportionately less risk in, say, Leningrad and Greece than in Bengal or Vietnam. The reduction in the birthrate, described below, is also likely to have increased female survival chances.

As far as mortality by age is concerned the evidence is mixed. Most famine victims have always been young children

---

[20] Das 1949, 94–95.

and those beyond middle age, but the greatest proportional increases in death rates have tended to be at ages where mortality is relatively low in normal times. A famine in the Puglian community of Orsara in 1764 increased infant mortality by three-quarters, while the death rate of those aged one to seven years rose sevenfold, and that of all other age groups rose four- to fivefold. In Berar in 1900, infant mortality doubled but mortality among ten- to fourteen-year-olds trebled. In Finland infant mortality doubled in 1868, and the death rate of the over sixty-five-year-olds tripled, while that of ten- to twenty-four-year-olds quadrupled, and that of twenty-five- to forty-four-year-olds quintupled. In rural Bengal in 1943, the pattern was similar to that in Berar or the USSR. The interesting differences between rural and urban Bengal was a reflection of the age distribution of migrants from the countryside—the main victims in urban areas. Figures 4.2a–4.2e, which provide more data on death rates in the above cases, highlight the generality of the famine gender gap, but show that an overgeneralization about deaths by age is not warranted.[21]

MISSING BIRTHS

That famines nearly always kill goes without saying; do they also affect the number of births? In a well-known essay, John Bongaarts and Mead Cain posited little impact on fertility since prefamine conceptions had a minimal risk of miscarriage.[22] In the longer run, they argued that fertility

---

[21] Figure 4.2a is derived from Adamets (2002, 332–33) and uses 1924 as a "normal" year.

[22] Bongaarts and Cain 1982.

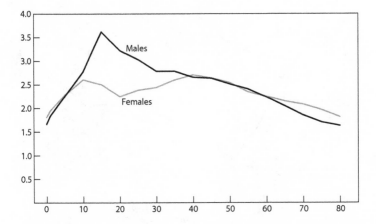

FIG. 4.2a. The USSR, 1922.

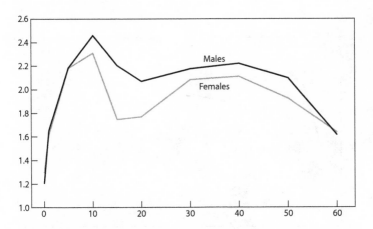

FIG. 4.2b. Rural Bengal, 1943–44.

should rise as couples sought to ensure against a repetition of famine through having more children. The reality is quite different. Famines almost invariably entail significant reductions in births and marriages. Without those reductions mortality would be higher. Indeed, reduced fertility is

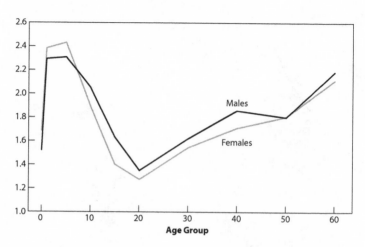

FIG. 4.2C. Urban Bengal, 1943–44.

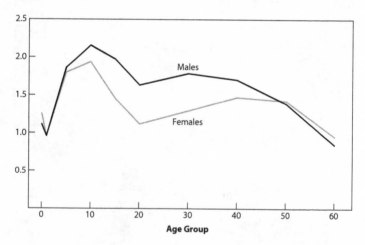

FIG. 4.2d. Berar, 1900.

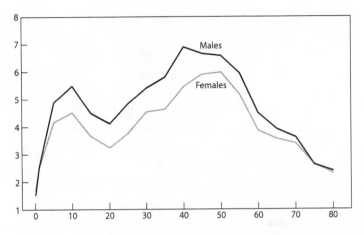

FIG. 4.2e.   Finland, 1868.

probably a more common symptom of famine than increased mortality.

Some demographers claim that averted births should be included in the demographic reckoning. In Ireland it has been estimated that "lost births" numbered about 0.4 million in the 1840s, whereas in China in the wake of the 1959–61 famine they have been reckoned as high as thirty million.[23] Such averted births are casualties of famine and should not be ignored. By the same logic, though, the reduction in deaths and rebound in births that often follow in famine's wake should not be ignored either.

Famines also usually entail a decline in the marriage rate, but this rarely accounts for the decline in births. In France in 1694, for example, the drop in the number of births below the prefamine norm was about six times the drop in marriages in the previous year. Reductions in the marriage

[23] Mokyr 1980, 246–49; Yao 1999; see also Razzaque 1988.

rate are likely to have been greatest in the lower socioeconomic groups, as in Bangladesh in 1974–75. In the wake of famines, marriages postponed during the crisis sometimes lead to a rebound in the marriage rate.[24]

There are several likely reasons for the decline in the birthrate. In the 1990s, nutritionists identified the link between the hormone leptin, which is lacking when food intake is low, and reproductive functioning. This sharpens the link proposed in the late 1970s by Rose Frisch between reduced body fat deposits and fecundity. Lower libido is also a likely factor. Testosterone levels depend on nutrition, and so are much lower in times of famine. One of those involved in the Minnesota Human Starvation Study, which used as test subjects conscientious objectors to military service during World War II, exclaimed after weeks of semi-starvation, "I have no more sexual feeling than a sick oyster." In blockaded Leningrad, scientist Elena Kochina continued to sleep next to her husband, but only because they had only one bed: "even through padded coats it's unpleasant for us to feel one another's touch."[25] This decline in libido had its compensation: it conserved energy better devoted to seeking food. In Ireland, the reduction in libido is reflected in the halving of the number of reported rapes in 1847–49 and, more poetically, in the line of a Kerry song saying that since the potato failed, "it was safe for young maidens to venture out alone." A further reason for a declining birthrate during famines is spousal separation: men are more likely to migrate to seek work (see chapter 3) or be fighting wars, and women more likely to migrate in order to beg.

[24] Lachiver 1991; Razzaque 1988.
[25] Keys et al. 1950, 2:839; Kochina 1990, 67.

The reduction in births in Athens between 1940 and 1942—from over twelve thousand to fewer than seven thousand—is striking, but the decline in births in besieged Leningrad in 1942 is probably unparalleled in history. The number of births recorded there dropped from 4,229 in January and 2,883 in February to a monthly average of only 86 in the last four months of the year. During 1942, the birthrate was 6.3 per thousand, or about one-quarter of the noncrisis norm. Moreover, during the first half of 1942 two-fifths of births were premature, and during the siege as a whole one delivery in four was stillborn or perished within a month.[26]

In the case of China in 1959–61, averted births are even harder to calculate than excess deaths, given the sizable fluctuations in births during the period straddling the crisis. As figure 4.1 makes plain, however, the recorded drop in births in 1960–61 was followed by an emphatic rebound in the following years. Births in 1962 exceeded those in any year since 1951, and in the following few years the birthrate was also higher than in any other year in the 1950s and 1960s. Indeed, the surplus over trend in 1962–65—insofar as any pattern can be detected from these data—far exceeded the deficit between 1959 and 1961. Should these births be left out of the account, should they be deemed births postponed at the height of the crisis, or was the rebound unrelated to the events of 1959–61?

A related effect concerns the sex ratio of births during famines. Since bearing males exacts a greater toll on mothers, and since malnourished infant males are less likely to survive than infant females, famines may, for physiological

[26] Stathakopoulos 2004, 161; Antonov 1947.

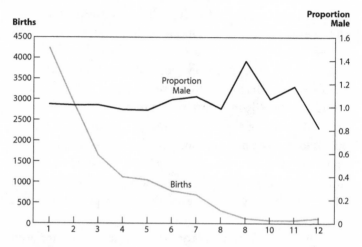

FIG. 4.3.   Leningrad, 1942: Total births and proportion male.

reasons, reduce the proportion of males born. In evolution-
ary terms, male fetuses could lose out because they require
more energy. Hard evidence on this issue is thin, though.
During the Leningrad siege-famine the proportion of females did not rise (see figure 4.3), although a recent study
of the long-term demographic impact of the Great Leap
Famine finds that it did in China in 1959–61.[27]

WHAT DO PEOPLE DIE OF DURING FAMINES?

The symptoms of some of the most common present-day
famine diseases—the swollen bellies and reddened hair of
protein-starved kwashiorkor victims, or the emaciated looks

[27] Cherepenina 2005, 60–61; Almond et al. 2007.

of children suffering from marasmus—are familiar from
the media. History is full of depictions of famine diseases
and their victims: "people [who] looked like they were from
Hades, while others looked like pregnant women" (Thessaloníki, AD 676–78), skin like "dirty parchment . . . drawn
tightly over the skeleton" (Ireland, 1847), young men "tot-
tering on their feet, and leaning on sticks as if ninety years
of age" (China, 1877), "lips that are mere skin, . . . eyes
glimmering dimly in hollow sockets" (India, 1896), children
"the colour of charred wood" (India, 1943), "puffy, glisten-
ing, albumen-coloured rubber balloon skins" (Bengal,
1943), and "skins sticking like paper to their skeletons while
the bones protruded out . . . body hair [sticking] out like
thick black pins all over their bodies" (India, 1943). Most of
these images refer to signs of starvation. Yet although the
lack of food is the ultimate reason for most famine mortality, infectious diseases rather than literal starvation account
for the majority of famine deaths.

Two broad classes of causes of death are responsible for
higher mortality during famines.[28] The first relates directly
to nutrition, and includes actual starvation. More often,
however, victims of this class succumb to nutritionally sensitive diseases brought on by impaired immunity, or poison-
ing from inferior or unfamiliar foods that would not have
been consumed in normal times. The second class is indirect, and relates to the disruption of personal life and the
societal breakdown resulting from the famine. It may stem
from increased mobility among the poor or the deterioration in personal hygiene as people grow weaker and more
despondent. Famines are also associated with outbreaks of

[28] Mokyr and Ó Gráda 2002.

seemingly unrelated diseases such as cholera, malaria, and influenza.

Das's graphic eyewitness account of the destitute living on Calcutta's streets in mid-1943 is apposite here. The victims that he and his assistants encountered had no regard for personal cleanliness. The prevalence of bowel complaints made them afraid of bathing, but bathing was pointless in any case, since they lacked a change of clothing. Their clothes accumulated the dirt of the streets; they answered calls of nature in alleyways and open spaces. Many relied on leaves to contain the gruel doled out in the public kitchens; this meant losing some, but they scooped up what they could from the pavement. Often they relied on contaminated rainwater for drinking; they ransacked trash cans and garbage heaps for leftovers. The rough, sometimes-unhusked *bajra* grain used in the gruel kitchens accentuated their bowel complaints.[29]

The Bengali famine and the Leningrad blockade-famine happened within a year of each other. The latter—the biggest ever in an industrialized economy—was the more intense of the two: about one-third of the city's population succumbed to it. Perhaps it would not have been so murderous had the Soviets airlifted more food in and moved more citizens out. But that was much easier said than done. One of the striking differences between the two famines is that although infectious diseases were responsible for most deaths in Bengal, few of Leningrad's 0.8 million or so victims perished of contagious diseases. This is all the more remarkable given that such diseases had been rampant in Russia during the famine of 1921–22, and endemic in

---

[29] Das 1949, 5–8.

nonfamine conditions. One of the first actions of the People's Commissariat of Public Health, established in 1918, was to make the notification of infectious diseases compulsory. Between 1918 and 1921 over six million cases were notified, and presumably many more were not. In Leningrad, seventy thousand cases of infectious disease in a population of less than one million were notified to the authorities. Yet little more than two decades later, according to the account of one *blokadnik,*

> How is the absence of epidemics to be explained, given conditions of acute hunger, shortage of hot water, lack of protection from cold weather, and physical weakness? Leningrad's experience proves that hunger need not be accompanied by the inseparable fellow travelers, infectious disease and epidemics. A good system of sanitation breaks down their comradeship, for not only during the winter months of 1941 but in the spring of 1942, when conditions were most favorable for outbreaks of disease, no epidemics occurred in Leningrad. The government set the people to cleaning streets, yards, staircases, garrets, cellars, sewer wells—in brief, all the breeding grounds where infectious disease might start. From the end of March to the middle of April, 300,000 persons worked daily cleaning up the city. Inspections of living quarters and compulsory observance of rules for cleanliness prevented the spread of communicable disease. The inhabitants were starving. Nonetheless, they fulfilled to their last days the social obligations necessary in a crowded community.[30]

[30] Pavlov 1965, 124–25.

Kochina, who also survived the blockade, noted in her diary the widespread presence of dystrophy on December 10, 1941, but a month later could still claim that there were no infectious diseases. The contrast with previous famines is indeed a striking one. The cold weather helped, given that the crisis was at its worst during winter 1941–42. As noted in Pavlov's account, patriotic zeal along with the energy and ruthless efficiency of the municipal authorities under Andrey Aleksandrovich Zhdanov were also factors. Zhdanov and the political leadership lived a little better than the people at large, but only a little better; many suffered permanent damage to their health. At the height of the famine, bronchopneumonia was diagnosed in three autopsies out of every four. Acute tuberculosis, scurvy, and pellagra were also present. Dysentery was inevitable, but there were only sporadic outbreaks of typhus and typhoid fever. Indeed, the numbers succumbing to typhoid fever, typhus, and dysentery—the classic famine diseases in temperate climates—were fewer in December 1941, at the height of the crisis, than in December 1940, before the blockade began.[31] Although the authorities managed somehow to keep the city free of infectious disease, the excess mortality was nonetheless enormous.

The success of the Leningrad authorities in keeping infectious diseases under control was replicated, although on a much smaller scale, in the Warsaw Ghetto, western Holland during the "hunger winter" of 1944–45, and Axis-occupied Greece.[32] As the death rate in the Warsaw Ghetto rose

---

[31] Kochina 1990, 52, 70; Salisbury [1969] 2000, 403; Brojek, Wells, and Keys 1946; table 4.1.

[32] Ó Gráda 1999, 99–101.

fourfold between 1940 and 1941–42, the proportion attributed to literal starvation shot up from 1 to 25 percent. Ironi-
cally, although the Nazis had created the ghetto in 1940 on
the false pretext of shielding the non-Jewish population
from typhus-infected Jews, the share of typhus in excess
mortality remained relatively small. Yitzhak Zuckerman, a
leader of the Jewish resistance, later reminisced, "People
often had high fever . . . [but] we had no cases of death from
typhus."[33] On the Greek island of Syros in 1941–42 over
seven deaths in ten were attributed to starvation, hunger
edema, and general exhaustion or wasting of the body. Only
5 percent of deaths was attributed to gastro causes. Typhus
and typhoid fever hardly registered at all. There was free
vaccination against typhus, and the overall hygiene situation was good.[34] The share of typhus in excess mortality in
the western Netherlands in 1944–45 was also small.

A striking feature of conditions in the Netherlands before the *Hungerwinter* of 1944–45 is that despite the high
population density and the nonavailability of imports, the
Dutch fared relatively well in terms of food and well-being
until September 1944. Neither the birthrate nor the death
rate was affected. But popular memory of the war is heavily
conditioned by events in the western Netherlands in the
eight months or so before liberation in April–May 1945. By
the end of the war, half of the women in that part of the
country had stopped menstruating, and the average weight
loss was about 15 to 20 percent. The estimates of the total
number of deaths range from sixteen to twenty thousand
out of a national population of over nine million. In this

[33] Zuckerman 1993, 494–95.
[34] Hionidou 2006, 190–219.

TABLE 4.1
Number of cases of disease in Leningrad,
December 1940 and 1941

Disease	Dec. 1940	Dec. 1941
Typhoid fever	143	114
Dysentery	2,086	1,778
Typhus	118	42
Scarlet fever	1,056	93
Diphtheria	728	211
Whooping cough	1,844	818

Source: Pavlov 1965, 124 (from a report of the
Leningrad Health Service, January 5 1942)

"modern" famine, in which infectious diseases were largely
kept at bay, infants and elderly males without family support suffered the most.[35]

The pattern described applies to modern famines occurring in relatively developed economies in abnormal conditions. Even before 1939, both the Dutch population and the
Jews of Warsaw were almost entirely literate; they had access to clean running water for drinking and washing, sufficient changes of clothing and bedding to ward off lice, and
stone housing that was relatively easy to keep clean; they
also had good cooking facilities for what food there was,
and received good medical advice. Measures that prevented

[35] Trienekens 2000.

the spread of infectious disease had become part of their daily routine, and must have continued to do so during the war. Unlike the Russians in 1918–22 and Bengalis in 1943–44, they were able to use the preventive measures implied by the findings of Louis Pasteur and Robert Koch.

Meanwhile, in sub-Saharan Africa, infectious diseases remain endemic in noncrisis years, and they still increase the death toll from famines.[36] In the emergency refugee camps of eastern Sudan in 1985, children aged less than five years were severely undernourished, but they were more likely to succumb to measles, diarrhea/dysentery, respiratory infections, and malaria than to starvation. Malnutrition and disease increased in these refugees after they arrived at the camps. In 1985, there were epidemics of cholera in Somalia and Ethiopia; in the Sudan, "acute gastroenteritis" and "001" were the official euphemisms for the same disease.[37]

It follows that the causes of death from famines in sub-Saharan Africa today have much more in common with Ireland in the 1840s or India in the 1890s than with famine-affected regions of Europe in the 1940s. Why is this so? Part of the answer is the cost of medical care: extreme poverty is responsible for children catching deadly diseases even when their parents are familiar with the modes of transmission simply because they cannot afford the minimal needs for prevention. Thus, in Thane, near Bombay, a woman who had already lost two children through waterborne illnesses pointed out that "to boil water consistently would cost the equivalent of US$4.00 in kerosene"—a third

---

[36] Salama et al. 2001; Waldman 2001.

[37] Shears et al. 1987; http://www.davidheiden.org/dust.htm (accessed September 7, 2007).

of her annual income.[38] Another part of the answer must be that while knowledge may have spread at least to medical personnel and officials, behavioral patterns and consumption were subject to a great deal of inertia. It is not enough for people in some sense to "know" what causes disease; they have to be *persuaded* to change their behavior. Even more important is that the associated remedies must have been difficult to effect in the existing crisis conditions. In sub-Saharan Africa, the world's main remaining famine-prone region, infectious and parasitic diseases alone are still responsible for nearly half of all deaths even in normal times, with diarrheal diseases accounting for nearly one in four of those. Another 13 percent are due to respiratory diseases. In Asia (excluding China) the same categories account for about one-third of all deaths.[39] In other words, in such places these diseases are endemic; little wonder, then, that they dominate during famines. Much mortality in both Africa and Asia—both in crisis and noncrisis times—could be prevented by low-cost primary health care such as immunization, prophylactics, and rehydration. In these underdeveloped areas, however, public health lags behind rather than leads medical science.[40]

In demographic terms, the Soviet famine of 1931–33 may have marked the beginning of a transition from "traditional" to "modern" insofar as the main causes of death were concerned. Traditionally, famine brought a disproportionate increase in deaths from infectious diseases. Yet in the Soviet case, while there was a big rise in recorded cases

---

[38] Bryceson 1977, 111.
[39] Murray and Lopez 1994.
[40] Mokyr and Ó Gráda 2002.

of typhus and typhoid fever, the *proportion* of all deaths due to infectious diseases was lower in 1933 (the first year in which the data were recorded) than in the immediate wake of the crisis in 1934.[41]

It is commonplace to argue that famines nowadays are rarely the product of food supply declines alone.[42] The ready availability—at a price, of course—of medical technology to prevent and treat infectious diseases such as typhus and dysentery compounds the anachronistic character of present-day famine. Even before the widespread availability of prophylactics, the revolution in hygiene spawned by Pasteur and Koch changed the character of famine mortality in different parts of Europe during World War II. In contrast, as noted above, even today much of sub-Saharan Africa has yet to undergo this "epidemiological transition."

Historical demographer Massimo Livi-Bacci observes that "in those cases where social organization, though sorely tried, nevertheless survives, increased mortality is imputable above all to the 'direct and final' consequences of starvation rather than to epidemic attacks."[43] While this is so, a better generalization might be that in places where infectious disease is endemic in normal times, it wreaks havoc during famines. Hence, measles is a big killer during modern famines in sub-Saharan Africa, since vaccination is lacking. The degree of "social organization" depends on economic development.

Moreover, the incidence of the different causes of death is likely to vary by age and gender. In Ireland in the 1840s,

[41] Wheatcroft 1983; Davies and Wheatcroft 2004, 430–31; Adamets 2002, 171–72.

[42] Sen 1981.

[43] Livi-Bacci 1991, 47.

nearly half of all reported deaths from starvation and one-third of deaths from diarrhea/dysentery were of children aged less than ten years, compared to only one-fifth of those succumbing to "fever." Females accounted for 50.4 percent of cholera victims and 47.1 percent of those dying of fever, but only 42.7 percent of those dying of diarrhea/dysentery and 41.4 percent of those who starved to death. In the case of northwestern England in the late sixteenth and early seventeenth centuries, Andrew Appleby inferred from the population age structure and seasonality of burials from local parish registers that the excess mortality in 1587–88 was mainly due to typhus, whereas in 1597–98 and 1623 most famine deaths were caused by starvation, not disease.[44]

During the Great Irish Famine, the graver the crisis, the higher was the incidence of starvation and dysentery/diarrhea, and the more likely they were to have been the proximate causes of death. Further, although the incidence of fever increased sharply in the worst hit regions, the proportion of famine deaths due to fever tended to be fairly constant across the island.

Little is known about the mechanics of mortality in China in 1959–61. Before 1949, infectious diseases "plagued the country and threatened many lives." In Frank Notestein's study of a large sample of rural Chinese households in 1929–31, of the five most important causes of death (out of sixteen) on which information was sought were smallpox, dysentery, typhoid, tuberculosis, and cholera (in that order).[45] Table 4.3, based on a study of Yunnan Province in southwestern China in the early 1940s, implies that infectious

[44] Appleby 1978.
[45] Notestein 1938.

TABLE 4.2
Main causes of excess deaths in Ireland in
the 1840s (%)

Cause	Ulster	Connacht
Hunger sensitive:	20.2	26.5
Dysentery/Diarrhea	11.8	16.3
Starvation	2.4	5.2
Dropsy	2.3	1.9
Marasmus	3.8	3.2
Partially sensitive:	49.7	40.4
Consumption	10.0	5.8
Others	39.7	34.5
Not very sensitive:	30.1	33.1
Fever	19.3	23.7
Cholera	2.3	3.7
Infirmity, old age	8.5	5.7
Total	100.0	100.0

diseases then played as big a role in Yunnan as they did in
Ireland on the eve of the Great Irish Famine. Perhaps the
most striking differences are the much smaller proportion of
prefamine Irish deaths attributed to dysentery/diarrhea
and cholera.

TABLE 4.3
Main causes of death in Ireland in 1840 and Yunnan
Province, China, in 1940–44 (% of total)

Cause	Ireland, 1840	Yunnan, 1940–44
Smallpox	4.35	6.73
Dysentery/diarrhea	1.04	14.09
Cholera	0.19	11.97
Fever (incl. Typhoid)	12.69	12.08
Other infectious (incl. measles, scarlet fever)	12.36	6.66
Convulsions	5.00	7.25
Coronary, respiratory	15.23	12.66
Digestive	11.44	5.54
Infirmity, old age	19.08	6.16
Total violent and sudden (incl. external)	3.32	2.32
Other and unspecified	15.25	14.44
Total	100.0	100.0

Sources: Mokyr and Ó Gráda 2002, table 1; Chen 1946, tables 25
and 26

Although Yunnan was relatively poor even by Chinese
standards, the comparison suggests that infectious diseases
should also have bulked large in 1959–61. Yet popular accounts of the Great Leap Forward famine emphasize starvation rather than disease. By implication the Chinese famine

of 1959–61 was, like those in Leningrad, the western Netherlands, and Greece during World War II, a modern famine
in terms of a marked transition: proportionately far fewer
victims died of infectious diseases than in 1917–22. Could
the Maoist campaigns to improve water quality and personal hygiene as well as impose mass inoculation against
infectious disease have had such a dramatic effect within
the space of a few years, thereby altering the causes of
death during the 1959–61 famine? A graphic and unset-
tling account of conditions in Fenyang in Anhui during
the famine refers to *e si* (death by starvation); other accounts
refer to dropsy (i.e., hunger edema) and hepatitis (probably linked to the consumption of unhealthy or contaminated foods), but do not mention classic famine-related epidemics.[46] But the issue surely requires further dispassionate
investigation.

LONG-TERM IMPACTS

Famines often wreaked demographic devastation in the
short run, but what of their long-term impact? Let us consider their broad economic impact first. Because famines
usually leave nonhuman inputs relatively unscathed, they are
likely to shift income distribution in labor's favor. Farmers
in turn are prompted to shift away from labor-intensive to
more land-intensive cultivation and output. This is what
happened in England in the wake of the Black Death; the
rise in the land-labor ratio led to higher wages and reductions in crop yields per acre. In Ireland after the 1840s,
these adjustments were accentuated by the persistence of

[46] Bernstein 1983; Ó Gráda 2008.

emigration after the famine and the rise of livestock prices relative to those of grain. Still, where population recovers in the wake of famine, the effects just described are unlikely to be permanent.

History suggests that malnutrition and disease in so-called normal times were more potent positive checks on population growth in the long run than the Third Horseman. One reason for this is that famines were probably not frequent enough to fulfill their Malthusian mission. A second is that famines offered no more than an ephemeral "remedy" to overpopulation unless survivors "learned" from the tragedy that they had escaped, since the resultant demographic vacuum would quickly be filled. In the case of Qing China, Malthus himself conceded that famines "produce[d] but a trifling effect on the average population."[47]

Recent scholarship tends to downplay the demographic impact of famine in the longer run.[48] Despite histories of enormous excess famine mortality, famine had little apparent impact on demographic trends in India, China, or the Soviet Union. Even in post-1850 Ireland, emigration rather than hunger was decisive in keeping population from rising again, and the rate of natural increase in the wake of the crisis was highest in those regions worst hit by famine. The collapses in the birthrates of Russia and Europe today are having a much greater demographic impact than the famines of the past. The populations of Africa and India are still growing robustly despite past famines; that India's population grew twice as fast in 1900–1940 as it had grown in 1860–1900 was only in part due to the attenuation of

[47] Malthus 1872, 255.
[48] Menken and Watkins 1985; Fogel 2004.

famine mortality. Finally, China's one-child policy has had a much bigger impact on population trends than the series of famines that came to an end with the disaster of 1959–61.

Nonetheless, it would be rash to deny entirely the claims made over two centuries ago by pioneering Swiss demographer Johann Heinrich Waser:

> The crisis caused by pestilence can be compensated within a decade. Damages caused by famine and starvation have had more severe consequences, however, because after those catastrophes the impoverished, worn-out and discouraged people are in want of the dearest necessities of life and will need years to recover. Whoever is not in the highest degree careless will think twice before he gets married, and due to the fact that children will not be considered the blessing of God but rather a burden of married life, the population will increase very slowly.[49]

Waser would have understood the well-known reluctance of the postfamine Irish to marry. The catastrophe of the 1840s supposedly taught them to strive for higher living standards through an end to the subdivision of farms, and marrying later and less. Smaller farms, instead of being divided up, were sold off or else passed on to neighboring relations. The shift allegedly exacted a price in increasing intrafamilial tensions as brothers competed for farms, and their sisters for dowries. There is evidence, certainly, of a decline in nuptiality as well as increasing emigration and literacy— proxies for "modernization." Yet such a "shock therapy"

---

[49] Cited in Braun 1978, 324.

interpretation of postfamine Ireland does not square with all the evidence; in particular, the propensity to marry was slowest to change in Ireland's poorest counties. There is tentative evidence, too, of a preventive check at work in eighteenth-century Finland through higher proportions of men and women never marrying.[50]

There is stronger evidence, in the recent past at least, of the prudential demographic response highlighted by Waser. Family planning programs in India and Bangladesh were given fillips by the famines of 1943–44 and 1974–75, respectively. In drought-prone northern Ethiopia, it is claimed that growing ecological stress and food insecurity prompted shifts, at least for a time, in the demographic behaviors and attitudes of farming communities in the 1980s and 1990s. These included a significant increase in the acceptance rates of family planning services; changing attitudes toward early marriage and having a large number of children; an actual reduction in fertility; increased out-migration (particularly by young people); and an increasing involvement on the part of farmers in activities generating income outside of agriculture.[51]

The impact of famine on the health and life expectancy of surviving cohorts has been the focus of a considerable medical literature in the recent past.[52] There is increasing evidence of a close link between health and nutrition in utero and in infancy, on the one hand, and adult health and longevity, on the other. This implies that famines should have

[50] Connell 1968; Walsh 1970.
[51] Caldwell 1998, 693; Ezra 1997; compare Hill 1989.
[52] See, for example, Barker 1992.

long-term demographic and health effects.[53] A pioneering
1976 study comparing birth cohorts in and outside the area
affected by the Dutch *Hungerwinter* found that deprivation
during the last trimester of pregnancy and in the first three
months after birth reduced the risk of obesity in adult
males, while deprivation in the first trimester increased
adult male obesity rates. A more recent Dutch study focusing
on women found a significantly increased risk of obesity in
the daughters of women pregnant during the crisis. The
children of women who were pregnant during the famine were also more likely to develop late-onset diabetes, resulting in an imbalance of blood sugars. Yet another recent
Dutch study suggests that women exposed to malnutrition
as children are now at increased risk from breast cancer.
This finding does not square with the received wisdom that
reduced food intake (up to a point) cuts the risk of cancer,
prompting the researchers to speculate that the famine
might have disturbed hormonal factors in young females.
Recent analyses of the impact of fetal malnutrition in Leningrad on the risk of heart disease later in life found that
starvation, or the stress that accompanied it, particularly at
the onset of or during puberty, led to an increased vulnerability to cardiovascular disease in later life.[54] Research in

[53] True, the evidence is not all one-way. A major study of the Finnish
famine of 1868 found no difference between the life expectancies of cohorts born before, during, and after the crisis, concluding that malnutrition before birth and during infancy was unlikely to be "crucial" to adult
health (Kannisto, Christensen, and Vaupel 1997), while a recent study of
people born during the Dutch Hungerwinter of 1944–45 could establish
no connection between exposure to famine conditions and life expectancy
to age fifty-seven years (Painter et al. 2005).

[54] Ravelli, Stein, and Susser 1976; Elias et al. 2004; Stanner et al. 1997;
Sparén et al. 2004; Lumey 1998.

Saint Petersburg—where famine was more intense in 1941–43 than in either the Netherlands in 1944–45 or even China in 1959–61—indicates that the siege reduced the life expectancy of children who survived it, with an increased incidence of arteriosclerotal damage being the main contributory factor.[55]

There is also some evidence that being conceived at the height of famines increases the likelihood of suffering from mental illness in later life. A study of children born in the Netherlands during and after the *Hungerwinter* found that the incidence of schizophrenia was much higher in those conceived when the crisis was at its peak. The incidence of neural tube defects among this cohort was over twice as high (3.9 per thousand versus 1.7 per thousand) as for those born between August and October 1945. A much larger study of subjects born before, during, and after the 1959–61 famine in the badly affected Wuhu region of China's Anhui Province has also found that children conceived during the crisis stood a much higher risk of schizophrenia. Among those conceived at the height of the famine, the risk more than doubled (from 0.8 percent in 1959 to 2 percent in 1960–61). Why this outcome occurred is not clear; attributing it to exposure to toxic foods such as tree bark and tulip bulbs is pure speculation.[56]

Being conceived or born during famines also seems to affect expected height in adulthood. The impact of famine on the height of Leningrad children is evident in figure 4.4. Boys aged between ten and thirteen years in 1945 were about eight centimeters shorter than boys of the same age

[55] Sparén et al. 2004; Khoroshinina 2005, 208.
[56] St. Clair et al. 2005.

cm

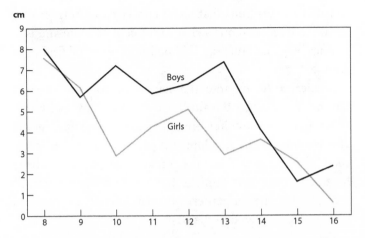

FIG. 4.4. Height "loss" of boys and girls in besieged Leningrad, 1945 versus 1939.
Source: Kozlov and Samsonova 2005.

in 1939; the gap for girls was less, but still substantial. The gap is all the more striking given the likelihood of a selection survival effect in favor of stronger children. Similarly, those born in Germany in the wake of World War II who endured hardships had a significant effect on their height in adulthood.[57] A recent study by two Chinese scholars suggests that the adult heights of those exposed to famine conditions in utero or shortly after they were born in China in 1959–61 were over an inch (three centimeters) less than they might have been otherwise.[58] The negative implications for health and life expectancy may be imagined. Yet another recent study of the long-run consequences of Great Leap Famine based on the 1 percent sample of the Chinese

---

[57] Kozlov and Samsonova 2005; Greil 1998.
[58] Chen and Zhou 2007; see also Cai and Feng 2005.

census of 2000 finds that being conceived or born during the famine reduced one's chances of being literate and economically successful in adulthood, and even of finding a spouse.[59]

Medical research into the long-term consequences of famine leaves open the further disturbing possibility that extreme malnutrition in utero or in early childhood adversely affected the mental development of those at risk. It is too soon to generalize from the tentative results of analyses based on a few recent famines, but the studies just described indicate that the longer-term human cost of famines has been underestimated in the past.

[59] Almond et al. 2007.

Chapter V

Markets and Famines

Everything is in plenty, everything is dear.

—*Remark overheard in Antioch, AD 362*

In times of crisis, mass opinion both educated and uneducated, likes to picture a small collection of scapegoats, a few enemies of society who should be "hanged on the lamp posts." This is a comforting view for society in general to take when the faults of society are shared by the majority of its members.

—*Leonard Pinnell, Bengal, 1943*

PROFITEERS

How food markets function during famines is both a sensitive and fraught subject. Do markets exacerbate or mitigate hardship? There is a view, associated in particular with maverick historian Karl Polanyi (1886–1964) that links market forces with the breakup of the social contract that bound ruler and ruled in precapitalist communities. Under feudalism, Polanyi argued, noblesse oblige had prompted the regulation of markets in order to prevent famines whereas under capitalism, markets were allowed free reign and "the people could not be prevented from starving according to the rules of the game."[1] An alternative generalization, more

[1] Polanyi [1944] 1957, 160.

widely accepted today, is that the authorities could not rely on markets to remove disequilibria speedily in "precapitalist" economies, where information was slow to travel and communications expensive. Nor were Polanyi's precapitalist economies famine free—far from it. The deregulation that he criticized occurred only when the ruling elites felt that it was safe to allow markets to replace traditional safeguards.[2]

Polanyi, of course, articulated the age-old suspicion that in times of famine or threatened famine, at least part of the blame rested on producers and traders in essential foodstuffs. Popular suspicions of merchants as profiteers and hoarders led to the pervasive sense that they benefited from free markets. Stories about how traders manipulated markets against the poor during famines are legion. As long ago as AD 362–63, the Roman emperor Julian accused the wealthy citizens of Antioch of creating a famine in a city where "everything is in plenty, everything is dear." Similar accusations were made against several citizens of Rheims in 1693 who held "large quantities of grain in their barns which they refused to expose to sale," and against "millionaire grain barons" in the Sudan in 1985 who, aided and abetted by corrupt officials, hoarded grain during that year's famine. William Laud's pithy judgment, referring to a near famine in England in 1632, that "this last yeares famin was made by man and not by God," was aimed at such miscreants.[3] Historian Stephen Kaplan eloquently describes popular feeling about the supply of food during famine, or at

---

[2] Persson 1999.
[3] Cited in Walter and Wrightson 1976, 31.

least during its early stages, in the following statement about hunger riots in mid-eighteenth-century France:

> In most of the cases the rioters, men and women, blamed their distress first of all on the merchant: anyone engaged, professionally or opportunistically, in the traffic of grain. The fact that the harvest might be patently bad or the supply notoriously short in a given area no more justified the maneuvers of the traders than it made the concomitant rises palatable. . . . Even in the midst of obvious scarcity, the consumers of each village, bourg, and town believed that if the grain "of the place" were properly used and honestly apportioned, there would be enough, albeit barely, for everyone at prices which would be onerous but accessible.[4]

In Ireland in the 1840s, the press was replete with accounts in the same vein. Thus, in October 1846 the *Waterford Freeman* claimed that "merchants [were] closing their stores, already counting their gains, and gloating over the misery by which they hope to enrich themselves." Some months earlier around Loughrea it was "well known that speculators have made large purchase of oats, and are overholding oat-meal in store at Galway to raise the price of that article, and realize exorbitant profits." In Westmeath, "1s 6d a stone [was being] demanded," while "in the large village of Portroe the provision dealers [were] charging £1–4–0 for a cwt. of oatmeal with two securities—and 20 percent for every day the notes remain unpaid after being due." In Carlow in January 1847, it was alleged that "the millers and

---

[4] Kaplan 1976, 192.

dealers united to spread alarm among the farmers to in-
duce them to bring their grain to market, which they were
always holding back in hopes of higher prices."[5]

In *De Officiis* (written in 44 BC), the Roman writer Cicero describes a trader from Rhodes who has imported a
large cargo of grain from Alexandria during a famine. The
trader knows that other traders have done likewise, but the
Rhodians don't know this yet, so should he in the meantime charge them "fabulous prices"?[6] It would be a surprise
if he did not; throughout history, merchants have combined
greed and deception—when they could. Histories of famine
often feature stories such as that of powerful rice merchants
who spread misinformation about the weather in eighteenth-
century China, usurers in western India in 1860 who allegedly engaged sorcerers to prevent the rains from falling, or
wealthy cultivators around Hubli in Maharashtra in 1896–97
whose barns were amply stocked, but who concealed their
grain, and sent their dependents to the nearest relief works.
Where information was thin and the poor ignorant, it is not
hard to imagine that merchants and large-scale producers
took advantage of their superior knowledge whenever
possible.[7]

The same themes frequently recur in literary allusions to
famine. A villainous character in Ben Johnson's *Every Man
Out of His Humour* (1599) speculates on "rotten weather,"
holding back his stocks of grain as the aggregate supply di-
minishes, and then "makes prices as he lists." He fools the

[5] Ó Gráda 1999, 135.

[6] Cicero 1913, Book 3 [50].

[7] In the case of the trader from Rhodes, it is market imperfections that
count.

public by being seen visiting the market almost daily, buying wheat for household use. Compassion for the starving poor is not part of his way of making a living: "he that will thrive, must think no course vile." William Shakespeare's *Macbeth* (1606) describes a drunken porter who dreams of opening the gates of hell for the "farmer that hanged himself on the expectation of plenty." In Ireland, both William Carleton's *Black Prophet* and Liam O'Flaherty's *House of Gold* feature reviled grain merchants who brag about having kept the poor alive in times of famine.[8] In Alessandro Manzoni's *I Promessi Sposi* (*The Betrothed*), a character in the street complains at the height of a famine in Milan in 1629–30, "There's no famine at all really. . . . It's profiteers, cornering the market." "And bakers," adds his companion, "hiding their stocks of grain. Hanging is the only thing for them." People rush to the bakers demanding bread at the (low) decreed price; the bakers protest, caught between the decree and the rising costs. Manzoni's hero, the gullible Renzo, joins the rioters in Milan and is lucky to escape with his life.[9]

Interventions by those in power on behalf of consumers only lent further credence to the age-old suspicion that the producers and traders exacerbated famines by hoarding or exporting their foodstuffs. Whether the accusations reported above are fictional or not, they represent the popular conviction that but for the merchant-speculator, there would be enough food to tide everyone over the crisis. Throughout the ages governments, bowing to popular pressure, have felt forced to intervene. Big price fluctuations were a threat

---

[8] Carleton [1847] 1972; O'Flaherty 1929.
[9] Manzoni 1972, 106–7.

to public order, and price stability therefore had a public good aspect to it. In ancient Rome, politicians courted popularity by supplying grain to the citizenry at below cost—or even free—and promising to eliminate "artificial" shortages. The tradition was continued into the early modern era by the Roman *annona*, which aimed at ensuring the city a regular supply of bread. This entailed keeping prices relatively high in times of plenty, in order to keep them low when the harvest failed. Many other cities adopted variants of this strategy of storage and trade restrictions. Such measures may have insulated urban consumers to some extent, but at a considerable cost in output foregone in the countryside. The most extreme version of such regulations is probably the *maximum général* forced through in 1793 by the sansculottes, the working-class radicals then virtually in charge of the city of Paris. This entailed controlling the prices of all commodities deemed necessities. The measure (further discussed below), which lasted for a year and brought legal trading in foodstuffs virtually to a halt, was backed by the threat of the guillotine against those who profiteered in the eyes of the law.[10]

Although the *annona* and the maximum général represented attempts by those in power at preventing famine, another common strand in the people's complaints describes the ruling classes as the beneficiaries of famine. Hence, to cite only three examples separated by space and time: in Kashmir in AD 917–18, the rivers swelled with corpses even as "the king's ministers and his guards became wealthy, as they sold stores of rice at high prices"; in Iran in 1870–72, "senior bureaucrats, landlords, grain dealers and high-ranking

---

[10] Virlouvet 1985; Reinhardt 1991; Aftalion 1990.

religious officials who engaged in hoarding and market manipulation" were blamed for famine; and in Malawi in 2002, trading cartels linked to the political elite were accused of large-scale embezzlement and price-fixing.[11]

The danger to order and stability was greatest in the towns, and so regulation rose in line with urbanization. Since ancient times, towns relied on public warehouses, price controls, prohibitions against hoarding, barriers to entry during crises, and export prohibitions to generate supplies in times of famine. Convinced that speculation was the source of all trouble in AD 362–63, Roman emperor Julian imposed price controls. When the scarcity persisted he imported grain from nearby cities, but this seems to have been purchased by merchants who resold it outside Rome at a higher price. In Thessaloníki in AD 676–78, the authorities ordered that houses suspected of concealing grain be entered and searched—as would happen again in Bengal in 1943.[12]

The list of rulers who sought to mitigate famine by controlling the trade in foodstuffs stretches from ancient times to Ethiopia's Dergue in the 1980s. Long before the annona, in pharaonic Egypt (where the dry climate eased the problems of storage) and Han China (ca. 200 BC) public granaries were used as a defense against famine. In ancient Rome, the *curator annonae* also held stores of grain but relied on rented storage space. The post-1664 Manchu Qing dynasty built up an elaborate system of granaries in China, managed directly by the state. The authorities also encouraged gentry- and community-operated granaries in places

[11] Okazaki 1986, 192.
[12] Stathakopoulos 2004, 356.

where the resources required to operate them existed. The system was subject to abuse by corrupt officials, and moreover, grain storage on a large scale was always inherently difficult and costly. In Russia, Alexander I and Nicholas I sought unsuccessfully to eradicate famine (in 1822 and 1834, respectively) by creating a system of granaries, to be filled in good years and emptied in bad.

In 1693 Louis XIV's secretary of state, Count Pontchartrain, employed a different strategy, seeking to prevent middlemen from making "futures" grain purchases, and barring merchants and bulk purchasers from attending the market before a certain hour. Pontchartrain prohibited exports and subsidized long-distance trade within France. During the European famine of 1816–18, the second-to-last to straddle several European borders, prohibitions or restrictions against grain exports were also common. As always, the aim was to alleviate hunger by attempting to increase supplies and force prices down. The ban did little for those with no purchasing power, and the balkanization of markets prevented food from moving to the worst-affected areas. Thus, the controls imposed by some Swiss cantons prevented grain from moving to famine-threatened highland zones, which were forced to import from farther afield at a higher cost. Some cantons faced mass starvation as a result, while in others prices hardly rose. In 1936, famine in Henan was exacerbated by the failure of the civil authorities to allow corn across the boundary that separated the area under their control from that controlled by Mao's Communists. In Kenya in the early 1980s, balkanized grain markets almost led to famine.

Finally, under Ethiopia's Dergue small-scale traders feared for their safety because the actions of a handful of leading traders in shifting grain from the famine-stricken Wollo Province into Addis Ababa had made all middlemen scapegoats for the famine of 1974. The Dergue targeted grain merchants as class enemies, executing many in front of village crowds in the provinces. Within a decade of the revolution, the number of grain dealers had fallen from twenty to thirty thousand to less than five thousand.[13] The campaign against merchants and middlemen seriously constrained the functioning of markets into the 1980s, and may have contributed to the 1984–85 famine.

Sometimes, rulers opted to encourage rather than restrict trade. In Edessa, "[the governor] gave an order than every one who chose might make bread and sell it in the market. And there came Jewish women, to whom he gave wheat from the public granary . . . and they made bread for the market." In AD 1024, the inhabitants of a famine-stricken town on the Volga "bought bread from the Bolgars." In AD 1316, a year of extreme famine, the English king guaranteed the safety of merchants from Genoa and Venice who brought corn from southern Italy, while in AD 1534 Rome avoided out-and-out famine with the help of grain imported from as far away as Picardy and Brittany.[14]

FRENCH *ÉCONOMISTES* AND ADAM SMITH

The intellectual case for unfettered markets as a means of alleviating rather than exacerbating famine was first widely articulated in eighteenth-century France. Writers such as

---

[13] de Waal 1997, 111.

[14] Drèze and Sen 1989, 138–46, 152–58; Wright 1882, 30b; Lucas 1930, 371–72; Sorokin [1922] 1975, 179; Bullard 1982, 281–82.

Claude-Jacques Herbert in the 1750s and A.R.J. Turgot in the 1760s led the charge, claiming that a prohibition on exports made French grain prices too low and variable, resulting in an underperforming farm sector. Free entry into a liberalized grain trade would arbitrage away any resultant excess profits. Competition between merchants would also eliminate excessive price differentials between different markets (as stipulated by the Law of One Price, which will be discussed below) and minimize seasonal fluctuations. Differences in geography and climate offered trading economies a form of insurance against harvest failures: *les accidents se compensent entre les royaumes* (shocks cancel one another out across kingdoms).[15] Supply shocks were bound to produce deviations from the normal price, but market forces were the surest way of minimizing them. Merchants, who bought when prices were low and sold when they were high, reduced seasonal price variations. State intervention, on the contrary, was more likely to produce uncertainty and speculative bubbles.

The *économistes* shifted the focus of public policy from consumer protection to creating incentives for producers to increase production, which would—in the end—benefit consumers as well. They placed their faith instead in Richard Cantillon's *"entrepreneurs"* and Turgot's *"négociants,"* just as English-speaking pro-marketeers would in Adam Smith's "inland traders," and David Ricardo's "patient, plodding, calculating merchants." Despite the radicalism of their project—a complete liberalization of a hitherto tightly regulated grain trade—it met with some legislative success from

---

[15] Persson 1999, 8 and chapter 1 passim.

the 1760s on. In France in 1763 and 1764, internal barriers to trade were abolished and foreign trade was partly liberalized. Yet a series of bad harvests led to the traditional pattern of popular unrest and the postponement of that Enlightenment project.

As governor of the Limousin (1761–74), Turgot—the most powerful and coherent exponent of the new liberalism—continued to encourage the free trade in corn. When placed in charge of the French economy in 1774, he immediately deregulated the trade in grain and flour. Within a year, however, he was relying on the king's troops to quell widespread riots against high prices and grain exports. The repression cost Turgot his popularity, and he was dismissed in 1776. For a few more decades, whenever crisis threatened, economic theory was powerless in the face of calls for direct action. Still, in due course, its logic led to deregulation. Strict regulation eventually gave way to pragmatic reliance on markets in most of Europe.

In France, the issue continued to be widely debated in the decades before the revolution, and the view that free trade in grain mitigated the damage done by famine was gaining in influence. The revolutionaries of 1789 established free trade in grain, but in September 1793, under pressure from the Parisian sansculottes, the radicals in control of the Paris Commune imposed price controls on food and other necessities. The maximum général led to huge queues outside shops, which were soon emptied of supplies. With shopkeepers reluctant or unable to restock, empty shelves and black markets were inevitable. As the crisis intensified, the Commune leadership claimed that only the threat of the guillotine would force the hand of hoarders; others accused legislators in turn of being part of a "foreign plot" to starve Paris. The guillotinings of the more moderate Georges-Jacques Danton (April 5, 1794) and the radical Maximilien Robespierre (July 27, 1794) were both linked to the political struggles generated by the food crisis. Some historians blame the famine of 1794 for the removal of the maximum général after Robespierre's downfall; Richard Cobb held that the death rates of the period indicted the free market policies introduced in the wake of Robespierre's overthrow. Others contend that, on the contrary, the maximum général was deterring farmers from growing the corn that the bakers needed to produce bread.[16]

Smith addressed the problem of famine in book 4 of *The Wealth of Nations*. He blamed (wrongly, as it happens) the catastrophic famine of 1770 in Bengal and Bihar on the meddlesome policies of the East India Company, and counseled confidence in the grain trader as the best palliative for a dearth or harvest failure. Smith believed that free markets minimized the inconveniences of dearths by ensuring both intertemporal and interregional arbitrage. Corn merchants were best placed "to divide the inconveniencies of [a scarcity] as equally as possible through all the different months, and weeks, and days of the year."[17] Their optimal selling strategy would be to even out consumption over the harvest year; those who hoarded supplies too long would be forced to sell at a loss. Moreover, by reallocating grain from areas in relative surplus to those in relative deficit, the market mechanism is likely to produce a net reduction in the damage done by any harvest failure.

Edmund Burke's *Thoughts and Details on Scarcity*, presented in a draft form to British prime minister William

----

[16] Aftalion 1990, 170.
[17] Smith [1776] 1976, 533–34. See also Rothschild 2001.

Pitt in November 1795, was another influential tract in the transition toward freer markets. Written at a time when grain prices were high and worries about a French invasion widespread, Burke seems to have intended to publish *Thoughts* in the form of letters addressed to English agronomist Arthur Young, but it appeared posthumously in 1800. In anticipation of Malthus and against the radical thinker Tom Paine, Burke—by this time a rather reactionary thinker— argued that poor relief in times of famine was not the responsibility of politicians: "the people maintain them, and not they the people." Statesmen might prevent evil, but they could do "very little positive good in this, or perhaps in any thing else." Tampering with food markets even in normal times was risky, claimed Burke; doing so during a famine, when tempers are high and suspicions run deep, was "always the worst." Burke also condemned the age-old remedy of state or municipal granaries as costly, and liable to result in waste and corruption.[18]

In *The Question of Scarcity Plainly Stated*, prompted by the near famine of 1799–1800, Young argued that the harvest shortfall was "great and real [and] a very high price a necessary consequence," against critics who blamed artificial manipulation by hoarders and speculators.[19] But Young, a defender of the landed interest, did not fully trust merchants' judgment in the matter of predicting the size of the harvest, and as secretary of the Board of Agriculture urged the necessity of a national agricultural census.

Europeans did not have a monopoly on the case for deregulation, though. Several officials in mid-eighteenth-century China objected to state meddling with the grain market.

[18] Burke [1795] 1960, paragraph 4.4.17.
[19] Young 1800.

In the late 1740s, the governor-general of Guangdong and Guangxi criticized measures such as price ceilings (which he believed would result in higher prices due to the cost of evading them), pressuring hoarders (which would reduce the stores necessary for later in the agricultural season), and preventing peasants from using grain as collateral when seeking loans. Such criticisms betrayed a fair understanding of market forces; their articulation is perhaps less surprising, given recent research suggesting that Chinese markets were no less integrated than European ones at this juncture.[20]

Although most promarketeers focused on the short-run effects of deregulation, some also held that it reduced the likelihood of famine in the long run. This was because the regional specialization resulting from free trade would increase the aggregate output, and therefore would reduce the risks attendant on any proportionate harvest shortfall.[21]

Finally, a further benefit of free markets, not articulated by Turgot or Smith, concerns the market for labor. As already noted in chapter 3, labor migration arguably limited the damage wrought by poor harvests, since it lessened the pressure on food and medical resources in regions where the crisis was deepest. This is probably true even when the poorest lacked the resources to migrate. In Ireland in the 1840s, emigration was an inefficient form of famine relief, insofar as it did not help those most at risk directly. Nonetheless, famine mortality would surely have been higher without the safety valve of emigration, with more people competing for scarce food supplies.[22]

[20] Dunstan 2006; Keller and Shiue 2007.
[21] Persson 1999.
[22] Ó Gráda and O'Rourke 1997.

MARKETS AND FAMINES IN PRACTICE

Whether merchants were (or are) as omniscient and flexible in times of famine as Smith and his French predecessors claimed remains a contested, empirical issue. Not all of Smith's contemporaries agreed with him.[23] And many others since have argued that markets do not work as smoothly as he implied.

The performance of markets during famines may be judged from spatial and intertemporal perspectives. The spatial aspect concerns the movement of foodstuffs from less to more disadvantaged areas. Markets "failed" when they failed to arbitrage away price spreads bigger than those justified by transport costs. In such cases, food markets flouted the Law of One Price, first articulated by Richard Cantillon in the 1720s. Cantillon, a pioneer in economics, described the Law of One Price as both an equilibrium condition and an adjustment process:

> The difference of prices in the capital and in the provinces must pay for the costs and risks of transport, otherwise cash will be sent to the capital to pay the balance and this will go on till the prices in the capital and the provinces come to the level of these costs and risks.[24]

Cantillon's point is that prices may well deviate from their equilibrium values, but market forces will eventually arbitrage away significant deviations.

[23] Rashid 1980.
[24] Cantillon [1755] 1931, 151.

Most populist critiques of how markets worked during famines focused on the intertemporal aspect. They held that traders often, if not always, tended to underestimate the size of the harvest in poor years, and thus engaged in "excessive" storage. The claim implies an asymmetry in speculators' expectations about the state of the harvest: they tended to be too pessimistic when there is a harvest shortfall.

The empirical evidence on the spatial dimension is mixed. An implication of the Law of One Price is that as long as transport costs do not rise, the coefficient of variation in prices across regional markets should fall during famines.[25] An analysis of grain markets during four famines in preindustrial Europe produced some evidence of slightly greater market segmentation (in the sense of higher coefficients of variation) during famines, but evidence too in most cases of a quicker-than-normal response to emerging disequilibria. During these famines, markets certainly worked better than might have been expected on the basis of a reading of qualitative and fictional accounts.[26]

The contrasting outcome in the maize markets of Botswana and Kenya in years of crisis in the early 1980s is also apposite here. In Botswana, where the average price of maize meal rose from 3.53 to 4.74 pula per bag between August 1980 and April 1983, the coefficient of variation across eighteen markets fell from 0.07 to 0.05. In Kenya, however, where the average retail price of maize rose from 2.42 to 4.61 Kenyan shillings per kilo between January and

[25] The coefficient of variation is the standard deviation divided by the average. Less formally, the Law of One Price implies that price variability across markets should not increase when the average rises.

[26] Ó Gráda 2001, 2005.

November 1984, the coefficient of variation across eighteen markets trebled from 0.15 to 0.45.[27] Further perspective is obtained from the situation in what would later become Germany-Prussia in 1816–17. In these years, poor harvests led to high prices along with excess mortality in northern and western Germany, while harvests in East Prussia were bountiful. Trade between different parts of Germany-Prussia was far from free, though: in Friedrich List's oft-cited account, "numerous customs barriers cripple trade and produce the same effects as ligatures which prevent the free circulation of the blood."[28] Under the circumstances, the spatial variation in prices was bound to increase, and it did.

In India during World War II, policymakers gave provincial administrators control over grain flows within their jurisdictions. This helps explain why in mid-May 1943, the maund (about eighty-two pounds) of rice that could be had in Cuttack (Orissa) for 6.5 rupees cost over double that in Bareilly (Uttar Pradesh) and over four times as much in Chandar-Puranbazar (Bengal).[29] Within the province of Bengal in 1943–44, the coefficient of variation of rice prices increased sharply above the average of the preceding years (from 0.210 to 0.337). The rise was only in part due to the near quadrupling in prices in Calcutta in 1943 (excluding Calcutta, the numbers are 0.219 and 0.299). The outcome is described in figure 5.1a. In an important study of the Bangladesh famine of 1974–75, Martin Ravallion found evidence of "significant impediments" to trade between the capital city, Dhaka, and its main sources of

---

[27] Drèze and Sen 1989, 138–46, 152–58.
[28] As cited in Henderson 1984, 22–23.
[29] *Star of India*, May 13, 1943.

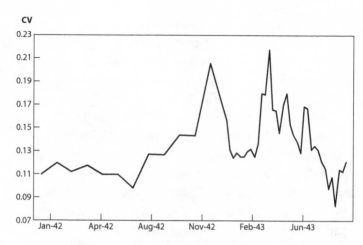

FIG. 5.1a.   Regional variation in rice prices in Bengal, 1942–43.

supply.[30] Figure 5.1b describes the coefficient of variation in the wholesale price of medium-quality rice across Bangladesh between July 1972 and the end of 1975; the spike in late 1974 reflects the balkanization of markets at the height of the crisis.[31]

Recent research on famines in Sudan and Ethiopia in the mid-1980s suggests that they too were exacerbated by the weak spatial integration of markets. According to Joachim von Braun and Patrick Webb, price explosions, price controls, and market disruptions were "commonplace," resulting in sharply rising marketing costs and making price trends in

[30] Ravallion 1987.

[31] Note too the implication that retail margins rose, albeit briefly, during the crisis. The Bangladeshi data are taken from Alamgir (1977) and the Bengali data from the Pinnell Papers (British Library, India Office Records, Mss. Eur. D911/8, "Further Information Desired by the Commission on 3rd Sept. 1944: Prices").

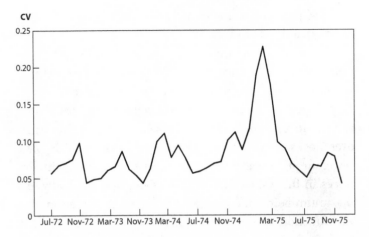

Fig. 5.1b. Rice prices in Bangladesh, 1972–75.

subregions often dependent on conditions in those same subregions alone. Regional prices in Ethiopia in normal times moved in tandem, but in the mid-1980s and again in 1988, the prices of sorghum and teff (the staple crop of the Ethiopian highlands) in Dessie, the capital of Wollo Province, soared above levels in other regional capitals. Von Braun and Webb link such anomalies to restrictions on private traders buttressed by quotas and roadblocks.[32] Trends in the spreads of teff and sorghum prices across ten of Ethiopia's provinces before and during the famine tell a somewhat different story, however. The rise in the coefficient of variation of teff prices from an average of 0.24 in 1981–83 to 0.28 in 1984 and 0.34 in 1985 was significant, but much less than the rise in Kenya (see above) over roughly the same years. The coefficient of variation of sorghum prices

[32] Webb and von Braun 1994, 47–55; see also von Braun, Teklu, and Webb 1999, chapter 6.

changed little during the same period: 0.43 in 1981–83, 0.41 in 1984, and 0.45 in 1985.[33]

What of the evidence on intertemporal arbitrage? Direct evidence on quantities stored is elusive, but sometimes something may be inferred from price data. Holders of grain expect to be rewarded for the opportunity cost of storage. In an uncomplicated world where there are no carryover stocks from one year to the next, this would imply a sawtooth price seasonality pattern in equilibrium, with low prices in the wake of the harvest giving way gradually to a maximum before the new harvest comes in. Moreover, in a well-functioning market seasonality would be expected to produce the same proportionate increases in prices in bad years as in good ones. If, though, some farmers and traders begin to hoard in the wake of a poor harvest, so that the proportion of the crop delivered to market in the wake of the harvest is less than in noncrisis years, the result would be proportionately higher prices early in the season—and therefore a less than proportionate rise between then and when the following harvest's crop is imminent. Hoarding during famines, in other words, implies smaller increases than usual from seasonal trough to peak.[34]

In the case of grain, in reality this presumption is complicated by the presence of carryover stocks from one harvest to the next. This produces considerable variation or "noise" in month-to-month and seasonal price movements. Yet research into a series of famines in preindustrial Europe—France in the 1690s and 1700s, Ireland in the 1840s, and Finland in the 1860s—shows that the seasonal rise in prices during famines dwarfed that in noncrisis years. In the case of the

[33] Derived from Kumar 1990, 200–201.
[34] Ó Gráda 1993, chapter 3; Ó Gráda and Chevet 2002.

potato in Ireland during the 1840s, where storage was not a complication, the outcome was the same: a much sharper seasonal increase during famine than in normal years. Such findings do not rule out excess hoarding, but surely they make it less probable.

Research on twentieth-century famines contend that on the contrary, speculative hoarding can exacerbate famine situations. Amartya Sen's influential analysis of the Great Bengali Famine of 1943–44 (which will be explored in chapter 6) builds on the finding of the official Famine Inquiry Commission, which argued that the rise in food prices was "more than the natural result of the shortage of supply that had occurred." Sen blamed farmers and grain merchants for converting a "moderate short-fall in *production* . . . into an exceptional short-fall in *market release*," and found that the famine was due in large part to "speculative withdrawal and panic purchase of rice stocks . . . encouraged by administrative chaos." Such speculation exacerbated the deterioration in the exchange entitlements of the poor, already hit by inflationary rises in the price of food. By ruling out food availability decline (FAD) as the fundamental factor in Bengal in 1943–44 (and by extension in other twentieth-century famine situations), Sen made room for an interpretation that places near-exclusive stress on market failure and public policy errors. Ravallion's brilliant study of the 1974 Bangladeshi famine broadly corroborated that of Sen. He found that excess mortality was, "in no small measure, the effect of a speculative crisis." Rice prices rose dramatically because merchants had badly underestimated a harvest that turned out to be normal. Prices then fell back just as fast.[35]

[35] Sen 1981; Ravallion 1987, 19.

In the instances mentioned above, food markets were not subject to drastic governmental interference. In twentieth-century Western Europe, however, where famine was an exclusively wartime phenomenon, price controls and rationing were the norm. Black markets followed, almost as inevitably as night follows day. In the Soviet Union of 1918–19, "war communism" prohibited trade in foodstuffs, but semi-legal markets flourished. Working-class households obtained half or more of their food through means other than rationing. The famine in occupied Greece in 1941–44 followed the naval blockade imposed by the Allies in the wake of Greece's occupations by the Italians and the Germans in April 1941. A food scarcity quickly ensued, and it assumed crisis proportions within months. In Greece price controls were nothing new in times of food shortage; their introduction even before the German invasion had led to panic purchasing and hoarding, and the rationing of foodstuffs from 1941 on led to intensified black market activity. Short-term price movements on the black market were sensitive to rumors about the war's progress. The regional variation in prices also rose sharply—a sign that the various black markets were far from integrated, partly because the effectiveness of these markets was hampered by hyperinflation. The authorities sometimes took drastic action against the black marketers, including public executions, but in vain. For most of those involved (apart from a few major operators) the markets were a means of survival.[36]

In general, such markets probably mitigated rather than exacerbated crises. A black market in ration cards (which entitled people to various food items, including some they

---

[36] Adamets 2003, 78–81; Hionidou 2006, 87–108.

may not have wanted) may well have increased welfare. And insofar as the evasion of price controls encouraged farmers to increase agricultural output, the impact of black markets may again have been benign. Still, the same may not apply to illegal trades in foods, which should have been ceded to—or requisitioned by—the authorities for redistribution to those at most risk.

Finally, the long-run gains from better spatial and inter-temporal arbitrage are clearly evident in figures 5.2a–5.2c, which refer to the markets for grain in Pisa, Rome, and England. They describe year-to-year differences in the natural log of wheat prices over several centuries prior to 1800.[37] The reduced variability in the series—in Pisa and England from about 1600, and Rome from about 1700—implies reductions in the cost of transport and holding carryover stocks. These must have significantly reduced the vulnerability of the Italian and English poor in the early modern era. The coincidence in timing between reduced variability and the eradication of famine is also striking. Both may have been functions of a third factor, however—namely, economic growth or technological change.

The above analysis has focused on how free markets might benefit the poor by supplying food where and when the demand for it is greatest. "Need" and "demand" are not the same things, though; it is easy to imagine how markets might allow outsiders, armed with the requisite purchasing power, to attract food away from famine-threatened areas. Well-functioning commodity markets are a mixed blessing when the distribution of income moves against the poor, as

---

[37] The price data are taken from Malanima n.d. (Pisa); Reinhardt 1991, 509–65 (Rome); Clark 2004 (England).

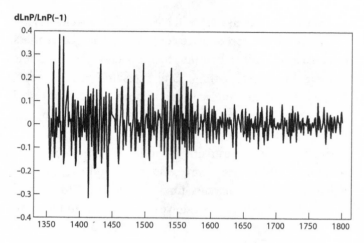

FIG. 5.2a. Year-to-year variation in the price of wheat in Pisa, 1350–1800.

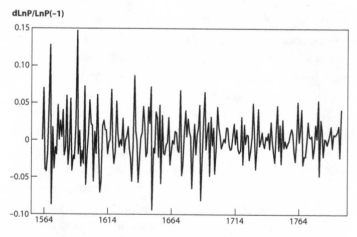

FIG. 5.2b. Year-to-year variation in the price of wheat in Rome, 1564–1797.

dLnP/LnP(-1)

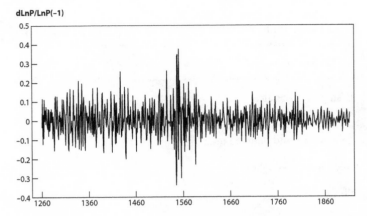

FIG. 5.2C. Year-to-year variation in the price of wheat, England 1260–1914.

highlighted by Sen in *Poverty and Famines*. Much depends on the extent to which such exports are used to finance cheaper imported substitutes (e.g., maize for wheat).

Much also depends on the speed with which food markets adjust. Today, long-distance movements of foodstuffs during famines, by air and fast ships, are routine. The international media, for example, first began to focus on the crisis in Niger in mid-July 2005. A week later, the Irish charity GOAL had chartered a humanitarian airlift into that troubled country. In earlier centuries such a rapid reaction could not be relied on. Table 5.1 makes the point for the case of the Irish famine. Although comparing prefamine (1840–45) and famine (1846–50) quinquennia captures the slump in production, it also suggests that imports largely made up for the shortfall in production. Yet this ignores the lag between the failures of the potato in 1845 and 1846 (with an accompanying reduction in grain acreage), and the arrival

Table 5.1
Irish food supplies, 1840–45 and 1846–50 (in 1,000 kcal/day)

Supply source	1840–45	1846–50
Irish production (less seed and horse consumption)	32.1	15.7
Less exports and nonfood uses	−11.8	−3.1
Net domestic supplies	20.3	12.6
Plus imports	+0.2	+5.5
Total consumption	20.5	18.1

Source: Ó Gráda 1994, 2000; after Solar 1989, 123.

of large quantities of imports of maize in spring and summer 1847. Treating 1846–50 as a unit muffles the serious food availability problems in 1846–47 in particular, and ignores the time it took to turn the export surplus into a deficit. Exporting wheat in order to import maize was fine in principle, if it could be done speedily, but that was not the case in Ireland in late 1846 and early 1847.

It was a similar story in nineteenth-century India. During the Orissa famine of 1867, the balance of trade responded too slowly and weakly to mitigate the damage done. At the time the pro–free trade *Calcutta Review* argued that in the event of a poor harvest, trade offered a cushion, since the affected region could import more and export less, and thus ensure itself against famine. Though fine in principle, in practice this mechanism worked too sluggishly. In an earlier era prohibitions on exports (and distillation too) would have been allowed, and probably would have provided some temporary respite against famine.

TRANSPORT

In the past, poor communications often exacerbated famine. The cost of overland transport was prohibitive, and market integration was accordingly poor. Coastal communities were at a relative advantage. Caesarea in Cappadocia (today's Kayseri in central Anatolia) in the second half of the fourth century AD was vulnerable to famine, prompting Gregory of Nazianzus to observe that "cities on the sea coast easily endure a shortage of this kind . . . but we who live far from the sea profit nothing from our surplus . . . since we are able neither to export what we have nor import what we lack."[38] The Edessa famine of AD 500 described by Joshua the Stylite happened in a town two hundred miles from the coast.

It is perhaps no coincidence that England's last famines took place in a region where the roads were "nothing but a most confus'd mixture of Rockes and Boggs."[39] The rivers of Cumberland and Westmoreland were not navigable, and their ports, such as they were, undeveloped. In the following decades mining and shipping opened up the region. In Scotland in the 1690s, a famine wreaked havoc in the Highlands and Aberdeenshire, but the west of Scotland was largely spared (because of its nearness to Ireland). "While the province of Murray and some of the best lands of the east coast of Buchan and Formartine abounded with feed and bread,"

[38] Cited in Garnsey 1988, 22.
[39] Cited in Appleby 1978, 85.

further inland in Monquhitter the population fell by half or more.[40] Yet even in the eighteenth century, the cost of shipping grain from the Baltic to western Europe amounted to half its price in a port like Amsterdam. Not only were communications expensive; they were also slow. Thus, the bulk of grain shipped from distant ports to a famished Ireland in the wake of a disastrous harvest in 1740 began to arrive only in spring and summer 1741.[41]

Marx noted in 1853 how the lack of transport was producing "social destitution in the midst of natural plenty, for want of the means of exchange," citing evidence before an 1848 parliamentary committee that the lack of roads in India meant that "when grain was selling from 6 to 8 shillings a quarter at Khandesh, it was sold at 64 to 70 shillings at Poona, where the people were dying in the streets of famine, without the possibility of gaining supplies from Khandesh."[42] In 1864 there was famine in Mexico City, "while the farmers of the Bajio—*less than two hundred miles distant*—are at their wits end to know how to dispose of their superabundant harvest." In China in 1877–78, efforts at getting food to a devastated Shanxi Province miscarried because of poor overland communications between it and the eastern ports, "where food was arriving in abundance."[43]

The introduction of railways, Marx predicted, would lead to the expansion of agriculture and the avoidance of "frequently recurring local famines.[44] During the following decades, railways did not rid India of famine but they alleviated

---

[40] Tyson 1986.
[41] Cullen 1999.
[42] Marx 1973, 321.
[43] Cited in Walford 1879, 120; Watt 1961, 76.
[44] Marx 1973, 321.

regional imbalances like those described by Marx. By 1880, nine thousand miles of railway had been constructed in India, of which over two thousand was state owned. Indeed, in the wake of the Bombay Famine of 1876–78, an official inquiry suggested extending the system by a further five thousand miles. The majority of India's railways were built to exploit the commercial potential of the subcontinent, but some were built into drought-prone areas to provide rapid famine relief or to frontier areas for military defense.[45] Were it not for the construction of six thousand miles of railway line in the previous few decades, the Chinese famine of 1920–21 would have been much more deadly.

During the famine of 1926–27 most of the food destined for Katsina in northern Nigeria was shipped by camel and donkey from the railhead at Kano, about eighty miles away. But in 1933 when tribal leaders from Zimbabwe's remote Sabi Valley warned of imminent famine, they were told that "if they bestirred themselves they would probably find a European motor-lorry owner . . . who would be willing to carry the grain to their areas at a modest rate." A decade later, however, wartime requisitioning shunted French West Africa "back into the age which preceded the era of roads," with disastrous results.[46]

CONCLUSION

The historical record suggests that the integration of markets and the gradual eradication of famine are linked. Wheat price data from a wide range of European markets highlight

---

[45] Maharatna 1996, 272–73; McAlpin 1983.
[46] Cited in Iliffe 1990, 88–89; see also Iliffe 1987, 158–59.

the coincidence between reductions over time in the amplitude of year-to-year fluctuations and the frequency of documented famine. So well integrated were European grain markets in the 1840s relative to earlier that "price movements do not help much to localize the crisis."[47] Smoothly functioning markets did not cause the elimination of famine, however; both were functions of economic development. In backward economies where markets were thin and slow to adjust, ruling elites relied on a variety of strategies in order to ensure the supply of food. Clearly such schemes had some success; they would not have persisted for so long otherwise. But this came at a cost. A well-documented case in point is the Roman *annona*, part of the regulatory framework in the Eternal City since classical times. This institution brought Rome immunity or near immunity from famine in the early modern era, although presumably at the cost of production and income foregone in its rural hinterland.

Recent research indicates that the "failure" of food markets per se was not responsible for famines, at least in early modern Europe. At the same time, it should be emphasized that markets were no panacea: again and again, market forces lacked the power and speed to override severe harvest failures in backward economies. In Ireland in the 1840s, as in France in the 1690s and Finland in the 1860s, the catastrophic nature of harvest failures overwhelmed functioning markets. Moreover, in nineteenth-century Ireland and India a dogmatic faith on the part of the ruling elite in markets as a mechanism for relieving famine cost millions of lives.[48]

[47] Solar 2007, 91.
[48] And compare Garenne et al. (2002) on Madagascar in the early 1980s.

CHAPTER VI

Entitlements: Bengal and Beyond

This matter is primarily one for the Ministry of that
self-governing province.

—*Leo Amery, secretary of state for India, August 1943*

The problem is . . . to decide how much shipping can be spared, even
for so serious a situation . . . without injury to the all-important task
of defeating the enemy and bringing the war to an early conclusion.

—*Leo Amery, October 1943*

BENGAL

IN THE HISTORY OF FAMINES IN BENGAL several dates stand
out: 1769–70 (when, allegedly, one-third of the population
perished), 1873–74 (when major famine was averted through
proactive public policy), 1896–97 (when the strict operation
of the Famine Codes did not prevent significant excess mortality), 1943–44 (when over two million Bengalis perished
in a famine that prompted Nobel Laureate Sen's reorienta-
tion of famine studies), and 1974–75 (when a combination
of civil war and harvest failure led to Bengal's last famine).

Today, the Great Bengal Famine of 1943–44 is the most
notorious of all Bengali famines.[1] It was unexpected; a few

---

[1] It has been the focus of an extensive scholarly literature (e.g., Sen
1981; Greenough 1982; Bowbrick 1986; Brennan 1988; Mitra 1989; Goswami 1990; Basu 1984; Devereux 1988; Kumar 1990; Dyson 1991, 1996;
Maharatna 1996; Tauger 2003). This chapter draws on Ó Gráda 2008.

years before it struck, a retired colonial administrator confidently declared that in India, "the old famine of history, with its dreadful death roll, is not likely to recur."[2] From the turn of the century on, Bengal suffered fewer and smaller mortality peaks. This had not been due to rising incomes—real wages hardly grew—but to a combination of fewer adverse weather shocks, better access to foreign supplies, and more effective social safety nets. In Bengal too, however, the era of famines would end with a bang rather than a whimper.

The famine, which cost the lives of over two million out of a population of sixty million or so—most of them in the east of the prepartitioned province—led native son Sen to refocus famine analysis from a Malthusian toward a distributionist perspective. Sen's fresh and highly influential approach, culminating in *Poverty and Famines: An Essay on Entitlement and Deprivation* (1981), grew out of the claim that in Bengal, shifts in the exchange entitlements to rice—the staple of the region—occurred in the absence of any significant FAD per se. There was no "remarkable over-all shortage of foodgrains," but wartime conditions led to disrupted communications, widespread panic, and a fettered press. War-induced expectations led producers and grain merchants to convert a "moderate short-fall in *production* . . . into an exceptional short-fall in *market release*." The famine thus was due in large part to "speculative withdrawal and panic purchase of rice stocks . . . encouraged by administrative chaos."[3]

This chapter provides a brief history of this paradigmatic disaster, and describes its implications for the broader

[2] Blunt 1937, 184.
[3] Sen 1981, 63, 76.

analysis of famines. The famine was presaged by a series of adverse shocks. First, there was a war on. Rangoon, the Burmese capital, had fallen to Japanese forces in March 1942, and in the following months fears grew that the Japanese, even though already militarily overstretched, would soon invade Bengal. In April 1942, the Japanese sank a destroyer and several merchantmen in the Bay of Bengal, and bombed Calcutta in December 1942. Other sporadic air raids followed. As a result, the usual supplies of rice from Burma, albeit a small proportion of the aggregate consumption, were cut off. In addition, on military advice officials removed rice and paddy deemed surplus to local requirements from coastal districts such as Midnapur, Bakerganj, and Khulna. They also requisitioned and sank boats capable of carrying ten passengers or more in order to prevent their use by any invading Japanese soldiers. This "boat denial policy" compromised the livelihoods of two of Bengal's most vulnerable groups—commercial fishermen and boatmen— and increased transport costs. Military considerations also meant giving urban workers, particularly those in war-related industries, priority over others, so that public agencies and Calcutta factory owners competed with other consumers. More than half of India's war-related output was produced in Calcutta by an army of workers numbering up to one million, "made up to a considerable extent of a volatile class recruited from outside Bengal." Concern for the city's "priority classes" accounted for the forcible requisition of rice from mills and warehouses in and around the city in late December 1942.[4]

---

[4] Braund 1944, 25; Greenough 1982, 108–11.

Second, parts of coastal west Bengal, including important rice-growing areas, were hit by a major tsunami on October 16, 1942, resulting in a significant loss of life as well as the destruction of standing crops, livestock, and paddy stores. State censorship shielded the full horrors from the public at first; the Bengal government's announcement of the disaster was not published in the London *Times* for over two weeks. Months later, animal fodder in the coastal area was still almost nonexistent, and the cattle were "poor specimens, with ribs protruding."[5] Third, there were rumors from western Bengal in November 1942 that a fungus had struck the autumn-winter *aman* crop, which normally accounted for three-quarters of the total rice output.

The initial jump in the price of rice in spring 1942 was in part a reflection of the failure of the *aus* (or summer paddy) crop in mid-1942 and the fall of Rangoon. Nevertheless, abnormal price rises in late 1942 were blamed on speculators bent on hoarding rice and prompted official measures to "break the Calcutta market." These measures produced long queues rather than more rice, and in March 1943 the government put an end to price controls in order to secure supplies for the city. Prices continued to increase—a maund (about eighty-two pounds) of rice costing about five rupees on the eve of the crisis, cost nine rupees in January 1943, twenty-one rupees in April, and thirty rupees in July.[6] Other crops were also subject to price hikes, but the price of rice rose much more than that of other food grains in 1943.

There were demands for rationing in Calcutta and other urban centers as early as January 1943, and in mid-February

[5] *Statesman* (Calcutta), March 28, 1943.
[6] Maharatna 1996, appendix D.

the Bengal legislature debated a demand for supplementary funding that included provision under the heading "Famine" for relief measures in the cyclone-affected areas. In another debate in March one deputy insisted that Bengal be declared a "deficit province," while another reckoned that the "estimated production" of rice was 23 percent short of needs and the "shiploads of wheat" promised some months earlier had never materialized. In late March, a correspondent for the Calcutta *Statesman* newspaper reported that a "large proportion" of the population of the coastal districts hit by the tsunami faced "something akin to starvation." By early April, public employees were receiving rationed food in Dacca and the authorities were promising to provide rationed food for the poor in isolated Chittagong, where the threat of invasion was greatest. In May the situation in Calcutta was "fast getting desperate."[7] Yet despite pleas and warnings from officials, opposition politicians, and the media, the authorities in Calcutta and Delhi held off declaring a famine, and ministerial spokesmen in the House of Commons in London downplayed the severity of the crisis. This was mainly because the wartime context dictated a policy of "creating confidence," and because the food supplies needed to sustain the traditional relief mechanisms of public works and smoothly functioning food markets were lacking.

By May 1943, destitute migrants were already pouring into Calcutta in the thousands and making the city's streets their homes. An outbreak of cholera led officials to blame the deterioration in public health on "the daily influx of a

[7] *Statesman*, January 28, February 19, March 10, March 28, April 3, April 5, and May 13, 1943.

large number of poor people from the surrounding districts."
The migrants' habit of queuing for hours for food in front
of controlled shops led them to "indulge in unhygienic
practices and create unhealthy conditions in the localities
where shops are located." The poor were also blamed for
the appalling state of the city's garbage cans. Meanwhile,
the Ministry of Civil Supplies announced that laborers' food
rations in Calcutta in the future would consist of equal
shares of *atta* (a kind of wheat flour) and rice in order to
release rice for the rural areas. Urban workers were expected
to "cheerfully bear this sacrifice" for the sake of those in rural
areas who required assistance "very badly."[8]

The immigration into Calcutta prompted the creation of
a system of government-funded soup kitchens, the first of
which opened in early July. It aimed to sell rice at six annas
per seer (slightly over two pounds) to the very poor. The responsible minister, Huseyn Shaheed Suhrawardy of the
Muslim League, just back from discussing Bengal's needs
with the central government in New Delhi, made the first
sale. Meanwhile, "growing economic distress" in the city was
producing a considerable increase in pickpocketing, house-
breakings, and "thefts by servants" in the city.[9]

Still, the British authorities and their local representatives blamed local politicians for failing to stop "profiteer-
ing and bad distribution." Relief came too late, as hunger
gave way to disease and mass mortality across much of
the province. Mortality peaked in the second half of 1943.
The prospect of a good *aman* crop in late 1943 and a drop in

[8] *Statesman,* May 15, 1943.
[9] *Statesman,* July 11, 1943.

the price of rice prompted many of the surviving migrants to return home from the cities, but excess mortality on a significant scale continued well into 1944.

When the famine struck, Bengal was even more dependent on rice than Ireland had been on the potato in the 1840s. Rice occupied up to nine-tenths of the cultivated area, with jute accounting for another 7 to 8 percent. Moreover, while the potato had offered the prefamine Irish poor a dull but nutritionally adequate diet, rice consumption in Bengal was about four seers (about eight pounds) per week per adult male equivalent, or at most two thousand kilocalories daily. Given the gap between the rich and the poor, this implied barebones subsistence for many.

On the eve of the famine Bengal's economy, like Ireland's, was mainly rural and agricultural. Peasant cultivators, either owners or renters of land, were more dominant in Bengal, particularly so in east Bengal, "home to a predominantly smallholding society overlaid by various rentier and creditor groups." At the same time, the Bengali peasantry was by no means an undifferentiated homogeneous class, and the presence of commercial farmers and substantial landholders entailed sharecropping and wage labor.

Since the publication of Sen's account, the relative importance of shocks to the food supply and the extent of market failure in Bengal has been a controversial issue, with ramifications for the study of famines far beyond Bengal in the early 1940s. In what follows, first I review the food supply situation before and during the famine, then I look at the functioning of food markets, and finally I discuss the incidence of the famine by occupational group and region. The chapter concludes on a comparative note.

FOOD SUPPLY AND MARKET FAILURE

Long after the crisis became a famine, the official position in London, Delhi, and Calcutta was that Bengal contained enough food to feed everybody. Suhrawardy, a leading light in the Muslim League and minister for civil supplies in Bengal from April 1943 on, based his policy during the following crucial few months on the premise that there was enough food in the province and his responsibility was to allocate it equitably. Prices, he maintained, bore no relation to the true supply position in Bengal; there was no need to fear "any ultimate shortage of foodgrains."[10] Again and again, Suhrawardy maintained that the food supply problem was "psychological." This prompted influential Hindu nationalist opposition spokesman, Shyama Prasad Mookerjee, to caricature him as telling people, "Don't get panicky. I am sitting here as the civil supplies minister and telling you there is plenty of foodstuffs. We have statistics which we do not want to publish. Everything will be alright. Do not get panicky." Mookerjee accused Suhrawardy of minimizing "the gravity of the situation."[11]

In May 1943, Suhrawardy, spurred on by the authorities in Delhi and London, asked newspaper editors to preach the "doctrine of sufficiency and sufficiency and sufficiency . . . *ad nauseam*" against the "psychological factors" of "greed and panic." A media propaganda campaign aimed at "outcasting the hoarder" was buttressed by an official determination to prove "statistically" that Bengal contained enough food.

[10] *Statesman,* May 4, 1943.
[11] S. P. Mookerjee, cited in Batabyal 2005, 108.

Yet the propaganda also described the government as "rushing grain ships to India, even from rationed Allies, even at the expense of munitions"—an assertion that would have been more convincing had the public been given "some general idea of the quantum of supplies coming forward instead of an occasional photograph of the unloading of a wagon."[12]

In August, Suhrawardy admitted for the first time in public that distress was widespread, and certain to become more acute in the following months.[13] He announced that rationing would be introduced in Calcutta and the industrial areas in October, meaning that Bengal was "in effect . . . being organized on a famine basis." But there was little he could do; he might appoint an expert to devise a form of gruel that would contain as little rice as possible, but the Indian Famine Codes could not be applied because Bengal lacked the food needed to provide the prescribed rations. The rest of India, Suhrawardy said, was gradually realizing Bengal's parlous state, but the omens were not so good: in the seven months beginning in December 1942 the rest of India had sent Bengal only a paltry forty-four thousand tons.[14]

The escalating crisis prompted the *Statesman*, hitherto a defender of official policy, to take a more critical stance. Realizing that the crisis menaced Bengal "in many ways," and that months of "this penury and disintegration" were likely to follow, it published several graphic photographs of the

[12] *Capital* (Calcutta financial weekly), February 25 and March 4, 1943; *Statesman*, May 14, 1943 (report of press conference presided over by Suhrawardy).

[13] Ghosh 1944, 18. Much of the detail in this and the following paragraphs has been culled from the *Statesman* newspaper.

[14] Mansergh 1973, 43.

famine and instituted the practice of reporting information on the numbers who had died. When Suhrawardy held out the hope that prices would soon fall, the *Statesman* doubted whether people would trust him, given his "earlier disingenuousness or ill-informed propagandistic optimism."[15]

The position taken by the official Famine Inquiry Commission's *Report on Bengal*, published in the famine's wake in May 1945, did not stray far from the line taken in public by Suhrawardy and Secretary of State Leo Amery. It found that although the "total supply, including the carry-over, was probably smaller in 1943 than in any of the preceding 15 years," nevertheless the likely supply shortfall was about three weeks' requirements. This finding has been recycled repeatedly since, but it bears noting that those responsible for the *Report on Bengal* placed less trust in the underlying data than some of its later interpreters. The only agriculturalist on the five-member commission strongly rejected the calculation just summarized, while its chair, Sir John Woodhead, a former Indian Civil Service official in Bengal and a safe pair of hands as far as the colonial authorities were concerned, confided to a senior India Office official that "sometimes I thought that our estimate of the shortage of 1943 was on the low side . . . the figures were so inaccurate—I mean the available data—as to make an accurate estimate impossible."[16] Yet he preferred to rest the *Report*'s case on unreliable data. Wallace Aykroyd, the nutritionist on the commission, later conceded that the output estimate had been generated after the event, and that at the time of

---

[15] *Statesman*, October 12, 1943.

[16] BL, OIOC, Mss. Eur. D714/67, letter from Woodhead to Sir David Monteath, assistant director, India Office, Whitehall, July 10, 1945.

the famine itself, it was impossible to know what the real situation was.[17]

The quality of Bengali agricultural statistics in the early 1940s is probably too poor to support contemporary or historical assessments of the aggregate food supply. Much has been made of the data, nonetheless. Supporters of the position taken in the *Report on Bengal* have emphasized the limited extent of the 1942–43 shortfall relative to the 1937–38 to 1941–42 average; detractors focus on the significant proportional reduction (32 percent) in the size of the aman crop of 1942–43 relative to 1941–42. The regional pattern is also of interest. The biggest declines in the aman harvest were registered in the Burdwan, Bankura, and Rajshahi in the west and northwest of the province. This geographical pattern is consistent with the claim that the aman harvest of 1942 in West Bengal was badly damaged by the fungus *Bipolaris oryzae*.[18]

The poor state of the aman crop in late 1942 also generated a good deal of contemporary commentary in the media, the Calcutta legislature, and confidential official memoranda and correspondence. While the authorities stressed sufficiency and maldistribution, censored reports from east Bengal were telling "impressive stories" of impending famine from March 1943 on. And although wartime uncertainty surely increased the incentive to hold on to precautionary stocks, the "surmise" regarding carryover stocks of rice suggested by officials in May 1943 was immediately pounced on by two widely respected academics at a meeting organized by the opposition in Howrah. Regional food commissioner

[17] Aykroyd 1974.
[18] Tauger 2003.

Henry Braund, hoodwinked at first into dismissing the crisis as the result of panic and "hoarding," realized by April or May that there was an "intrinsic" shortage, and later admitted as much.[19] Spokesmen for London and Delhi were the last to accept the widespread conviction that food supplies were short in Bengal. It is surely telling that by early April 1944, when the worst was over, the authorities worried about the impact of overpessimistic expectations on the disposal of available rice stocks. This prompted the editor of the *Statesman* to muse,

> Memories remain fresh of the long dismal period last year when Authority in Calcutta, in New Delhi, and in London was profuse in subsequently falsified assurances that no serious danger impended, that enough food for harassed and bewildered Bengal and for India existed, and that the only need was greater trustfulness on the public's part and minor redistribution of stocks of grain. Over-optimistic and provenly erroneous assertions such as these, from persons presumably in a position to know the truth, have their inevitable psychological sequel.[20]

In linking famine to speculative hoarding, Sen's interpretation echoed both the colonial authorities in 1943 and their supporters, and the *Report on Bengal*. It scarcely needs pointing out that the hoarding hypothesis suited the authorities since it undermined demands to divert shipping

---

[19] *Statesman*, May 16, 1943. According to Braund (1944, 30), as early as March 1943 "villagers, cultivators, traders, and jotedars were all predicting shortage."

[20] *Statesman*, April 2, 1944.

and food supplies from the war effort to relieve Bengal. Local politicians were divided on the issue. Supporters of the Fazl ul-Huq coalition, which fell in April 1943, stressed the precarious food supply situation, but the more pro-British administration led by the Muslim League that replaced it, and particularly the influential Suhrawardy, clung to the line that hoarding was the main problem.[21]

In the sectarian bear pit of Bengali politics, the hoarding hypothesis suited the Muslim League, since major "hoarders" were more likely to be members of the mainly Hindu landowning and merchant classes. Bengali Muslims were poorer and less educated than Hindus, but well mobilized politically. The poorest strata among the peasantry were disproportionately Muslim, and Muslim leaders prominent in 1943 such as Abul Kashem Fazlul Huq, Suhrawardy, and Khwaja Nazimuddin had cut their teeth on populist communal politics in the 1920s and 1930s, supporting pro-peasant land reforms and controls on moneylending. Hindu politicians were more likely to represent landlord and trading interests as well as the genteel and literate bhadralok. "The Hindu section of the traders is dominant in the internal economy of Bengal," noted P. C. Joshi in People's War. Lending money at interest was forbidden by the Koran, so moneylending was mainly in the hands of Hindu banias (traders), mahajans (usurers), and landowners. The Bengal Moneylenders' Act of 1940 had hit them hard.[22] While the Muslim League was criticized at the height of the crisis for giving contracts to one of its prominent supporters, the Hindu Mahasabha attacked the government and "big firms,

[21] Gupta 1997, 2019–20.
[22] People's War, November 14, 1943; Chatterji 1994, 106.

particularly non-Bengalis," for holding on to excess stocks. The pro-*bhadralok* Mahasabha also claimed that repeated warnings against hoarding only served to create panic "specially among the poor middle class people who were obliged to keep small stocks to meet the present abnormal situation."[23] During the famine communal rioting took on an economic hue, with Muslim wrath directed particularly against Hindu and Marwari traders and moneylenders.[24]

The official line on hoarding was supported by the local Communist Party, legal only since 1942 and an enthusiastic supporter of the Allied war effort. The Communists saw Mookerjee and his followers as representing the selfish interests of Hindu traders and hoarders. According to *People's War*, "Dr. Shyamaprosad [Mookerjee] gives the lead, the Hindu hoarders pay the cash and call the tune, [and] the Fifth Column gives the cadres." Mookerjee, leader of the Hindu nationalist Mahasabha, represented Hindu communalism and in particular its more "genteel" *bhadralok* component. Yet Asok Mitra, a witness to the famine, accused the Communists of ignoring what they must have known, given their access to information: that hoarding was a "mere fleabite" relative to official culpability.[25]

The nature of the hoarding does indeed matter. If it entailed merely increasing prices in order to make a smaller harvest last the whole season, then it would have thereby reduced privation and deaths. If, on the other hand, it was based on an exaggerated view of scarcity, the release of a

[23] *Statesman*, May 22, 1943; Chatterji 1994, 136.

[24] Compare Greenough 1982, 160.

[25] *People's War*, November 14, 1943; Mitra 1989. See also Gupta 1997, 2030–36 (evidence of party members to the Famine Inquiry Commission).

disproportionate amount of food later in the season would have led to losses and even bankruptcies. Malthus had made the point as follows in 1800:

> The man who refuses to send his corn to market when it is at twenty pounds a load, because he thinks that in two months time it will be at thrity, if he be right in his judgment, and succeed in his speculation, is a positive and decided benefactor to the state; because he keeps his supply to that period when the state is much more in want of it; and if he and some others did not keep it back in that manner, instead of its being thirty in two months, it would be forty or fifty.
>
> If he be wrong in his speculation, he loses perhaps very considerably himself, and the state suffers a little; because, had he brought his corn to market at £20, the price would have fallen sooner, and the event showed that there was corn enough in the country to allow of it: but the slight evil that the state suffers in this case is almost wholly compensated by the glut in the market, when the corn is brought out, which makes the price fall below what it would have been otherwise.[26]

What can price movements in 1942–44 tell us? First, between mid-1942 and mid-1943 the nominal price of rice trebled while the real price doubled. This is a relatively modest increase compared to rises in the price of food grains during famines elsewhere. Thereafter it rose more rapidly, especially in East Bengal. Second, excessive hoarding on a grand scale should have been followed by plummeting prices as hoarded supplies were released, but this did not

[26] Malthus [1800] 1970, 14–15.

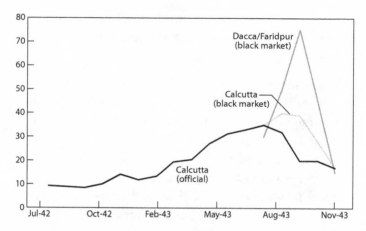

FIG. 6.1.   Bengal rice prices, July 1942–December 1943 (rupees/
maund)
Source: Maharatna 1996, 291; Brennan 1988, 544.

happen. The quoted price fell from thirty rupees per maund
in late August 1943 to twenty rupees a month later, but that
fall was a "mirage" caused by official price ceilings being
reported as market rates (see figure 6.1). In early September in Manikganj (in the Dacca district), price controls drove
all rice out of the municipal market, but it was fetching forty
rupees on the black market; a month later it cost sixty to
seventy rupees. By October 1943, according to the Communist organ *People's War*, rice was costing eighty rupees per
maund in Chittagong.

In reality, market prices fell to ceiling levels only in December 1943, as growers reaped "the largest paddy crop
ever seen in the province." All of a sudden, the huge queues
outside public rice stores disappeared. The real price during the first half of 1944, however, was still higher than before the crisis. The "glut" predicted by a government official

in April 1943, whereby the "large imports from outside" in the presence of "adequate internal stocks" would result in "a steep fall in prices" that only hoarders would have themselves to blame, just never materialized.[27] A plausible interpretation of price movements in 1943–44 is that far from hoarders holding back grain for speculative gain, many producers were forced to reduce off-farm sales in order to satisfy their own needs.

The most telling direct evidence against the claim that speculators held back a disproportionate share of the 1942–43 harvest was the disappointing outcome of Suhrawardy's "food drive" of June–July 1943. This high-profile campaign, involving one hundred thousand committees and thirty thousand full-time workers at its peak, located only one hundred thousand tons of rice held in hoards of four hundred maunds and over throughout Bengal. Asok Mitra, then a young Indian Civil Service officer, told of how he and a police officer raided some warehouses in East Bengal at the height of the famine. Finding little grain, they nonetheless arrested one owner "just to create an atmosphere against hoarding," and walked him handcuffed around the village before locking him up. Pressed to furnish disaggregated data on the outcome of the drive, Suhrawardy was forced to admit that he had no statistics, but the general picture was that in most places, a deficit had been reported.[28]

Critics berated ministers for excluding Delhi and Howrah from the drive. A separate drive against hoarders in Calcutta and Howrah was carried out amid considerable

[27] Gupta 1997, 1938 (Major-General Wood to H. Braund, April 23, 1943).

[28] *Statesman*, July 13, 1943.

publicity over a weekend in early August, but it produced
similarly disappointing results. An editorial in the nationalist *Amrita Bazar Patrika* noted that had it produced significant hoards rather than the proverbial "horse's egg," ministers would have shouted this from the rooftops. Instead,
they were forced to admit that in Calcutta consumers had
not engaged in large-scale hoarding and that stocks in the
hands of traders were in line with the figures they had declared to officials. Suhrawardy had to concede that stocks in
hand were "not considerable." A confidential memorandum
forwarded by the viceroy, Lord Linlithgow, to Amery few
weeks after the urban drive tellingly summarized:

> The much-heralded "anti-hoarding" drive in the Ben-
> gal districts and in Calcutta has achieved very little that
> is positive. The Bengal Government themselves do not
> claim that it is more than a "food census," disclosing
> stocks in the districts amounting to rather more than
> 300,000 tons. The Bengal Government emphasises
> that this is "stock," and is in no sense "surplus," except
> to a negligible extent. In Calcutta itself practically no
> stocks were disclosed which would be classified as
> "hoards," or were held in contravention of the Foodgrains
> Control Order.[29]

There followed Suhrawardy's admission in the Bengal assembly that "for five months he had declared that there was no
shortage of foodgrains," adding the weak excuse that "mere
insistence on shortage would not help any one." By mid-
October the *Statesman*, which had supported the Muslim

---

[29] Lord Linlithgow to Leo Amery, September 1943 (Mansergh 1973,
4:197).

League ministry and Suhrawardy since April, was berating
politicians in London, Delhi, and Calcutta for their "dis-
graceful" record of "false or ignorant prophecy," noting how
they had "proclaimed that food-shortage in India and Bengal was practically non-existent."[30] Across the province, the
rice discovered in hoards represented only a small fraction
of the annual supply. The failure of the "drives" left the
poor with a foreboding sense of calamity, because the actual
shortage was much worse than they had realized or been
lulled into believing.[31]

Leonard Pinnell, director of civil supplies in Bengal until
April 1943, was a key witness to the unfolding famine. Pinnell patriotically supported the line that there was no shortage, and employed an ineffective combination of compul-
sion and moral suasion to keep prices down. Tensions
between him and Fazl ul-Huq's Krishak Praja (Peasants'
People's Party) coalition were high, with ministers accusing
Pinnell of being more concerned with the war effort than
the plight of the Bengali people.

By spring 1943, Pinnell recognized that his anti-hoarding
campaign was not producing the desired results and that the
damage to the 1942 aman crop was significant. Torn between patriotic duty and an increasing realization that the
crisis was escalating, his stance in public remained as before.
Ian Stephens, editor of Bengal's main English-language
daily, later described Pinnell and a colleague as "two unhappy but not dishonest men working to a brief they didn't
believe," whose inept performance convinced Stephens that
a catastrophe was inevitable. The tension proved too much

[30] *Statesman*, September 14, September 28, and October 12, 1943.

[31] Ó Gráda 2008; see also Gupta 1997, 2061 (letter from N. N. Sircar
to Lord Linlithgow).

for Pinnell, who suffered a nervous breakdown in April 1943 and resigned. In material prepared for the Famine Inquiry Commission in the following year, though, he vehemently contested the charge that "Bengal itself is to blame for the trouble owing to the failure to deal with a ring of speculators and hoarders who conspired to hold the Province to ransom." In other words, the speculative hoards that underpinned the entitlements hypothesis did not exist. In oral evidence to the commission, Pinnell also denied the presence of significant stocks in the hands of traders. His offers of large rewards to informers came to nought; on an inspection of the Calcutta Rice Mills in March 1943, he found that stocks were "very negligible"; and he insisted if merchants outside Calcutta had been holding on to rice, officials on the spot "would have known about them."[32] Pinnell's colleague, Henry Braund, was also originally a propagandist for the "sufficiency" line. In a confidential account of the famine written in 1944, he too admitted that "looking back, that the adoption of the psychology or gospel of 'plenty' in Bengal was a mistake."[33]

WINNERS AND LOSERS

Another, indirect way of checking for the existence of a FAD is to identify which groups lost and which groups (if any) gained during the famine. Marx's quip that the Great Irish

[32] Gupta 1997, 2019–20, 2034–36. In their evidence to the commission, representatives of the Krishak Praja repeated their attack on the position taken by the authorities at the height of the famine, insisting that a bold, timely confession that there was a shortage would have helped secure outside help.

[33] Braund 1944, 142.

Famine "killed poor devils only" also holds for Bengal, but the FAD and entitlements approaches imply different categories of poor devils. The latter implies a reduction in the real wage, a tendency for labor to shift from other sectors to agriculture, and an improvement in landlord incomes. The former results in reductions in the agricultural labor force, the real wage, and rent. In other words, *both* "entitlements famines" and "FAD famines" hurt wage earners and net consumers of food. A key difference is that whereas the former predicts that rice producers should fare relatively well, the latter predicts that they too suffer. Everyone suffers when there is an overall shortage of food—there are no "winners"—while all but the producers suffer when the retail shortfall is caused by market imperfections.

In seeking to identify winners and losers in Bengal, Sen and several other historians of the famine have exploited the pioneering statistical survey conducted in 1944–45 by the Indian Statistical Institute.[34] Based on the economic condition of nearly sixteen thousand randomly selected families in 386 villages, the survey highlighted the precariousness of existence in Bengal on the eve of the famine. It found that average holding size was too small to provide the rice necessary for subsistence, and that those groups most affected by the famine were already under pressure even before 1943. It also found that the famine's impact was uneven regionally, and that subdivisions with proportionately more families on below-subsistence holdings were more vulnerable to the famine.

Consistent with the entitlements view, the survey confirmed that the landless suffered most. Yet it showed that landholders were not immune either. One of the most in-

[34] Sen 1981, 70–85; Mahalanobis, Mukherjea, and Ghose 1946.

teresting tables in the Indian Statistical Institute survey—
reproduced below, with minor alterations, as table 6.1—
suggests that the occupational status of 0.7 million families
out of a total of over 10 million deteriorated between January 1943 and May 1944, in the sense that they were forced
to shift from their former occupation (e.g., farmer) to an
inferior one (e.g., laborer), while the status of 0.24 million
improved. Those engaged in agriculture accounted for the
lion's share of those who lost status. While this is hardly
surprising given their numerical predominance, it is not so
easy to square with a normal harvest plus a relative increase
in the price of rice.

Less well known is the survey of destitute migrants in
Calcutta conducted by anthropologist Tarakchandra Das at
the height of the crisis in September 1943. It found that
while day laborers accounted for the highest proportion of
destitutes, over one in five was a cultivating owner (11.7
percent), tenant (6.5 percent), or cultivator combining own-
ership and tenancy (3 percent). "None of these units," according to Das, "worked as day labourers on a hire basis. All had
enough land to maintain themselves throughout the year."
A third study, conducted in five villages in East Bengal, also
found that agricultural laborers suffered most, but neither
landholders nor petty traders escaped. During 1943, the
proportion of families owning no land rose from 29.9 to
36.7 percent.[35]

Evidence on land transfers during the famine is also of
interest. In 1940, Bengal contained 16.4 million landholders. In the wake of the famine, 2.7 million sales of whole or
part-occupancy holdings were recorded. The sales, which

---

[35] Das 1949; Mukerji 1965, 178 (tables 63 and 64).

TABLE 6.1
Change in occupational status in Bengal, 1943–44

[1]	Number of families (100,000s)				Percentage of families experiencing change January 1943–May 1944		
	January 1943	Change between January 1943 and May 1944					
		Better	Worse	Ambiguous	Better	Worse	Ambiguous
	[2]	[3]	[4]	[5]	[6]	[7]	[8]
Occupation group							
Agriculture	33.3	—	2.5	—	—	7.51	—
Agriculture and labor	17.1	0.4	1.5	—	2.34	8.77	—
Agricultural labor	17.3	0.7	0.6	—	4.05	3.47	—
Noncultivating owner	6.2	—	0.2	0.1	—	3.23	1.61
Fishing	1.3	—	—	0.1	—	—	7.60

(*Continued*)

TABLE 6.1
Continued

	Number of families (100,000s)					Percentage of families experiencing change January 1943–May 1944		
	January 1943	Change between January 1943 and May 1944					
		Better	Worse	Ambiguous		Better	Worse	Ambiguous
[1]	[2]	[3]	[4]	[5]	[6]	[7]	[8]
Occupation group								
Craft	5.1	—	0.3	0.1	—	5.38	1.96
Husking paddy	1.7	0.7	—	—	4.12	—	—
Transport	0.7	—	0.1	—	—	14.29	—
Trade	6.9	—	1.6	0.2	—	23.19	2.90

Profession and service	6.8	0.1	0.1	0.1	1.47	1.47	1.47
Nonagricultural labor	1.0	—	0.1	—	—	10.00	—
Other productive occupations	2.2	0.1	—	—	4.55	—	—
Living on charity	2.8	0.4	—	—	14.29	—	—
Total	102.4	2.4	7.0	0.6	2.34	6.84	0.59

Source: Mahalanobis, Mukherjea, and Ghose 1946, table 4.5.

dwarfed those of the prefamine period, and involved mainly peasant smallholdings, were disproportionately concentrated in East Bengal. A microsurvey of land transfers in one village in East Bengal found that as many as 54 families out of a total of 168 disposed of part or all of their holdings in 1943. While some of the land was transferred in order to repay old debts or buy land elsewhere, thirty-nine of the fifty-four transfers were prompted by "scarcity and food purchase."[36] In sum, the shift into agriculture and the rise in rent predicted by a pure entitlements model did not occur, and the plight of agriculturalists and those combining agriculture and labor, as revealed by these surveys, is more consistent with a FAD.

Although the harvest shortfall was severest in the west, the crisis was worst in the east, a rice deficit region where the living standards were lowest to begin with, the cessation of imports from neighboring Burma had a disproportionate impact, and the proximity of fighting on the Arakan front and the disruption to communications due to the "denial" policy wreaked havoc.

CONCLUSION

At the height of the Bengal famine, an editorial in the Calcutta *Statesman* pointed to the uncanny similarity between official reactions to incipient famine in Bihar and Orissa in 1866 and Bengal in 1943. In both cases the authorities denied that there was a genuine dearth, "large stores being in the hands of dealers who are keeping back stocks out of

---

[36] Mukerjee 1947, 309.

greed"; they refused to recognize "advancing calamity"; and in both cases disaster followed. In the case of Bengal, the lack of convincing evidence for significant speculative hoards and the socioeconomic backgrounds of the "losers" support the case for a dearth. A major difference between the two famines, though, is that in 1943 the authorities were engaged in a global war that they were in some danger of losing. When the *New Statesman and Nation* first raised the specter of famine in India in January 1943, the *Economist* responded with a concise statement of British wartime priorities: "The best way to end the famine is speedy victory and, however hard the decision, food ships must come second to victory ships."[37] And wartime priorities made Bengal starve in the second half of 1943.

A shortcoming of Sen's classic account is its overreliance on the *Report on Bengal*, and failure to take account of once-confidential correspondence between London, Calcutta, and Delhi in 1943–44. Some of this material has long been in the public domain; some remains unpublished. Its version of the events does not support that in the *Report*. Thus, as early as November 1942 it reveals Linlithgow, conveying his serious worries about "the food situation" to Amery, after receiving "most urgent representations" from the governor of Bengal, John Herbert. A month later, Linlithgow continued to be greatly exercised by a picture that continued to be "nasty."[38] And yet, in January 1943, despite accumulating evidence of a poor harvest in Bengal, we see Linlithgow in-

[37] "Food for India," *Economist*, January 30, 1943, 141; *New Statesman and Nation*, January 23, 1943, 51–52.

[38] British Library (India Office Library), Mss. Eur. F125/11, Linlithgow to Amery, November 30, 1942, December 22, 1942.

sisting to Chief Minister Fazl-ul Huq that "he simply must produce more rice out of Bengal for Ceylon even if Bengal itself went short!" and hoping that he might "screw a little out of them."[39]

As late as July 1943, when famine deaths were already commonplace, and starving country people were fleeing in their thousands to the main towns and cities, Amery, the secretary of state for India, informed fellow members of Parliament in faraway London that there was "no overall shortage of foodgrains," and the "present difficult situation" was due to "maldistribution." By then, Amery was blaming not merely speculation by a handful of major players but a psychosis that had also gripped small traders and cultivators. The crux was "a widespread tendency of cultivators to withhold foodgrains from the market, to larger consumption per head as the result of increased family income, to hoarding by consumers and others."[40]

Herbert—hitherto a strong supporter of the "sufficiency" position—began to sound the alarm in early July. He pleaded in confidence with Linlithgow:

I must invoke all my powers of description and persuasion to convey to you the seriousness of the food situation in Bengal. Hitherto I have studiously avoided overstating the case and I have faithfully reported any day-to-day alleviation of the situation: I am now in some

[39] British Library (BL), Oriental and India Office Collections (OIOC), Mss. Eur. F125/12, Linlithgow to Amery, January 22, 1943.

[40] *Hansard* (Commons), ser. 5, vol. 390, col. 1774, July 1, 1943; *Hansard* (Commons), ser. 5, vol. 391, col. 216, July 14, 1943.

doubt as to whether I have not erred in the direction of understatement.[41]

Herbert's report that the "food drive" had located only one hundred thousand tons in stocks of four hundred maunds or more was interpreted by Linlithgow as evidence of "how much is in fact available." While Herbert was insisting that Bengal needed imports, Linlithgow was still arguing that there was enough in the province. Further reports of the rapidly deteriorating crisis forced Linlithgow to change his tune. By mid-July he was demanding food imports as a matter of extreme urgency, no matter "how unpalatable this demand must be to H.M.G." and realizing its "serious potential effect on military operations." On the verge of retirement, he hoped that he could announce imminent food imports in his valedictory address to the New Delhi legislature. Amery, now also convinced that disaster was looming, took Linlithgow's plea seriously and argued the case at a meeting of the war cabinet on July 31. Relying on military rather than humanitarian rhetoric, he advised that unless help was forthcoming, India's role as a theater of war would be compromised.[42] But the war cabinet held, against all the evidence, that "the shortage of grain in India was not the result of physical deficiency but of hoarding," and insisted that the importation of grain would not solve the problem. Amery pleaded in vain with the cabinet to reject

[41] Sir John Herbert to Lord Linlithgow, cited in Batabyal 2005, 90, 93.

[42] Amery (1988, 912) noted in his diary in September 1943 that "the sight of famine conditions cannot but cause distress to the European troops and anxiety to the Indian troops as to the condition of their families in other parts of India."

the position of the minister for war transport, who offered merely 100,000 tons of Iraqi barley and "no more than 50,000 tons as a token shipment . . . to be ordered to Colombo to await instructions there." Ministers hoped that on the strength of this measly offer, but "without disclosing figures," the viceroy would announce that supplies were on their way as required. Amery conceded that he "might be compelled by events to reopen the matter within a very few weeks."[43] Just a week later, General Claude Auchinleck, commander in chief of British forces in India, echoing Amery's request, pleaded with the chief of imperial general staff in London: "So far as shipping is concerned, the import of food is to my mind just as if not more important than the import of munitions."[44] To no avail: on September 24, the war cabinet decided that it would not be possible to divert ships to lifting grain for delivery in India before the next Indian harvest.

As the crisis worsened by the week, Linlithgow, clearly affected by the mounting tide of criticism within Bengal, declared that "it will have to come back on His Majesty's Government." But London continued to prioritize military requirements and "the food situation nearer home." Amery confided to the viceroy that "famine in Greece has been, I imagine, even worse than in Bengal and one of the most urgent needs of the immediate future will be the shipping of food into Greece to help the insurgents, of whom something like 50,000 are under arms today and playing a really important role in the whole war effort." In a letter to the incoming viceroy, Lord Wavell, Amery recognized the "natural

[43] Ó Gráda 2008.
[44] Mansergh 1973, 44–217 passim.

and widespread feeling here that somehow or other the ultimate responsibility rests with us and that this country could
or should have done more."[45] Yet he continued,

> As to that, you know as well as I do the military preoc-
> cupations of the War Cabinet and the difficulty of di-
> verting shipping from the first duty of winning the
> war. As you will remember, the last War Cabinet deci-
> sion was that the matter should be reviewed at the end
> of the year. I am not sure that that is not leaving things
> too late and, if you can manage at an early date to visit
> Bengal yourself, or, even apart from that, feel that you
> should weigh in with a strong demand for earlier
> consideration, I hope you will do so.[46]

Even as late as October 1943, London needed convincing
that "everything has been done within India to extract
hoarded supplies and get them to the starving districts." In
an exasperated response to London's reluctance to supply
more grain in early 1944, Wavell warned that the famine
was "one of the greatest disasters that has befallen any people
under British rule and [the] damage to our reputation both
among Indians and foreigners in India is incalculable."[47]

Concerns about war morale also explain why the Bengali
authorities were so reluctant to operate the Famine Codes,
even though classic famine symptoms were present, and
why the full extent of the crisis remained largely hidden
from the outside world for so long. By the same token, the
war accounts for the muted, kid-glove tone of the *Report on
Bengal* and its refusal to criticize the authorities in London

[45] BL, OIOC, Mss. Eur. F125/12, Amery to Wavell, October 21, 1943.
[46] Ibid.
[47] Moon 1973, 54.

for leaving Bengal short. It would be naive to think that the wartime context did not influence the composition of the commission and its final report. The "denial policy" and ensuing disruption of internal markets, the cutting off of Burmese imports, the support for incompetent local politicians who would not ask awkward questions, and the inevitable impact of the war on expectations about future supplies were also the products of war.

To summarize, the heavy focus in the literature on hoarding is misplaced. The extensive hoards as described in ministerial propaganda were mainly mirages. Not that this was just another example of FAD à la Malthus, however: in Bengal in 1943–44, Mars played a much bigger role than Malthus. As economic historian Lance Brennan has emphasized, earlier harvest failures in Bengal, in 1936 and 1941, had not led to famine. But wartime priorities deprived the Bengali poor of the food they so badly needed, disrupted food markets (to some extent), inhibited free speech, and delayed the public proclamation of famine conditions. The conclusion seems inescapable: the two million and more who perished in Bengal were mainly unwitting, colonial casualties of a struggle not of their making—that against fascism.

A "no FAD" interpretation of the Bengali famine implies that it was akin to a zero-sum game, with the shift in the relative price of food distinguishing winners from losers. The main losers in Bengal—unskilled workers, petty artisans, landless farm laborers, and their dependents—were no different from those most at risk during famines generally; but evidence that food producers and speculators in stocks of food made comparable gains seems doubtful. Sen and others have described the famine as the product mainly of bureaucratic bungling and accompanying market failure. I see it instead as largely due to the failure of the British authorities, for war-strategic reasons, to make good a genuine food deficit.

Nevertheless, Sen's emphasis on entitlements transcends its original focus on Bengal. It is a useful and timely reminder that *any* famine resulting from a serious harvest shortfall will *also* generate an entitlements crisis in the sense of Joshua the Stylite's account of famine in Mesopotamia a millennium and a half ago: "Everything that was not edible was cheap, such as clothes and household utensils and furniture, for these things were sold for a half or a third of their value, and did not suffice for the maintenance of their owners, because of the great dearth of bread."[48]

The sharp deterioration in the entitlements of wage earners and their dependents during the Bangladesh famine of the mid-1970s is evident in figure 6.2, and is reflected in the distribution of famine deaths by socioeconomic status. As in Ireland in the 1840s, although it is difficult to identify any major class of winners, landless and near-landless rural laborers were much more likely to perish than were farmers.[49] Note, too, that claims that famines in India resulted from maldistribution rather than from a literal lack of food are not new. A report on the famine of 1860–61 described Indian famines as "famines of work [more] than of food," and the Indian Famine Commission of 1880 portrayed this process in the following words: "As a general rule, there is abundance of food procurable, even in the worst districts in the worst times; but when men who, at the best, merely live from hand to mouth, are deprived of their means of

[48] Wright 1882, 29b.
[49] Razzaque 1989; Alamgir 1977; Ó Gráda 1999, chapter 4.

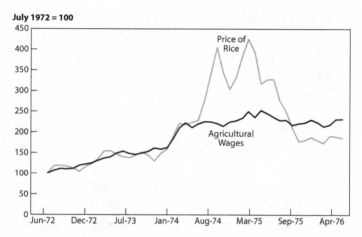

July 1972 = 100

Fig. 6.2.   Nominal agricultural wages and the price of rice in Bangladesh, 1972–76.

earning wages, they starve not from the impossibility of getting food, but for want of the necessary money to buy it."[50]

The relative importance of FADs and entitlement shifts independent of harvest size has probably shifted during the past century. Accounts of famines in places ranging from the Soviet Union in the 1930s to Biafra/Nigeria in the 1960s, and from China in the 1950s to Ethiopia in the 1970s, highlight the role of politics and institutional factors rather than "economic" causes. Nonetheless, it is too soon to dismiss entirely the role of FADs in twentieth-century famines. In three of the case studies highlighted by Sen—Bengal in 1943–44, and Bangladesh and Ethiopia in the 1970s—subsequent research indicates significant FAD problems.[51]

[50] Famine Commission 1880, appendix 1, 205, cited in de Waal 1997, 22; see also Davis 2001, 27.

[51] Goswami 1990; Basu 1984; Kumar 1990; Devereux 1988; Dyson 1996.

1980 = 100

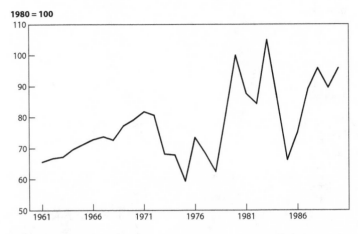

FIG. 6.3.   Cereal production in Ethiopia, 1961–90 (milled rice equiv-alent, in m. metric tons).

Figures 6.3 and 6.4 (based on Food and Agriculture Orga-nization [FAO] data) imply that both the Ethiopian famines of 1973–74 and 1984–85 as well as the Bangladeshi famine of 1974 followed series of poor harvests.

Famines dramatically highlight and usually magnify social inequalities in the societies in which they happen. It is hardly possible to imagine a famine that might not have been—or could not be—alleviated by more generous transfers from the rich to the poor. Markets, moreover, are unlikely to tilt the balance in favor of the poor. Unfettered markets merely make the most of existing resources, given their initial distri-bution across a community, but that is the limit to their opti-mality. Even if they work like clockwork, they cannot override mismatches between entitlements and market position. For those, in Bengal, whose survival required the urgent redistri-bution of resources or entitlements, as well as beyond, the efficiency or otherwise of markets mattered little.

FIG. 6.4.   Cereal production per head in Bangladesh, 1965–85.

Taken together, the findings described above do not rule out a further role for markets in exacerbating these crises; as Sen reminds us, highly integrated markets might allow inhabitants of less-affected areas, armed with the requisite purchasing power, to siphon food away from famine-threatened regions. Much depends on the extent to which such exports are used to finance cheaper imported substitutes (e.g., maize for wheat) and the speed with which food markets adjust. Finally, as already noted in chapter 3, the widespread conviction that famines make the rich richer, may well have a basis in their relatively easier access to credit, particularly during famines. In the past this presumably gave the rich the edge in purchasing land, housing, livestock, and other property forced on to the market during crises.

CHAPTER VII

Public and Private Action

They ne'er cared for us yet: suffer us to famish, and their store-houses crammed with grain; make edicts for usury, to support usurers; repeal daily any wholesome act established against the rich, and provide more piercing statutes daily, to chain up and restrain the poor.

—*William Shakespeare*, Coriolanus

And I'm sure it crossed your mind
What it is you have to find
Find a man to lead you through the famine
With a flair for economic planning

—*Tim Rice*, Joseph and the Amazing Technicolor Dreamcoat

FEEDING THE STARVING

The state of nature in which all households grow their own food, and have only themselves and the gods to blame for famine, has always been the exception. Since the dawn of history the landless or semi-landless poor have been present, as have the farmers, merchants, and rulers who exacted rents, profits, and taxes from them. When disaster struck, the poor expected others to help them. Help involved providing food, foregoing customary exactions, or reducing rents and taxes. The urban poor, more vulnerable to shortages, were particularly dependent on the authorities during famines, and represented a threat to rulers who seemed not to care. As for the rich, they were nearly always in a position to do more than they did.

The conviction that the rich could and should relieve the poor in times of threatened famine is an age-old one. It is famously reflected in the chant of the hungry poor who marched on Versailles in October 1789—"*Allons chercher le boulanger, la boulangère et le petit mitron* [let's find the baker, his wife, and the baker's boy!]."[1] Failure to deliver led to anger, or worse. So Emperor Nero's failure to guarantee the citizens of Rome their grain supplies from Africa in AD 68 led to his downfall and suicide, while Venice's Pietro Loredan (1482–1570) was reviled as the "famine Doge" and the "millet Doge." The *grande princesse* mentioned in Jean-Jacques Rousseau's *Confessions* who responded to news that the poor had no bread with "*qu'ils mangent de la brioche*" (then let them eat cake) was identified, quite wrongly, as Marie-Antoinette, whereas in Ireland, exaggerated stories about Queen Victoria's stinginess during the 1840s led later generations of Irish nationalists to remember her as the "famine queen." Again, the secretary of state for India who rationalized British inaction in Bengal in 1943 on the grounds that "the matter in Bengal is primarily one for the Ministry of that self-governing province," was berated by a left-wing parliamentarian, who asked, "Could there be anything worse than disclaiming responsibility?"[2] Today, Swaziland's Mswati III, the ruler of a tiny country suffering from serious food shortages and an HIV/AIDS epidemic, spends more than double his country's health budget on an execu-

[1] Kaplan 2008.
[2] *Hansard* (Commons), ser. 5, vol. 392, cols. 396–99, September 23, 1943.

tive jet, and earns the condemnation of the media and the International Monetary Fund.

Elites have long accepted a moral obligation to relieve those most at risk during famines, though their commitment to noblesse oblige presumably was sharpened by threats of civil unrest and the spread of infection, from which the wealthy were not immune. The earliest documentary evidence of famine relief comes from ancient Egypt and stems from the desire of the rich to be remembered for their good works. A stela (commemorative pillar) dating from the thirteenth or fourteenth dynasty (ca. 1700 BC) proclaims: "I gave bread to the hungry, clothes to the naked, sandals to the barefoot; I gave corn to the entire country, I saved my city from starvation. Nobody did what I have done." An even earlier stela boasts: "I was a great provider for their homes in the famine year; I fed those I did not know in the same way as those I knew."[3]

In ancient Greece and Rome, members of local oligarchies prevented food crises (which were frequent) from developing into famines (which were rare). In 123 BC, civil unrest provoked by food shortages prompted the populist Gaius Gracchus to enact the first *lex frumentaria*, which guaranteed all citizens grain at subsidized prices. In late classical Rome and Constantinople, public action in times of crisis was a key part of the imperial moral code. Constantine, the first Christian emperor, began the practice of using the churches as channels of aid, while Julian II ("the Apostate") supervised the distribution of revenue and grain during a severe famine in Antioch in AD 362–63. Julian

[3] Vandier 1936, 19, 105.

also cut back the size of the court, reduced taxes, and distributed uncultivated land to smallholders.

In early imperial Rome the role of the elite was central, but historians have detected a sharp decline in private philanthropy in the late empire. Stathakopoulos's comprehensive listing of famines in the late empire contains only two mentions of action by the rich. In Rome the authorities took action only as crises became grave, usually through supplying grain or, less often, remitting taxes. Sometimes such measures came too late. As the authorities increasingly took a backseat, the Roman church played an increasing role, emerging as an institution centrally involved in charity and relief in the later fourth century.[4]

In India, too, both the Mughal ruling classes and the East India Company conceded a duty to act in times of crisis. Typically, they prohibited food exports and regulated food prices in urban markets. Adam Smith castigated the East India Company for its antimarket stance, but ignored relief measures that also included (albeit always inadequate) food distribution depots and regional migration schemes. In 1837– 38, the company "acknowledged its responsibilities more openly." It offered work to the able-bodied on the assumption that the aid would reach others through them, and also granted limited relief in the form of food rations to those unable to work; in this instance, the breakdown of "law and order" was the spur.[5]

In pre-Reformation England, the bulk of the responsibility for relief of the poor fell on the church. With the dissolution of the monasteries in the 1530s, new policies for helping

[4] Garnsey 1988, 82–86; Stathakopoulos 2004, 65–66; Holman 2001.
[5] Ahuja 2002; Loveday 1914, 40–42; Sharma 2001.

the poor in the event of harvest failure were needed. These were codified in Elizabeth I's *Book of Orders* (1586), prompted by "her majesty, observing the general dearth of corn, and other victuals, groune partly through the unseasonabless of the year when passed, and partly through the uncharitable greediness of the corn-masters but especially through the unlawful and overmuch transporting of grain to foreign parts."[6] In further legislation passed in 1598 and 1601, Parliament enacted a compulsory system of poor relief that was administered and financed at the local (parish) level. When prices rose, exports of grain were prohibited and a census was taken of stocks. Local magistrates were charged with overseeing the supply of grain in the market, inspecting grain stocks in the hands of dealers and producers, and fixing delivery quotas if deemed necessary. They were also charged with trying to regulate the price of grain. Policies to control the supply of grain were reinforced by a decentralized system of poor relief funded by a compulsory tax on property (or poor rate). Relief was relatively generous, and the law operated in a way that kept the cost of identifying the needy low and free riding to a minimum. Its poor law set England apart from its continental neighbors and probably softened its formerly harsh demographic regime.[7]

Famine prevention and relief were recognized as a key responsibility of the Chinese bureaucracy—a reflection of the Confucian tenet that to "feed" people is to better "educate" them. The variety and generosity of relief in Qing China under the Yongzheng and Qianlong emperors (1723–96) is

---

[6] As cited in, for example, *Remains Historical and Literary Connected with the Palatine Counties of Lancaster and Chester*, vol. XLII [1857], 604.

[7] Walter 1992; Solar 1995.

well documented. Grain allocations accounted for a significant percentage of central government spending; indeed,
some claim that relief was more generous in China than in
the West, and taxes and rents were more likely to be reduced
in hard times.[8] Perhaps so, but famine mortality in eigh-
teenth- and nineteenth-century China greatly exceeded that
in the West. Moreover, an abiding problem in China was
the venality of village chiefs and regional administrators. At
first sight, the finding that during the reign of the Kangxi
emperor (1662–1722), the size of a province's grain stocks
varied inversely with the amount of relief granted is what
one would expect of a well-functioning relief mechanism
responding to the scale of shortages facing the provinces
and their relative backwardness. Yet it turns out that in crisis after crisis, the richest provinces received a disproportionate share of the relief. Carol Shiue explains how the
central bureaucracy, which devoted a significant portion of
aggregate expenditure to grain allocations, relied on corrupt
local agents to identify and relieve those most at risk. The
allocation reflected a moral hazard problem arising out of
asymmetrical information, which periodic monitoring of
grain stocks and penalties against officials mitigated, but
did not eliminate the problem.[9] Incompetence and neglect
increased the risk of famine. The flooding that resulted in
famine in central China in 1906 was the product of years of
neglect of systems of drainage and communication long in
existence.[10]

Historical sources on famine are also full of references to

[8] Will 1990; Li 2007; Bengtsson, Campbell, and Lee 2004, 92.

[9] Will 1990; Shiue 2004, 2005.

[10] Kirton 1907, 86.

private philanthropic activity. In the Syrian city of Edessa in AD 499, local grandees set up infirmaries, and "many went in and found shelter in them," while the Greek soldiers built shelters for the poor, which they paid for out of their own pockets.[11] In the Nasik district of Maharashtra in 1802–4, "private charity was also active, and merchants distributed dishes of grain and cooked food." They were simply taken out and knocked on the head to save them from starvation During the Irish famine of 1740–41, Dubliners "gave willingly gold and silver, flour and coal, to support the miserable people, making no distinction between Protestant and Papist . . . and farmers gave permission for bushes and hedges to be cut down and used for firewood," while in rural areas some landed proprietors provided food and work. Two well-known architectural structures dating from that time—the "folly" at William "Speaker" Connolly's Castletown and the (recently restored) obelisk on Killiney Hill near Dublin—owe their existence to landlord-funded relief schemes. A century later the Irish were the first beneficiaries of "globalized" famine relief, much of it through the auspices of the Roman Catholic Church and the Society of Friends. Some aid was in-kind, in the form of imported and unfamiliar maize (see below). But private acts of charity were unequal to the task of relieving a major and enduring famine. As a northern Indian philanthropist put it in 1837, "Private charity may do much to alleviate individual suffering, but the relief of hundreds for an indefinite period, comes only within the means of governments."[12]

[11] Wright 1882, 32b.

[12] Cited in Sharma 2001, 170–71. On Ireland in 1740–41, the best source is Dickson 1997.

In the past, religion and ideology also influenced the stance on relief in various ways. In the *Arthasastra* of the Indian sage Kautilya (third to fourth century BC), a monarch's responsibility for his people's welfare was made explicit. In Confucianism, disasters such as famine were the product of human failure, and the elite had a responsibility to prevent them by conquering nature through flood and drought control as well as storing foodstuffs in anticipation. In Judaism, the tithe was originally intended *exclusively* as a means of supporting the poor, *not* as a support for the religious institution. In Christendom, the original redistributive intent of the tithe was reflected in the fact that it was deposited in a tithe barn (or *grange aux dîmes*), whereby the village poor could monitor, if not control, its allocation and availability in times of dearth. This progressive aspect was recognized by Marx, who in *Das Kapital* interpreted the commutation of the tithe in England as the "tacit confiscation" of "legally guaranteed property of the poorer folk." In late classical Rome, as noted earlier, the Christian church played a more active role, especially in urban areas.[13] In sum, Christianity, Confucianism, and other ethical traditions acknowledged an obligation to help those immediately at risk.

In early sixteenth-century Europe, the harsh economic climate and the Reformation provoked much controversy about the reform of poor relief. The mainspring was Germany and Martin Luther, who along with his supporters strongly condemned begging, and distinguished between the deserving and undeserving poor. But the Spanish-born humanist Juan Luis Vives, who addressed his influential *De Subventione Pauperum* to the mainly Catholic burghers of

---

[13] Li 2007, 13–15; Marx 1967, 721; Stathakopoulos 2004, 62–65.

Bruges in 1526, also opposed begging. Vives acknowledged the city's obligations toward its poor, but argued for the suppression of mendicancy, the expulsion of vagrants, and compulsory labor for those seeking relief. Relief should be financed through a combination of philanthropy and taxes on the rich. His ideas were rejected by the more traditionalist mendicant orders. Similar in spirit was the decree passed by the Venetian Senate in 1529. It also distinguished between the deserving and undeserving poor, and invited shipmasters "to take on board whatever number of [robust and hardy] poor they choose . . . and give them half the normal pay." The decree was provoked by a famine that had sucked the countryside dry of grain, and attracted mass immigration into Venice. Fearing contagion from fever and plague, the authorities erected four hospitals in which immigrant invalids were provided for, and urged institutional and individual donors to assist the poor.[14]

On occasion, famine or the threat of famine also prompted lasting institutional reforms. The Elizabethan Poor Law, the municipal schemes of poor relief that followed in the wake of Vives's *De Subventione Pauperum*, and the Indian Famine Codes are in this category. The Great Irish Famine hastened the repeal of the Corn Laws and the reform of cumbersome legislation governing the Irish land market, while the "Great Drought" of 1877–78 prompted the Dutch to put in place an extensive meteorological data network that outlasted their stay in Indonesia.

Luther and Vives distinguished between the deserving and undeserving poor, but Malthus and his followers denied the innate right of any of the poor to subsistence. In the words

[14] Pullan 1963–64; Chambers and Pullan 2001, 304.

of Thomas Wilson, editor of the fledgling, dogmatic *Economist*, "It is no man's business to provide for another." That was in the context of the Great Irish Famine of the 1840s. The *Economist* also invoked utilitarianism in its campaign against the Irish poor: relief during the Irish famine would only shift resources from "the more meritorious to the less."[15] The issue of rights apart, the Malthusians focused on the moral hazard implications of ignoring the impact of overgenerous relief on the economy at large in the short run and the likelihood of more famines in the longer run. Economist Nassau Senior allegedly "feared that the [Irish] famine . . . would not kill more than a million people, and that would scarcely be enough to do much good," claiming that more lives saved now would mean more deaths later. A providentialist version of Malthusianism saw famine as a divine plan to alleviate overpopulation.[16]

During the Great Irish Famine, a prominent parliamentarian spoke of times "when it was more difficult to do nothing than to do something, although the trying to do something were almost certain mischief." Yet Senior approvingly described the "something" as "experiments made on so large a scale, and pushed to their extreme consequences in the sufferings which they inflict, that they give us results as precious as those of Majendie"—a reference to the live dissections conducted by French physiologist François Magendie. A more sympathetic observer referred to Irish famine policy as "a sort of Majendie experiment made on human beings—not on cats in an air-pump, or on rabbits

[15] *Economist*, January 30, 1847.

[16] Woodham-Smith 1962, 375–76 (citing Senior); Gray 1997; Ó Gráda 1999, 6–7.

with prussic acid."[17] In Ireland and the Netherlands in the 1840s, Malthusian dogma constrained both private charity and the public purse. Critics of the stance of British policymakers during the Irish famine, both then and now, castigated them for not doing more. Accusations of tightfistedness were common; for example, the guardians of Fermoy's workhouse in November 1846 pleaded with ministers "who gave twenty million to emancipate the slaves, who were never so much to be pitied as the people of this country are at present." Radical nationalist John Mitchel's dramatic claim that Ireland had "died of political economy" in the 1840s was thus by no means entirely untrue; policy at the time was constrained by a stance that was obsessive about the moral hazard implications of relieving the starving, the providential nature of the failure of the potato crop, and fiscal prudence even in times of the extreme humanitarian crisis.[18]

In India, too, the same orthodoxy constrained relief policy until the 1880s. Although the Orissa famine of 1866 prompted an inquiry that "effectually called attention to the responsibilities which rested on government in famine years," and relief in Rajputana in 1868 and Bihar in 1874 was relatively generous, in the late 1870s the old principle of "less eligibility" was enforced in a draconian way in Bombay and Madras, and wages on the public works were barely enough for subsistence. Backed by a viceroy who believed that the goal of a "life at any price" was utopian, Sir Richard Temple, the governor of Bombay, obsessed about "depen-

---

[17] Senior cited in Ó Gráda 1993, 127–28; "Deplorable State of the Kilrush Union," *Illustrated London News*, December 15, 1849.

[18] Ó Gráda 1993, 127–28.

dency," "demoralization," "the bread of idleness," and "the resources of the state" during a famine that killed five million people.[19] He later changed tack, claiming that the real problem was the reluctance of the poor to seek aid from the state, but Temple was rationalizing a policy that emphasized short-term budgetary constraints. Although unsure whether a daily diet of a pound of grain was enough to sustain life, Temple supported experimentation with such a diet "in the interests of financial economy" in Madras, and the policy was implemented against the protests of local officials.[20] A late statement of the Malthusian position in its starkest form is to be found in a memorandum submitted to the viceroy of India in 1881:

> If we are to secure that a class of men—so low in intellect, morality, and possessions, the retention of which makes life valuable, as to be absolutely independent of natural population checks—shall be protected from every cause, such as famine or sickness which tends to restrain their numbers by an abnormal mortality, they must end up by eating every other class in the community.[21]

Thereafter, recognition that inadequate relief was responsible for much of the excess mortality in the late 1870s concentrated policymakers' minds on the need to focus primarily on saving lives. This led to the introduction of the Indian Famine Codes, the "first written statements of famine policy in the modern era."[22] The codes inaugurated the first famine

[19] Ahuja 2002, 354.
[20] Digby 1878, 2:172; Hall-Matthews 2007.
[21] Cited in Ambirajan 1976, 8.
[22] Hall-Matthews 2005, 216.

early warning system, and set out strict conditions under which relief should be introduced. Although intended to provide no more than "what is required to maintain life and health," this did not preclude a gradual relaxation of the budget constraint on relief expenditure. Thus, Temple had allocated about 50 million rupees to public works and "gratuitous relief" in 1876–78, while the authorities spent 171 million and 165 million rupees in 1896–97 and 1899–1900, respectively.[23]

The codes have been much praised. They were guided by the "enlightenment" principles that the authorities should not interfere with the grain trade or compromise economic activity in other ways, and that relief should not give rise to more permanent dependency. In combating famine, though, "it must be laid down as a first principle that the object of State intervention is to save life and that all other considerations should be subordinated to this."[24] Following this diagnosis, the relief policy embodied in the Indian Famine Codes placed most emphasis on the creation of large-scale employment through relief works.

The code drafted in 1880 set down a procedure to watch for signs of distress in rising prices, and establish "test works" and soup kitchens. It sought to minimize delays in providing relief, realizing that delays cost lives. Numbers applying for relief were monitored, and if they rose rapidly famine was declared. If the famine was extensive, a commissioner was appointed. Public works, providing employment at low wages on infrastructural projects, were central,

[23] Bhatia 1967, 96, 261; Klein 1984; Ambirajan 1976; Hall-Matthews 2005.

[24] Hall-Matthews 1998, 125.

allied with adequate medical care. Although in practice the measures taken may have been too timid and miserly, the codes "formed part of a move, however hesitant, toward greater state responsibility."[25] Gradually, the qualifications for relief were eased; according to the official 1900 famine inquiry there was less reluctance to seek relief in 1900–1901 than in 1896–97. In 1900–1901, the numbers on relief exceeded six million at one point (in August 1900). As before, most of the relief was through public works: about one out of six were relieved with food at the peak. A self-congratulating Lord George Nathaniel Curzon, viceroy at the time, claimed that the excess mortality of 0.5 million (his estimate) was modest in the circumstances: "In the entire history of British famines, while none has been so intense, in none have the deaths been so few." The reality was quite different—an excess death toll of between 3 and 4.4 million.[26]

India was spared major famine between the 1900s and 1943–44. The Great Bengal Famine, which was discussed in some detail in the previous chapter, was unexpected. Here we are concerned with the link between the famine's wartime context and relief measures. Due to the war, the authorities in Bengal and India generally were more worried about "creating confidence" than saving lives by invoking the Famine Codes. The contrast with 1936, when West Bengal suffered a severe drought but no famine, is striking.[27]

For Pinnell, director of civil supplies during the rice procurement crisis in 1943, the famine was "a personal

[25] Arnold 1988, 115.
[26] Maharatna 1996, 15.
[27] Sen 1981, 78–83; Brennan 1988, 543.

failure." Although privy to reports that the aman harvest of late 1942 was poor, at first Pinnell supported—as "any officer with a sense of responsibility to India as well to his Province in a common danger" would do—the official line that there was no overall shortage of food. Later, he would bitterly regret not forcefully making the point at the first All-India Food Conference in December 1942 "that there was definitely going to be a shortage in Bengal." His patriotism instead led him to emphasize the presence of ample carryover stocks, and the upshot of the conference was a determination "to bring out any hidden surpluses."[28] Pinnell's continued support for the case for adequate food supplies led the editor of the Calcutta *Statesman* to describe him and a colleague as "two unhappy but not dishonest men working to a brief they didn't believe," and their inept performance convinced the editor that a catastrophe was inevitable.[29]

Only on July 28, 1943, did the authorities announce a plan to assist privately-run gruel kitchens, which the government would supply at subsidized rates. The gruel was distributed only once a day—barely enough to hold body and soul together—in over five thousand gruel kitchens. In order to prevent abuse, it was distributed simultaneously at all centers, for an hour at noon. When a new viceroy, Lord Wavell, arrived in Bengal in October 1943, he found a situation still "grim enough to make official complacency surprising," with thousands of destitutes from the countryside camped on Calcutta's streets and in open areas. He initially rejected demands for an official inquiry into the famine on

[28] Brennan 1988; Pinnell 2002, 97.
[29] Cited in Ó Gráda 2008.

the grounds that its findings would probably embarrass the authorities in London.[30]

MEANS OF RELIEF

Over the centuries, governing elites have employed a variety of famine relief strategies: the maintenance of public granaries, institutionalized care through poor laws, improvised soup kitchens, workfare, and subsidized migration schemes.[31] Elites often relied on local agents (the clergy, private philanthropists, and political leaders) to identify and relieve the neediest, but such delegation frequently leads to principal-agent problems of corruption and red tape in the affected regions. Some of the historical controversies about the optimal form of famine relief—such as the choice between public works or soup kitchens, or between centralized or decentralized bureaucracies—have a distinctly modern ring to them. The record suggests the importance of the historical and institutional context.[32]

The storage of food stocks against the eventuality of famine goes back to the Old Testament (Genesis 41:54–57): "All Egypt would have perished unless the king, by [Joseph's] advice, had ordered grain to be stored many years before the famine came." Joseph's wisdom in laying up supplies not only sustained Egypt but also helped relieve seven years of famine in neighboring countries. Whether the pharaoh's

---

[30] Moon 1973, 35.

[31] For more on relief policy, see Ravallion 1997; Webb 2001.

[32] Brennan 1984; de Waal 1997; Drèze and Sen 1989; Hall-Matthews 1998; Waldman 2001; Toole, Nieburg, and Waldman 1988.

warehouses really had the capacity to guard against seven poor harvests in succession is doubtful, however. If the experience of other storage experiments is worth anything, the risks due to vermin, rotting, and theft should not be underestimated.

Municipal granaries were also a key element in the battle against famine in early modern Europe. The *chambre d'abondance* of Lyons, established in 1643, was modeled on the *abbondanzas* of Genoa and Florence. Its aim was to maintain a reserve stock of wheat in order to smooth price fluctuations and ensure a subsidized supply of bread for the poor as the need arose. The city administration named local merchants as directors, whose task it was to keep the warehouse stocked with grain purchased at a distance from local markets. This arrangement capitalized on the skills and contacts of the merchants. Still, the city had no dedicated building for the purpose, and rented premises to store its grain. Short of space, it was often forced to sell old grain at a loss. The high cost of transport was another problem. As a result, several times the *chambre d'abondance* was caught napping, most seriously in 1693. In the wake of that crisis it was resolved to maintain a stock, but again by 1707 there was hardly anything in store.[33]

Nevertheless, during the crisis of 1709–10, the *chambre d'abondance* managed to locate corn. Its early efforts ended in disaster: the weather first prevented grain purchased in the south from being shipped north, and then three barge loads were confiscated by the authorities in Valence, whereupon several other port towns held on to Lyons grain in their warehouses. Soon, however, Valence was forced to make

[33] Monahan 1993, 33–36.

restitution, and the *chambre d'abondance* began to sell corn at a loss to the city's bakers. It sent one of its directors to Italy to buy wheat in May 1709; after much effort and expense, the first supplies arrived four months later. As a result, by March 1710 its debt had risen from almost nothing in Easter 1708 to over two million livres two years later—a sum considerably more than the city's entire annual revenue on the eve of the famine. The grain arrived too late for many, and more could not afford the high prices being charged, but whether the city's merchants would have supplied the city in such volume unaided must remain a moot point. At the end of the crisis the directors found themselves with excess stocks of wheat, which they again sold at a loss.

Confining the poor to large prisonlike institutions has frequently been a key feature of famine relief. Such a strategy was seen as minimizing the spread of infectious disease and a deterrent to vagrancy. It also was more likely to separate the deserving from the undeserving, and addressed the likelihood that the most at risk were homeless. The Venetian famine of 1528–29 prompted the construction of four hospitals to house vagrants. In France the *hôtels-dieu*, refuges for the sick and elderly poor in normal times, were heavily relied on in times of famine or threatened famine. In Finnish folklore the famine of 1868 connotes begging, substitute foods, and perhaps above all, the workhouse; "to be carried to the workhouse means the same as death." The workhouses were a product of the famine. The neo-Malthusian workhouse system introduced in England in 1834 aimed at reducing welfare dependence—a classic example of what economists dub the moral hazard problem—by imposing the principle of "less eligibility" through the "workhouse test."[34] In Ireland, a system of workhouses closely modeled on that in England catered at first mainly for the very young, the elderly, and the temporarily out-of-work. Already in place in 1845–46, it was transformed to confront the catastrophe of the Great Famine. About one famine death in four—about half of them due to infectious disease—occurred within workhouse walls. The proportion of deaths from infectious diseases varied across workhouses; predictably, the level of background poverty mattered. But even allowing for background poverty, measures of the competence of workhouse management, such as the date of the workhouse's opening or the percentage of inmates dying from infectious disease, suggest that the quality of management varied considerably from workhouse to workhouse.[35]

Public works have been another common means of famine relief. In principle, the aim of such works was to fulfill the double function of being productive and incorporating the principle of "less eligibility." Effective food-for-work schemes require a competent bureaucracy to organize them, though. During the extensive Indian *chalisa* famine of 1783–84, the ruling nabob reportedly gave employment to forty thousand people on public works in Lucknow, but evidence for similar schemes in the precolonial era is lacking. In northern India in 1837–38 the East India Company organized "works of public utility," focusing in particular on roads as a means of widening markets and facilitating military movements. The works reconciled a political imperative to maintain

---

[34] Ó Gráda 1999, 50–51.

[35] Guinnane and Ó Gráda 2002. For excellent case studies, see Ó Murchadha 1995; Eiríksson 1996a, 1996b.

peace and tranquillity in the short run with strategic goals in the longer run.[36]

Public works were also an important feature of relief during the European famine of 1816–17. In Britain, legislation enabled the government to lend money to companies investing in public works schemes. The projects, which were limited to severely affected parishes, focused on canal and road building as well as draining marshes. Elsewhere projects ranged from military fortifications to land reclamation. In addition, cities also organized their own public works schemes, such as new docks in Liverpool. In practice such spending had the added benefit of being countercyclical.[37]

The provision of employment through public works also featured prominently during the early stages of the Great Irish Famine. The cost of the works, which mostly consisted of small-scale infrastructural improvements, was to be split between taxpayers (namely, local large landowners and farmers) and the central government. Relief considerations constrained the size and location of the works. At their height in spring 1847 they employed seven hundred thousand people, or one in twelve of the entire population. But they did not contain the famine, partly because they did not target the neediest, partly because the average wage paid was too low, and partly because the works entailed exposing malnourished and poorly clothed people (mostly men) to the elements during the worst months of the year. Such works, in earlier times, had usually been confined to the spring and summer. In 1846–47 it was a different mat-

---

[36] Ahuja 2002, 356; Sharma 2001, 160–71.
[37] Post 1977, 63–64.

ter. An account in a Cork newspaper from one badly affected area is telling.

> Yesterday morning at daybreak, I saw a gang of about 150, composed principally of old men, women, and little boys, going out to work on one of the roads near this town. At the time the ground was covered with snow, and there was also a very severe frost. . . . The women and the children were crying out from the severity of the cold, and were unable to hold the implements with which they were at work, [and] most of them declared they had not tasted food for the day. . . . The actual value of the labour executed by these could not average two pence each per day, and to talk of task work to such labourers would be too ridiculous.
>
> I could not help thinking how much better it would be to afford them some temporary relief in their own homes during this severe weather, than thus to sacrifice their lives to carry out a miserable project of political economy.[38]

In Ethiopia in the 1980s, a series of food-for-work programs focused on road building, afforestation, digging wells, and land conservation. There were widespread complaints about how the participants were selected, and indeed the neediest would seem to have been disadvantaged. Female-headed households were underrepresented, and strong, healthy workers benefited most. Nor were most projects, conceived in conditions of urgency, likely to endure without periodic maintenance.[39]

---

[38] Cited in Ó Gráda 1999, 68.
[39] Webb and von Braun 1994, 108–13.

CORRUPTION

Because governing elites were often remote from those at risk, they relied on sub-bureaucracies and local gentry to identify worthy recipients of relief. Almost inevitably, there was a trade-off between the degree of delegation, on the one hand, and corruption and red tape, on the other. In Venice in April 1570, the problem was noblemen who were buying flour in public warehouses and then selling it as bread at a markup of over 100 percent. The senate reacted quickly by declaring that the flour should be given to the bakers who were supposed to bake it and then give it to the poor, but the bakers resold the flour instead of making bread with it. In seventeenth-century India, Mughal rulers such as Shahjahan and Aurangzeb allocated considerable sums toward relieving the destitute, but "the benefit of these grants was generally reaped by corrupt and unscrupulous state officials." In Qing China, as noted earlier, the venality and rapacity of village notables was taken as given by the central government; for a relief effort to have any hope of success, the central bureaucracy needed to bypass them at the local level. In Honan in 1942, one of a group of Canadian missionaries used relief funds to build a cottage for himself, and others closed ranks around the guilty party, who was reelected chair of the mission. Favoritism and nepotism also constrained relief: for example, missionaries of different persuasions (naturally) gave priority to saving their own coreligionists, while in Bengal in 1943, the middle-class Hindu *bhadralok* reserved the best of the food aid for themselves. In Bangladesh in the 1970s the ration system was "rife with corruption"; urban populations were privileged at the expense of the rural masses. In eastern Sudan in the 1980s, a U.S. physician wondered whether the money "for those Mercedes trucks" came from the United States, and had been intended for distribution as humanitarian aid. The physician recorded his outrage at "watching expensive modern materials go to an army, while in this camp we still lack cheap vitamin pills and other medicine to cure children with illnesses from the Middle Ages."[40] A report from a Bangladeshi newspaper in November 2003 described the plight of the elderly poor, on whom loan sharks and corrupt relief officials preyed. Government-allocated vulnerable group feeding cards, intended for free distribution, were being sold for thirty to fifty takas (US$0.60 to US$1.00) in remote northern districts hit by near famine. Moneylenders who charged a monthly rate of interest of 300 percent waited on the *aman* (November–December) harvest to get their money back.[41] Strict policing and greater political transparency have often been unequal to the seemingly Sisyphean challenge of ensuring that relief reached those most at risk.

Two final points about corruption and famine are worth making. First, it bears noting that although public action and human agency certainly mattered and continue to matter, they too are to a degree a function of the economic backwardness that makes famine more likely. Second, obsessing about corruption, particularly on the part of the

---

[40] Chambers and Pullan 2001, 111–12; Kaw 1996, 64; Christensen 2005, 114–15, 118; Brennan 1988, 560; Hartmann and Boyce 1983, 46; Heiden 1992, 168.

[41] Http://www.thedailystart.net/2003/11/07/d3110701022.htm.

poor themselves, is a recipe for inaction. In the past, officials and commentators hostile to famine relief have been
quick to focus on the inevitable accompanying corruption
as a means of reducing support for relief.[42]

NGOS AND THE GLOBALIZATION OF RELIEF

No man can be so inhuman and wicked, that when he sees
men languishing on the streets, and falling down from hunger,
he does not feel a pain in his heart to think how near he is to
the same suffering.

—*Giovanni Battista Segni*, Carestia e Fame

Until relatively recently, the most that famine victims could
hope for was *local* relief from either the public or private
sector. The Irish famine of 1740–41—possibly more murderous in relative terms than that of the 1840s—seems to
have elicited little support from across the Irish Sea. In
1822, however, the London Tavern Committee was created
to raise funds for famine relief in the west of Ireland. In the
1840s several similar ad hoc groups—the Central Relief
Committee of the Society of Friends, the British Association for the Relief of Extreme Distress in the Remote Parishes of Ireland and Scotland, the Dublin Mansion House
Committee, and others—were set up to solicit funds and
administer relief during the Great Irish Famine. News of
the famine reached the Choctaw Nation in Oklahoma, where
a tribal assembly contributed $170 toward relief. As the
telegraph and news media spread reports of the Great

---

[42] Compare Watts 1983, 391; Ó Gráda 1999, 48–55.

Northern China Famine of 1876–79, Chinese expatriates from far-flung corners of the world such as Peru, California, and the Sandwich Islands remitted money home, and merchants contributed flour sent by steamship. By then disaster relief was truly globalized. In Russia in 1891–92, members of the royal family and the aristocracy organized several relief committees to solicit donations from near and far; the "millers of America" sent a boatload of grain all the way from the Great Lakes. As a final example, a collection organized in London in aid of victims of the Midnapur cyclone of late 1942 raised the equivalent of 412,902 rupees, including donations from "a blind lady of 85, a blind and bed-ridden pensioner, . . . and many small children who had sacrificed their pocket money."[43]

Such ad hoc organizations were wound up once the crisis had passed. Band Aid and Live Aid are in this tradition. More recently, though, several agencies created to address particular crises have tended to transform themselves into more durable organizations. The British nongovernmental organization (or NGO) Oxfam, originally the Oxford Committee for Famine Relief, began as a fund-raiser for victims of the Greek famine of 1942. Its first appeal—"Greek Week" in the following year—raised £12,700 for the Greek Red Cross. Since then Oxfam has developed into a global confederation of twelve campaigning organizations supported by hundreds of thousands of regular donors. Concern Worldwide, an Irish-based NGO, grew out of famine relief efforts by Irish Holy Ghost missionaries during the Nigerian civil war in the late 1960s; its remit now ranges

---

[43] "The Famine in China," *New York Times*, April 16, 1878; Edgar 1893; *Calcutta Statesman*, April 6, 1943.

from advocacy and HIV/AIDS to education and microfinance. The British charity Comic Relief began as a response to the Ethiopian famine of 1984–85, but now raises money for the relief of poverty in both the United Kingdom and Africa. CARE International, which began as the Cooperative for American Remittances to Europe in 1945, today has agents at work in sixty countries.

NGOs have undoubtedly succeeded in raising global awareness of poverty and underdevelopment. The transition from ad hoc philanthropy to enduring bureaucracy has not been without its downside, however. In 1929, the American Red Cross sharply criticized the China International Famine Relief Commission on the grounds that

> a permanent organization involves continuing expense from one famine to the next for salaries and other items of upkeep; that inasmuch as the life of the organization depends upon receipts from relief contributions there must always exist, perhaps unconsciously, an urge to discover in every period a serious crop deficiency, a reason for calling on the public for contributions, before thoroughly exploiting the possibility of meeting the situation by more ordinary methods.[44]

The Red Cross also criticized the China International Famine Relief Commission for transforming emergency relief funds, donated in 1920–21 and later for the immediate relief of famine sufferers, into a revolving or endowment fund, and using the funds in ways not intended by the original donors. Another criticism aimed at relief organizations in general was their failure to cooperate by sharing information

[44] Nathan 1965, 18.

and coordinating activities in the field. [45] Such criticisms are still made of NGOs today.

Another tendency for such organizations has been to shift focus from disaster relief to development aid (including famine prevention)—a shift prompted by their bureaucratic need for continuous activity and funding. NGOs must balance the public's wish to relieve disasters as they happen and their own need for bureaucratic sustainability, which entails concentrating more on long-term projects than on famine relief per se. Thus CARE now focuses on "creating lasting solutions to root causes of poverty," while Concern Worldwide's mission now is "to enable absolutely poor people to achieve major improvements in their lifestyles which are sustainable."[46]

Third, many NGOs have become increasingly reliant on public funding, and have in effect been co-opted by governments as intermediaries to distribute food and development aid. This has reduced their reliance on private donations. In the early 2000s, one of Ireland's best-known third world charities, GOAL, was doubling up as relief administrator in Afghanistan, and about one-third of its grant aid was United States Aid for International Development funding; in 2007, Concern Worldwide relied on "governments and other co-funders" for half its income, and the Irish Department of Foreign Affairs announced a five-year public funding program that would double support for that agency from €60 million in 2003–06 to €148 million in 2007–11.[47]

---

[45] American Red Cross 1929, 22.

[46] Http://www.ethics.emory.edu/content/view/393/140/; http://www.concern.net/about-concern/index.php.

[47] Http://www.concern.net/documents/1083/Accounts.pdf.

Such developments have conditioned the role of NGOs in international famine relief efforts. Famines have allowed them to channel the basic decency of millions of ordinary people, as volunteers and donors. By the same token, far too often NGOs' reliance on the media has led them to overstate the extent or danger of famines. Well-known examples include the hyping up of a waning famine in Somalia in 1992 and wildly exaggerated estimates of the numbers "about to die" in central Africa in 1996.[48] Apocalyptic warnings in late 1998 that Sudan was on the brink of an "unprecedented calamity" were followed by more in 2002 that "only massive intervention now, with large-scale delivery of food aid," would prevent a disaster on the scale of Ethiopia in 1984 or Somalia in 1992. Yet the Sudanese famine of 1998 was a minor one, and there was no famine in 2002. The cell phone text message circulated by field workers in southern Africa in 2002—"Starving child found in Malawi!"—was their tongue-in-cheek response to agency claims of fifteen million victims spread across six countries.[49] The telltale signs of famine—migration, hospitals filled with the malnourished, and an increase in mortality—were lacking. An audit found NGOs guilty of greatly exaggerating the dangers in 2002–3, and warned that such claims would reduce the effectiveness of future appeals.

Demographer and activist Alex de Waal has more than once noted the tendency for humanitarian relief agencies to opt for the higher figure in any expert guess at the number

---

[48] de Waal 1997, 208.

[49] Nicole Itano, "Africa: The Famine That Wasn't," *Christian Science Monitor*, April 9, 2003. Available at http://www.mindfully.org/Food/2003/Africa-Famine-Wasnt9apro3.htm.

of predicted deaths. So often do the exaggerated figures get repeated that they sometimes achieve the status of a historical fact. Hence, a death toll of one million is frequently attributed to the Ethiopian famine of 1984–85, although expert opinion is that the true figure was roughly half that amount. In the case of Darfur in 1984–85, the subject of de Waal's doctoral dissertation, widely publicized predictions ranged from 0.2 to 2 million, against de Waal's estimate of an outcome of 95,000 deaths.[50]

Yet the overstated claims persist. In September 2004, UN agencies warned of a famine in Bangladesh within three months: "A million children face acute illness or death within weeks." Meanwhile, Mauritania "called for urgent aid to combat the largest locust plague to hit West Africa in more than 20 years." Aid agencies alleged that the area "may be on the brink of famine," and that farmers in the south of the country could afford a meal only every second day.[51] In August 2005, the Irish NGO GOAL described the crisis in Niger as "what some observers believe will be Africa's most acute famine for decades," while Niger's president accused NGOs of overemphasizing the problems faced by his country in order to improve their own finances.[52] On the other hand, in 2002 the president of Senegal apologized to donors for duping them into believing that five million risked starvation as a result of drought. The reports of looming famine had led to the appeal to international

[50] de Waal 1989, 1997, 2007.

[51] BBC Tuesday, September 21, 2004 (Pascale Harter, "Mauritania on Brink of Famine"); *Guardian*, September 29, 2004; de Waal 1997, 204–8; Howe and Devereux 2004.

[52] Http://www.goal.ie/newsroom/letdown0805.shtml; BBC Thursday, August 29, 2002.

donors for $23 million and the setting up of a government emergency relief unit.

In 2002, the reply of the World Food Programme (WFP) to such criticism was that its timely actions "averted" famine, while its critics countered that it had a vested bureaucratic interest in exaggerating the crisis in the first place. Was the crisis of 2002 a panic engineered by vested interests or an averted famine? FAO data reveal that, indeed, the cereal harvests in the main countries at risk were less than average, but such failures had not been unusual in the previous two decades, and output recovered well in Malawi and Zambia in 2003, although less so in Zimbabwe. Given the likely long-term costs of such tactics and the increasing dependence of NGOs on public funding in the recent past, independent monitoring of NGO activities is essential.[53]

A further problem with NGO actions is that their interventions have typically lagged behind, rather than led, media reports. Instead of being positioned to rapidly dispense previously accumulated reserves, they have used famines as a pretext for soliciting additional aid. Much of that aid has then subsequently been put to other uses. The crisis in Niger in 2005 highlighted this problem. When the world media first drew attention to it in July 2005, few NGOs— Médecins sans frontières being a well-known exception— had a presence in the country, and their information about the severity of the crisis and numbers at risk was all secondhand. Not only did the NGOs arrive late; the Irish agency Concern linked the publicity about Niger in late July and early August 2005 to a generic "Emergency Appeal

---

[53] Iriye 2002, 207.

for Sub-Saharan Africa," which invited donations "to help Concern's life saving work."[54]

This illustrates a third problem with NGO disaster relief: the dilemma facing agencies that spread their activities thin and wide. The Niger famine was localized and required expert local knowledge, and in September 2005 Médecins sans frontières was complaining that food was still not reaching the right places and people. Most agencies were, and remain, too small and thinly spread to offer effective assistance against famines. Instead of specializing in niche skills and geographic areas, NGOs want to be involved in every disaster. No doubt, some NGO expertise and experience is transferable from one disaster to another, but their lack of local contacts must constrain their effectiveness to respond fast in unfamiliar environments. Thus in Ethiopia in 1984–85, outside donors unknowingly abetted the brutal resettlement schemes of the Mengistu regime. Bob Geldof, the inspiration behind Live Aid, argued that "we've got to give aid without worrying about population transfers."[55]

In the past, then, the rivalry between NGOs, their tendency to follow rather than prevent disasters, and the lack of concern on the part of the public about where donations ended up being spent have combined to reduce the effectiveness of this valuable form of disaster relief.

FAMINE RELIEF AS STATE AID

One of the earliest examples of disaster relief as official foreign aid was that afforded by the United States to Venezuelan earthquake victims in 1812. Another U.S.-funded mea-

---

[54] See, for example, *Irish Times*, August 9, 2005, 1.
[55] *Irish Times*, November 4, 1985.

sure, the campaign mounted by the American Relief Administration (ARA) in the Soviet Union in 1921–22, is probably the most ambitious government-funded program on record. The ARA's involvement, in response to an appeal from writer Maxim Gorky "to honest European and American people," was on the condition of being given a free hand in the distribution of aid. The ARA spent $20 million on famine relief, for which the Soviet government later thanked it "in the name of the millions of people who have been saved."[56]

In the wake of World War II, the United States was to the fore again: food aid was an important part of the Marshall Plan. The explicit aim of Public Law 480, passed in 1954, was "to lay the basis for a permanent expansion of our exports of agricultural products with lasting benefits to ourselves and peoples of other lands." During the following half century, over one hundred million tons of U.S. maize and wheat were sent abroad as "Food for Peace," "creating thousands of jobs in the U.S. and abroad." Today the United States still accounts for the bulk of food aid worldwide. By offering a way around international antidumping agreements, Public Law 480 has allowed U.S. food producers to match philanthropy with self-interest for over half a century. Critics of the WFP's launch in 2002 of the "largest humanitarian operation in history" in southern Africa contended that it was prompted more by its huge stockpiles of U.S. maize than by any real or imminent danger of famine.[57]

Since the 1990s, the issue of genetically modified food

[56] Patenaude 2002; Adamets 2003, 168–75.
[57] See, for example, Oxfam 2005.

has added to the controversy, with European governments claiming that the U.S. insistence on genetically modified food was driven by the interests of agribusiness rather than genuine empathy with the world's poor. For impoverished countries, such as famine-threatened Zambia in 2002, the choice is a difficult one.

History warns us that foreign aid, even in the form of emergency food aid, is rarely disinterested. "Food is power," proclaimed Senator Hubert Humphrey referring to U.S. foreign assistance in 1974, "and in a very real sense, it is our extra measure of power." In that year, the United States held back aid to Bangladesh until it ceased exporting jute to Cuba; when U.S. food arrived it was "too late for famine victims." Controversy still surrounds the issue of "souperism" during the Great Irish Famine, when zealous proselytizers "sacrificed much of the influence for good they would have had if they had been satisfied to leave the belief of the people alone," and poisoned interfaith relations for decades to come.[58] In late nineteenth-century China spreaders of the Christian gospels were to the fore, and "every dole was accompanied by a sermon."[59] According to Jesuit missionaries in Ethiopia in the mid-1620s, "An empty stomach renders the mind very acute and their ears propitious . . . there was no one who did not accept the faith together with the food." In Kashmir in 1640–42, people "would even voluntarily agree to baptize their children believing that it would fetch them a piece of bread."[60] A leading ARA official described how food relief had been used as a weapon in the overthrow

[58] Hickey 2002, 263.
[59] Nathan 1965, 5.
[60] Pankhurst 1986, 38; Kaw 1996, 60.

of Bela Kun's Communist regime in Hungary in 1919; naturally, such comments fueled Soviet suspicions of the ARA, and prompted Vladimir Ilyich Lenin to order expulsion and arrest for "for the slightest interference in internal matters."[61]

Finally, although food aid in the form of rice or maize may relieve the poor in the short run, it brings with it the risk of collateral damage to indigenous agriculture in the longer run. Since the early 1980s, heavily subsidized exports of coarse grains and wheat from the United States and (more recently) the European Union to Africa's poorer economies have doubled, and now amount to 20 to 25 percent of all cereal production in the area. Foods distributed by the WFP (mostly originating from the United States) have more than doubled since the mid-1990s as well. Stipulations in the 1999 Food Aid Convention that food aid be "culturally acceptable," and where possible not interfere with indigenous food markets, are intended to counteract what amounts to dumping by another name on the part of the United States and the European Union. Toward this end, and under pressure from aid agencies and food producers in the developing world, recent World Trade Organization agreements commit the European Union to abolishing export subsidies, and the United States to end its trade-distorting export credit and food aid programs.

[61] Patenaude 2002, 41–42.

Chapter VIII

The "Violence of Government"

WAR BY ANOTHER MEANS

FAMINES THAT ARE DELIBERATELY engineered to kill are as old as history. In the Greco-Roman world military manuals explained how to destroy food supplies and poison water reservoirs, and siege-induced famines were not unusual—indeed, Julius Caesar relied on one to conquer Vercingetorix's Gauls at Alesia in 52 BC. The English poet Edmund Spenser was therefore describing an age-old ploy in the 1580s when he advised that "great force must be the instrument but famine must be the means, for till Ireland be famished it cannot be subdued." In 1628, after a siege lasting a year, the French Huguenot city of La Rochelle was brought to its knees by famine, losing four-fifths of its population in the process. In the 1820s in Natal, King Shaka's scorched-earth policy against neighboring tribes led to famine and, reportedly, instances of cannibalism.[1] In 1936 Edgar Snow, admittedly an *engagé* observer, blamed famine in the Chinese province of Henan on the Kuomintang for its refusal to allow grain to cross war lines to the Shensi area where Mao's Communists were in control.

All sides employed such famine-inducing tactics during World War I and II. During World War I, the requisitioning of grain and livestock along with the conscription of male

---

[1] Stathakopoulos 2004, 46–47; Maddox 1990.

labor in central Tanzania, then under German rule, led to the *mtunya* (literally, "scramble" in the Gogo language), which according to one colonial official, killed one-fifth of the indigenous population. An early academic assessment of the Allied blockade of 1917–19, which resulted in the deaths of hundreds of thousands of Germans, found that "no means could have been more effective" in breaking the morale of an enemy deemed a threat to European civilization. For several months after the November 1918 armistice, the Allies allowed shiploads of U.S. food to spoil in Dutch ports rather than risk a recovery in German morale. Only the fear of Bolshevism prompted an end to the blockade.[2]

The Nazi blockade of Leningrad (today's Saint Petersburg) in 1941–43 sought to starve the city into submission, and it is reckoned that Nazi policy toward Soviet prisoners of war resulted in the death through starvation and disease of about three million men. Meanwhile occupying Japanese forces, by hoarding food and putting their own needs first, inflicted a terrible war-famine on Vietnam. The massive aerial mining campaign conducted by U.S. B-29s against Japan in the closing months of World War II was tellingly codenamed Operation Starvation. Carl von Clausewitz, famous Prussian theorist of warfare, codified such actions in *On War* (1832): "If the assailant does not venture to pass by a position, he can invest it and reduce it by famine." Military tactics that singled out civilian populations were forbidden by the Fourth Geneva Convention (1949), but this did not deter a senior Ethiopian politician from revealing at the height of the famine of 1984–85 that "food is a major element in our strategy against the secessionists."[3]

[2] Starling 1920; Roesle 1925; Vincent 1982.
[3] de Waal 1997, 117.

Over the past century or so, almost without exception, famines in peacetime have been exacerbated by corrupt and rapacious governing elites. Sen's striking claim that famine and democracy are incompatible is a special case of the more general thesis that democratic institutions promote economic development.[4] The argument is that democratization reduces the incidence of famine by speeding up the spread of information and criticism, and penalizing governments that fail to avert disasters and prevent excess mortality. Even the half exceptions to Sen's claim seem few: perhaps Ireland in the 1840s (a free and sometimes vocal press, but only a middle-class franchise), India in 1972–73 (when famine killed 130,000 in Maharashtra), and Niger in 2005 (a semi-democracy) are in this category. An added caveat is that the causation between democracy and the absence of famine is not all one-way; in poverty-stricken, ethnically divided economies democracy may not be sustainable.

Can a free press guarantee that news of deficient harvests and relief measures are made public? This may hold in the case of the indigenous press, as in India today; typically, however, the attention span of the international media—and their readership—is too fleeting to monitor famines from start to finish. The investigative journalist who stays the course is the exception; more typical is the reporter who cut short his famine tour of India in Allahabad in early 1897 because "the Cretan crisis was in full blast, and absorbing the attention of the British public," or the television crews who arrived in Malawi in 2002 "like spectators at a car crash: to observe the tragedy, not to prevent it."[5]

[4] Sen 2001.
[5] Merewether 1898, 299; Devereux 2002, 72; de Waal 1997, 82–85.

In discussing the "political" famines of the twentieth century, economist Michael Ellman's distinction between FAD1 and FAD2 famines is apposite. Mortality during FAD1 famines is largely unavoidable, whereas alternative public policies could prevent or at least reduce the mortality associated with FAD2 famines. The war-induced famines just described would qualify as FAD2 famines. So would the famines in the Soviet Union in 1932–33 and 1947 as well as in China in the late 1950s, where ideologies of high-speed industrialization at all cost resulted in the deaths of many millions, while the Great European Famine of the 1310s is a clear case of FAD1.[6] FAD2 famines, though, range from those where different policies would have mitigated the damage caused by some exogenous shock (e.g., Ireland in the 1840s) to those where the famine was purely the product of human agency (e.g., Leningrad in 1941–43).

It is a great irony that the most deadly famines of the last century—including the worst ever in terms of sheer numbers—occurred under regimes committed, at least on paper, to the eradication of poverty. The history of the USSR (1917–89) is pockmarked by famine. Post-1949 China's remarkable record of achievements in terms of life expectancy and material progress will always be marred by the Great Leap Forward famine of 1959–61, resulting in the deaths of millions of people. Today, the people of the Democratic Republic of North Korea struggle to survive in the wake of a smaller famine. In all these cases, the extent of loss of life and the factors leading to famine are highly controversial: there is denial, on the one hand, and exaggeration, on the other.

---

[6] Ellman 2000; Barber and Dzeniskevich 2005, 4–5.

THE USSR

The Soviet Union was born amid famine. In the wake of the October Revolution, its cities fared worst at first. In Saint Petersburg in early 1918 Lenin proposed the death penalty for speculators, and armed detachments were sent to the countryside in futile searches for grain. In May 1918, Gorky described Muscovites as trying to survive on "bread that's half straw, herring heads, cotton-cakes, and the like," while "Petrograd [was] dying as a city."[7] World War I and the ensuing civil war had produced massive economic disruption.

The famine that followed in 1921–22, caused by a combination of civil war and drought, had its epicenter in the mid-Volga region, but extended to more than half the regions of the old czarist empire. Data for 1920–22 imply an output of cereals and potatoes only about one-half the levels achieved either before 1914 or during the rest of the 1920s. In the areas worst affected by famine (the northern Caucasus and Kyrgyzstan), the average wheat yield fell from forty to fifty poods per *desyatin* (roughly sixty to seventy-five kilos per hectare) before the war to ten to twenty poods in 1920 and only eight to nine poods in 1921 (at a time when seed requirements were about eight poods per *desyatin*). Civil war and the ensuing economic disruption, exacerbated by poor weather, were responsible; the added burden imposed by requisitions was small relative to the shortfalls in production.[8]

---

[7] Wolfe 1967, 71–73; Gorky 1968, 216–17.
[8] Adamets 2003, 45–75.

In desperation, Russia's new rulers made peace for the time being with representatives of the old order and sought outside help. Gorky helped found the All-Russian Famine Relief Committee, which attracted the support of Herbert Hoover's ARA. The relief effort mounted by the ARA in 1921–22 is probably unmatched in the history of famines. The number of people fed daily by the ARA at the beginning of May 1922 approached six million; the Russian authorities fed another two million, and other foreign relief organizations reached an additional one million. By mid-1922 Hoover's staff had handled 0.8 million tons of cereals, milk, other foods, and medical supplies and clothing, and mobilized resources worth $60 million, mainly from the central government. The Americans supplied the food, while the Soviets undertook to supply distribution facilities—transport, warehouses, labor power, and so on.

In a letter to Hoover in the wake of the crisis, Gorky claimed that "in all the history of human suffering I know of no accomplishment which can be compared in magnitude with the relief you have accomplished. . . . It will be inscribed in the pages of history as unique, gigantic, and glorious."[9] The help provided by the ARA dwarfed that supplied by other governmental and private agencies. The Bolsheviks, whose grip on power was tenuous at times in 1921–22, were understandably suspicious of ARA motives. Despite the massive relief effort, the excess mortality in 1921–22 was still enormous. A recent estimate puts the number of deaths at over six million, mainly from diseases such as typhus and relapsing fever.[10] Thankfully the 1923 harvest

[9] Cited in Wolfe 1967, 8.
[10] Adamets 2002, 64.

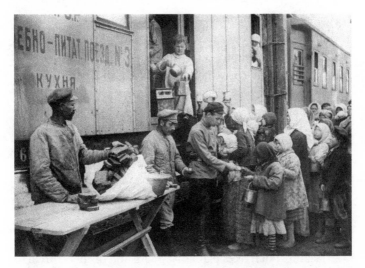

FIG. 8.I.   Famine relief in Russia, 1921. Photo by Topical Press
Agency. Courtesy Getty Images.

was good, due in part to the concessions granted to agriculturalists through the New Economic Policy.

The Soviet famine of 1932–33 was the second in a series
of notorious twentieth-century "socialist" famines. Denied
or downplayed at the time by both the regime—the authorities pointed instead to the scandal of unemployment
abroad—and some sympathetic outside journalists, it has
been the subject of heated controversy ever since.[11] Accounts such as Robert Conquest's passionate and influential *Harvest of Sorrow* (1986) or the relevant sections of *Le
Livre Noir du Communisme* (Courtois 1997) tend to argue
that the famine was deliberately engineered and politically
motivated, particularly against Ukrainians. Recent specialist scholarship denies this, regarding the "years of hunger"

[11] Davies and Wheatcroft 2004, 412–15; Engerman 2000.

instead as the outcome of a political struggle between a ruthless regime, bent on industrialization at breakneck speed, and an exploited and uncooperative peasantry. The recently released correspondence between Stalin and his right-hand man, Party Secretary Lazar Kaganovich, shows no signs of a plan to single out the Ukraine; to the contrary, on August 11, 1932, Stalin, while on vacation in the south, confided to Kaganovich his conviction that "we should be unstinting in providing money" to the Ukraine, if only for fear that it might be lost to Moscow.[12] The traditional verdict has been revised in several ways:

- Ellman's forceful analysis finds evidence for intent lacking, but makes plain that Stalin and his henchmen were culpable to the extent that they prioritized the balance of payments and fast-tracked industrialization over preventing mass deaths.[13] Without collectivization and its associated excessive grain procurements the famine would undoubtedly have been much less severe. Ellman notes, however, that there was nothing unique in the focus on targets other than famine relief; in 1943, the British government in India "was more interested in the war effort than in saving the life of Bengalis."[14] While Ellman's verdict has much to commend it (see chapter 6), Soviet famine deaths in the wake of forced migration to the Gulag had no equivalent in Bengal or elsewhere in India.[15]

[12] Davies et al. 2003, 181.

[13] Grain exports in 1932–33 totaled 1.6 million tons—that is, about 9 percent of the procurements and 3 percent of the output.

[14] Ellman 2002, 2007, 1172.

[15] Khlevniuk 2004, 68–82.

- Excess famine mortality was huge, although somewhat less than the 7 million claimed by Conquest or the 6 million Ukrainians claimed by *Le Livre Noir du Communisme*.[16] The latest estimates lie between 4 million and 5 to 6 million in the Soviet Union as a whole, of whom it is reckoned that 2.4 million perished in the Ukraine. Much hinges on assumptions about the underregistration of deaths at the time. In addition the Ukraine "lost" about 1 million births.[17]

- Although the literature about 1932–33 has focused largely on the Ukraine, the famine straddled a much larger area stretching from the northern Caucasus to the Urals. Proportionately speaking, the crisis was most severe in Kazakhstan, where collectivization wreaked havoc on a largely pastoral, semi-nomadic agriculture.[18]

- Much uncertainty surrounds grain output and requisitioning data. By the late 1920s, the harvest statistics had become a political football, with producers wanting underestimates in order to reduce obligations, and officials wanting inflated returns in order to impress the center. The grain harvests of both 1931 and 1932 were genuinely poor, though (see table 8.1). Robert Davies and Stephen Wheatcroft blame this mainly on collectivization and excessive procurements, while Mark Tauger places more stress on adverse weather conditions and plant

[16] Conquest 1986; *Livre Noir du Communisme* 1997.

[17] Adamets 2002, 165–68; Davies, Harrison, and Wheatcroft 1994, 77; Davies and Wheatcroft 2004, 412–15; Vallin et al. 2002.

[18] See, for example, Tauger 1990, 2001, 2006; Ellman 2002; Davies and Wheatcroft 2004; Olcott 1981.

diseases.[19] Nevertheless, the center insisted for a time on planned procurements, even requisitioning seed for the following season from recalcitrant kolkhozy (collective farms). Only late in summer 1932 did it begin to concede the gravity of the situation in the countryside.

- Grain procurements represented over two-fifths of the output in 1931–32. They were lower in absolute terms in 1932–33 than in any year after 1929–30 (table 8.1), but represented a lethal share of the harvest in a year of shortage. Yet rural consumption may well have been less in 1932–33 than in 1931–32. The increase in procurements between 1928–29 and 1932–33 outstripped the growth of the urban population, so the crisis was mainly a rural one.[20]

- Fear and terror distorted information flows. As late as July 25, 1932, Stalin seems to have believed that the harvest prospects were "undoubtedly good for the USSR as a whole while acknowledging problems in the Ukraine."[21] In the wake of the collectivization drives of 1929–30, the authorities and the peasantry engaged in an ultimately deadly game in which brute force, ignorance, and moral hazard all played a role. Moscow suspected the peasantry and its allies of concealing grain, while the peasantry in turn sometimes employed the strategy of exaggerating local privation.[22]

[19] Davies, Harrison, and Wheatcroft 1994; Davies and Wheatcroft 2004; Tauger 2001, 200.

[20] Allen 2003, 106–7.

[21] Davies et al. 2003, 167–68.

[22] Fitzpatrick 1994, 69–74.

- The famine brought an escalation of protest, crime, and civil disorder, culminating in Stalin's own draconian law of August 7, 1932, against the theft of socialist property.[23] It also generated attempted mass migration to urban areas, and even (as noted in chapter 2) instances of cannibalism.[24]

- The authorities engaged in famine relief to a greater extent than previously thought. Much too late, they adjusted planned procurements in the worst-affected regions downward and relaxed the restrictions on private trade. Tauger claims that they lacked the food to make relief effective.[25] But they never sought the outside help that would have mitigated mortality—as had been done in 1921–22.

- The 1933, 1934, and 1935 harvests were good ones, though not much better than those of the late 1920s. Recovery from famine conditions thus came relatively fast, and living standards were higher on the eve of World War II than before collectivization. Birth weight and height data capture the immediate and long-term effects of the famine, although they also suggest that World War II bore more heavily on the population than the "years of hunger."[26]

Famine struck the Soviet Union again in the shape of the blockade-famine of Leningrad in 1941–43.[27] At its peak during

[23] Davies el al. 2003, 14–15, 105; Fitzpatrick 1994, 73; Ellman 2007, 668–71.

[24] On migration, see Davies et al. 2003, 105. On cannibalism, see Davies and Wheatcroft 2004, 421–24; compare Patenaude 2002, 262–70.

[25] Tauger 2001; Davies and Wheatcroft 2004, 424–26.

[26] Allen 2003, 132–52; Wheatcroft 1993.

[27] Leningrad is today's Saint Petersburg; the famine, like Dmitry Shostakovich's Symphony no. 7, still bears the city's former name.

Table 8.1
Harvests and procurements in the USSR, 1927–34

Year	Total procure- ments	Rest of harvest (D)	Procure- ment share of harvest (%) (D)	Rest of harvest (T)	Procure- ment share of harvest (%) (T)
1927–28	11.1	51	17.9		
1928–29	10.8	52	17.2		
1929–30	16.1	46	25.9	46	25.9
1930–31	22.1	42	34.5	44.9	41.5
1931–32	22.8	33	40.9	31.2	42.2
1932–33	18.8	37	33.7	29.2	39.2
1933–34	23.3	42	35.7	44.7	34.3
1934–35	26.3	42	38.5	40.7	39.3
1935–36	28.4	47	37.7		

Sources: (D) Davies et al. 1994 290; (T) Tauger 2001, 438.

winter 1941–42, the city still contained 2.5 million people. An improvised ice road across Lake Ladoga was used to evacuate a further 0.5 million Leningraders during that winter, but only 262,500 tons of supplies made it across during that period. After initial mistakes, the authorities under an able and ruthless Zhdanov managed to control fraud, crime, and as mentioned earlier, infectious disease; as a result, the city never descended into disorder. The whole population was reregistered in October 1941, in order to minimize ration card fraud. The authorities erred in not evacuating more people before the Nazi noose tightened, in not dispersing the food stocks within the city, and in not reducing the daily food ration sooner than they did. In mitigation, the authorities dealt harshly with corruption, and the available food was spread as evenly as possible—at the peak of the crisis, even Zhdanov and his senior associates obtained only the military ration of a pound of bread, some cereal, and a bowl of fish or meat soup. Nevertheless, three-quarters of a million died.[28]

The last famine to strike Europe was the little-known Soviet famine of 1946–47, apparently resulting in the deaths of 1.0 to 1.5 million people. A drought reduced the 1946 harvest by one-sixth of an already low 1945 level, yet had the authorities focused less on building up stockpiles, allowed in imports, and relaxed procurement targets, the famine would have been attenuated, if not averted. In Ellman's definition, this was a FAD2 famine. The precise death toll is unknown, though clearly the famine was uneven regionally. Its epicenter was Moldova, where it led to the deaths of about 5 percent of the population, and where "the eating of corpses took place on a large scale."[29]

THE CHINESE FAMINE OF 1959–61

The Great Leap Forward famine is just as controversial as the 1932–33 Soviet famine, and is commonly described as the

[28] Salisbury [1969] 2000, 403; Barber and Dzeniskevich 2005, I, 11.
[29] Ellman 2000, 617n1.

worst man-made famine in history. Its demographic aspects have already been discussed in chapter 4. Much about it remains hidden. Reports of famine in China were widespread in the Western media in 1960–61, but never fully credited.[30] Almost a decade after the event, the eminent Harvard sinologist Dwight Perkins declared that a famine had been averted despite three poor harvests in succession; in the past such a shortfall "would have meant many millions of deaths in the areas most severely affected," but effective rationing and the railway meant that "few if any starved outright." Perkins was not alone in believing that the regime had "averted a major disaster."[31] Only with the release in the early 1980s of new demographic data by the post-Mao leadership, coupled with cryptic accounts in Chinese sources, could the full extent of the crisis be guessed at.[32]

Although well aware of the crisis—as gestures of solidarity, Mao reportedly ate no meat for seven months in 1960 and Chou En-lai cut his monthly grain consumption to seven kilos—the authorities also concealed and denied the true scale of the disaster from their own people. Moreover, nervous or overzealous local officials failed to reveal the true extent of the problem to the center. Grain continued to be exported during the famine—although exports were a small fraction (about 2 percent) of output—and was not imported on a significant scale until 1961.

The famine has been linked to policies pursued in connection with the Great Leap Forward, including the excessive procurements of grain from certain provinces (compare

[30] Compare Riskin 1998; Asian People's Anti-Communist League 1962.
[31] Perkins 1969, 166, 303, 303–19.
[32] See, for example, Bernstein 1983, 1984.

table 8.4), the forced diversion of agricultural labor from the countryside to industrial sites, the adoption of Trofim Denisovich Lysenko's erroneous ideas about the close cropping of seed, collective farming, the system of communal eating that eroded the incentive to conserve and economize on food, and an agricultural overspecialization that may have eliminated the insurance provided by even limited crop diversification. Dictatorship produced the crazy über-leftist policies and then the lack of relief. The proportions of output procured by the authorities were not huge relative to the landlords' share of output in a typical less developed country, or indeed in preindustrial Europe, or the shares procured in the Soviet Union in the early 1930s. A major difference, however, is that whereas landlords tended to relent in bad years, the Chinese authorities' share of output *rose* from 20.9 percent in 1958 to 28 percent in 1959.[33]

In China itself, the famine period was dubbed "the three bitter years" or, more euphemistically, "the three years of economic difficulty." The authorities stressed the problems caused by the cold war, and the withdrawal of Soviet experts and equipment in mid-1960 exacerbated the difficulties faced in 1959–61. True, the Soviets had departed suddenly, leaving a trail of unfinished projects and half-trained workers in their wake. Yet outside accounts of the famine highlight the different set of factors, all homegrown, listed above. In this version, the poor harvests of 1959 and 1960 were due to the misguided and overambitious policies associated with the Great Leap Forward, not to adverse exogenous shocks.

[33] The economics literature on the causes of the famine is considerable. See, for example, Kueh 1984, 1995; Lin 1990; Yang 1996; Yao 1999; Lin and Yang 2000; Riskin 1998; Han 2003; Li and Yang 2005.

The impact on output, population, and urban and rural consumption are outlined in table 8.2.

The truth, insofar as it can be inferred from the fallible sources available, is that the famine was due to a combination of natural and man-made causes. Liu Sha-ch'i, initially an enthusiast of the Great Leap Forward, later admitted that the disaster was "three parts nature and seven parts man."[34] Cold war analyses of the famine stressed the role of institutional forces even more. Those forces certainly compounded the impact of other factors. In particular, the extreme backwardness of the Chinese economy in the 1950s was surely also a factor. In 1950, the Chinese GDP per head (measured in international 1990 dollars) was less than that of most African countries in the late twentieth century; and on the eve of the Great Leap its GDP per head was less than half the African average today. Moreover, the Chinese GDP per head in 1950 was also only about one-fourth that of the UK GDP per capita in 1820—and therefore almost certainly much less than the Irish GDP per head on the eve of the Great Irish Famine (table 8.3). Indeed, Angus Maddison's historical national accounts database implies that China was one of the poorest economies anywhere during the past two centuries. To engage in radical economic experimentation in such an extremely backward economy was to risk disaster.

The history of famine in China before 1949 is also pertinent. Richard H. Tawney memorably described the position of the rural population in northern China in the early 1930s as resembling "that of a man standing permanently up to the neck in water, so that even a ripple is sufficient to drown him." Even more than Walter Mallory's depiction of China

---

[34] Houser, Sands, and Xiao 2008.

as "the land of famine" a few years earlier, Tawney's metaphor has been elevated to the status of cliché. So much so, that in a recent World Bank publication, it is described as "an ancient Chinese proverb."[35]

Between the mid-nineteenth century and the 1940s, major "tsunamis"—never mind "ripples"—were frequent enough in China to probably warrant Tawney's and Mallory's descriptions. In Tawney's own account in *Land and Labour in China* (1932), the famine of 1849 "is said to have destroyed 13,750,000 persons," while famines during the Taipeng Rebellion (1851–64) allegedly killed another 20 million, and the Great North China Famine of 1878–79 a further 9.5 to 13 million. The first two of these estimates are no more than speculative guesses; the third, often invoked by experts in the field, is more reliable. Famine mortality was probably lower in relative terms thereafter. Even so, Tawney noted that "in Shensi three million had died of hunger in the last few years," and in Kansu "one-third of the population ha[d] died since 1926 owing to famine, civil war, banditry, and typhus."[36]

Parts of China would suffer from devastating famines in 1936 and again in 1942–43. Theodore White's graphic accounts of the Henan famine of 1942–43 refer to telltale symptoms such as famine foods (cooked elm bark, leaves, straw roots, cottonseed, and water reed), suicides, beggars at every city gate, voluntary slavery, dogs eating bodies by the roadside, and even cannibalism. White reported parents tying children to a tree "so they would not follow them as they went in search for food"; "larger" children being sold

[35] Tawney [1932] 1964; Mallory 1926; World Bank 2001, epigraph to chapter 3.
[36] Tawney 1932 [1964], 76.

for less than ten dollars; and a mother who was charged with eating her little girl merely denying that she had killed it. Before leaving the city of Chengchow (Zhengzhou), the capital of Henan, White and a colleague were treated to a banquet by Kuomintang officials: "We had two soups. We had spiced lotus, peppered chicken, beef and water chestnut. We had spring rolls, hot wheat buns, rice, bean-curd, chicken and fish. We had three cakes with sugar frosting."[37] That was just a decade and a half before the Great Leap Forward

TABLE 8.2

Grain production, grain consumption, and mortality, 1958–65

Year	Grain production (% change)	Rural retention (% change)	Urban allocation (% change)	Death rate (per 1,000)
1958	2.5	–1.8	23.2	12.0
1959	–15.0	–22.6	14.0	14.6
1960	–15.6	–8.0	–35.0	25.4
1961	2.8	8.1	–16.5	14.2
1962	8.5	10.3	–0.3	10.0
1963	6.3	5.1	12.4	10.0
1964	10.3	10.3	10.1	11.5
1965	3.7	3.4	5.5	9.4

Sources: Lardy 1987, 381; National Bureau of Statistics 1999.

[37] "The Desperate Urgency of Flight," *Time Magazine,* October 26, 1942; "Until the Harvest Is Reaped," *Time Magazine,* March 22, 1943.

Table 8.3
GDP per head in China and other selected countries
(in 1990 Geary-Khamis $)

Country	Year	GDP per capita
China	1950	439
China	1955	575
Africa	1980	1,538
Chad	1980	339
Guinea	1980	551
United Kingdom	1850	2,330
China	1890	540
China	1870	530
China	1820	600
India	1942	679

Source: Http://www.ggdc.net/maddison/.

famine, which would bring the era of famines in China to a sensational end.

The role of the weather in 1959–61 remains controversial. On the one hand, Jasper Becker claims that "there were no unusual floods or droughts" in this period; and according to Jung Chang "of all the people I have talked to from different parts of China, few knew of natural calamities in their region." It is also true that while Beijing played down the famine, it played up the adverse weather, prompting one critic to quip that "the Communists call the natural calamities in every year unprecedented."[38] Still, although Chinese claims about natural calamities cannot be taken at face value, impressionistic accounts of drought and flooding are plentiful. They range from references to thirty inches of rain in Hong Kong over five days in June 1959, to a hurricane in July 1960 that ruined 777,000 *mu* (or about 130,000 acres) of crops in Shandung Province, to a drought in northern China that in 1960 resulted in eight of the twelve main rivers drying up for part of the year and, for the first time in living memory, it being possible to wade across the Yellow River.[39]

To make matters worse, China was struck by more typhoons in 1960 than in any year in the previous half century. Droughts brought locusts, while the rains brought wheat stripe rust. Sinologist Roderick MacFarquhar has described China in 1960 as "experiencing the worst natural calamities in a century," while economist Y. Y. Kueh has concluded that "the weather was the main cause of the enormous grain losses in 1960 and 1961."[40] Chinese agricultural statistics imply that the average cultivated area affected by disasters was much higher than normal. All this supports a contemporary report of a lecture to military students by a U.S. China expert:

> Nineteen hundred and fifty nine, gentlemen, was one of the most disastrous years as far as farming is concerned in Red China. Eighty percent of their best agricultural area was just damaged with everything—from rain, drought, pests. If you name it, they had it. They

[38] Chang 1991, 311; Chi 1965, 37.

[39] MacFarquhar 1983, 322.

[40] Dwyer 1974, 262–64; MacFarquhar 1983, 322; Kueh 1995.

had all kinds of disasters. It was the worst year in a century, in my opinion.[41]

Hard meteorological evidence is less conclusive. The annual rainfall data from Chinese weather stations do not highlight 1959–61 as exceptional. Although precipitation over most parts of eastern China was below normal in 1960 and particularly during the summer of 1960, with the Loess Plateau and northern China experiencing severe drought, the data imply that the 1960 drought was mild compared to 1972 and 1997. Data from several individual weather stations do point to abnormal weather, however. Between 1950 and 1988 (a period for which data are available for nearly all Chinese weather stations), July 1959 was the hottest July in Zheng Zhou (Henan), Chong Qing (Sichuan), and Wuhan (Hebei); August 1959 was the wettest August in ChengDu (Sichuan) and Lan Zhou (Gansu); while August 1960 saw hardly any rain in AnQing (Anhui), and likewise for Gui Yang (Guizhou) in July–August 1959. Figures 8.2a, 8.2b, and 8.2c describe the monthly rainfall (in millimeters) in three badly affected areas. In one (ChengDu), rainfall was very high, in the other two very low.[42] The issue, though, remains open. Meanwhile, it bears noting that two other periods of extreme weather in the recent past—that ending in 1929, and that of 1941–42—had also led to severe crop shortfalls and resultant massive excess mortality in China.

The varying severity of the famine of 1959–61 across China's provinces is also striking in this context. In several provinces the mortality rates were virtually unaffected in

---

[41] Smith 1960, 26.

[42] See also Hughes et al. (1994), where the famine period is an outlier.

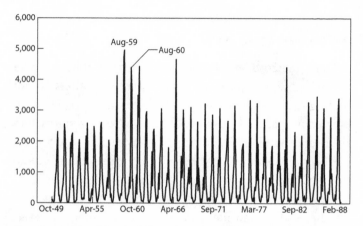

FIG. 8.2a. Monthly rainfall in ChengDu (Sichuan), 1950–88.

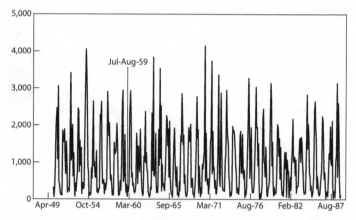

FIG. 8.2b. Monthly rainfall in GuiYang (Guizhou), 1950–88.

1959–61, while two provinces—Sichuan and Anhui— accounted for nearly one excess death in two, but only one in six of the prefamine population. Both provinces were in- famously famine prone in the past. In 1907 the *Guardian* placed Anhui at the epicenter of a major famine; four years

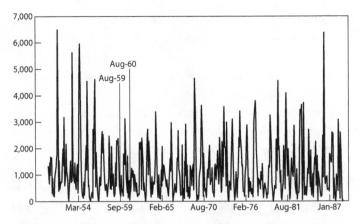

FIG. 8.2C.   Monthly rainfall in AnQing (Anhui), 1950–88.

later a U.S. account described Anhui's "fame of late years
[as] only the bitter fame of her sorrow," and in the 1920s
Anhui was the location of Pearl Buck's famine novel, *The
Good Earth* (1931).[43] Between the 1920s and the 1940s Sichuan was hit three times by major famines. The 1936 famine, the product of severe drought compounded by civil war,
killed up to five million people in Sichuan and led to reports
of widespread cannibalism, while it is estimated that another 2.5 million died in Sichuan in 1941. Henan, another
badly affected region in 1959–61, had been badly hit by the
famine of 1876–78, and two million died there in a major
famine in 1928–29. "Of all marks on my thinking," wrote
U.S. journalist Theodore H. White in 1978, "the Honan
famine [of 1943] remains most indelible." That famine
killed three to five million people.[44]

[43] Buck [1937] 1980.
[44] White 1978, 144; Ó Gráda 2008; "On the Yellow River's Banks,"
New York Times, October 25, 1942.

Anhui, Sichuan, and Henan were also economically backward even by Chinese standards in the 1950s. Given their fragile ecologies and poor track records, it is hardly likely that they would have escaped severe and repeated harvest shortfalls without a significant loss of life. It is also probable that radical economic experimentation was more likely to cause havoc in such places. Figures 8.3a and 8.3b contrast the patterns in four badly affected and five little-affected provinces.

That the famine was a product of economics and geography as well as politics is suggested by the power of economic variables to "explain" a significant proportion of the variation in the excess mortality during the famine. In a simple econometric analysis described in detail elsewhere, two variables—the estimated regional GDP per capita on the eve of the crisis, and the extent of crop loss during it—account for over two-fifths of the variation in the excess mortality across China's twenty-four rural provinces. Similarly,

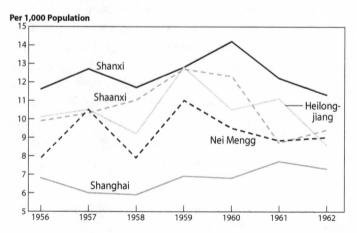

FIGURE 8.3a. Mortality in five less-affected provinces.

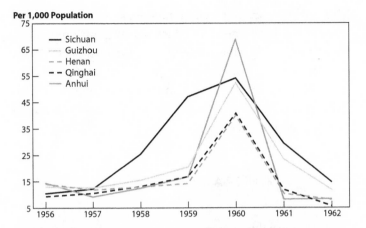

FIG. 8.3b.   Mortality in five worst-affected provinces.

TABLE 8.4
China grain output, state procurements, and
foreign trade (m. tonnes)

Year	Output [1]	Procurements [2]	Net rural availability [3] = [1]–[2]	Imports [4]	Exports [5]
1958	200	41.8	158.2		
1959	170	47.6	122.4	0.00	4.15
1960	143.5	30.85	112.7	0.06	2.72
1961	147.5	25.81	121.7	5.8	1.35
1962	160	25.76	134.2	4.92	1.03
1963	170	28.9	141.1	5.95	1.49
1964	187.5	31.88	155.6	6.57	1.82
1965	194.5	33.65	160.9	6.4	2.41

high birthrates during the famine were associated with high income per head and low reductions in grain production. Two "political" variables—the percentage of the population registered as party members on the eve of the famine, and the percentage of the population reliant on commune mess halls at the end of 1959—fail to improve the explanatory power of either regression.[45]

ETHIOPIA AND NORTH KOREA

Whether the Ethiopian famine of 1984–85 fits in the same category as those described above is a moot point, for in this case too, the policies of a totalitarian regime exacerbated the damage caused by harvest failure. The northern province of Wollo, epicenter of the crisis, had also been subject to famine in 1972–73. Then, the authorities had sought to suppress news of the crisis, and by the time a British television documentary made the "unknown famine" the focus of global relief efforts in mid-October 1973, the worst was probably already over. The estimated forty to eighty thousand deaths in 1972–73 were the product of a FAD in the affected region and callous official neglect.[46] The significant rise in the price of the staple foodstuffs in Wollo suggests that poor communications prevented the movement of grain from areas in relative surplus. In a rare case of regime change triggered by famine, the crisis

---

[45] Ó Gráda 2008. For more on party membership and communal dining variables, see Yang 1996; Lin 1990. For more on the famine more generally, see MacFarquhar 1997; Bernstein 2006; Riskin 1998.

[46] de Waal 1997, 106.

of 1972–73 undermined Emperor Haile Selassie's legiti-
macy and ushered in the revolutionary Dergue.

After 1975, the Amhara-dominated Dergue quickly transformed itself into a brutal dictatorship, combining dirigiste,
antitrader economic policies with a determination to stamp
out secessionist aspirations. By the time the harvest again
failed in Wollo in 1983 and 1984, the private trade in foodstuffs had been greatly reduced, and the resilience of the
farm sector shattered by low prices and forced collectivization. This time the crop failure was much more extensive
and protracted than in 1972–73; worst hit were nomadic cattle owners whose livestock lost three-quarters of their value
relative to grain. Yet the war waged by the Dergue against
secessionists in the northern provinces of Wollo and Tigray
was probably a more important contributory factor than its
ill-advised economic policies. The war disrupted farming and
caused mass movements of famished refugees, mainly to
Sudan and Somalia.[47]

The extent and causes of the disaster that struck the Democratic Republic of North Korea—a backward economy with
a population of about twenty-five million—in mid-1995 also
remain controversial. Its origins lay in rainfall "of biblical
proportions" that struck on June 26, 1995, and produced
twenty-three inches of rain in ten days. Satellite mapping
data suggest that two-fifths of North Korea's paddy fields
were damaged, and that the rice crop in the worst-affected
area in the west of the country suffered a loss of more than
half.[48] The resultant displacement of more than 0.5 million
people (according to the authorities) led to significant excess

---

[47] Kumar 1990; de Waal 1997, 117.
[48] Okamoto, Kamoto, and Kawshima 1998.

mortality, and age-old hallmarks of famine such as human flight from the worst-affected areas as well as sales of children and women near the Chinese border. Whether environmental degradation had left the country vulnerable to such rainfall is a moot point, although the persistence of lower output of both crops and livestock is suggestive. The relative importance of subsequent harvest failures, economic mismanagement and corruption, the "loss of socialist markets" (i.e., an end to subsidized imports from the Soviet Union), and despotic leadership in prolonging the crisis are disputed.[49]

Even the demographic contours of this crisis remain vague. Aid agencies argued that more bad weather had led to worsening conditions in the late 1990s, and some lent credence to unsubstantiated rumors of cannibalism. Journalistic claims that famine in North Korea had killed up to three million people became commonplace. In 2004, however, the U.S. Central Intelligence Agency judged that "massive international food aid deliveries ha[d] allowed the regime to escape mass starvation since 1995–96," and recent scholarship indicates a more modest demographic cost of between 0.6 million and one million. Those estimates combine excess deaths and "lost" births.[50] Although the timing and character of the mortality are still unclear, the persistence of the crisis suggests famine followed by endemic malnutrition rather than a pharaonic seven-year famine. The relatively low infant mortality rate (twenty-three per thousand) and high life expectancy (67.7 years for males and 73.9 years for females) prevailing in North Korea on the eve of

[49] Smith 2005, 66–74.
[50] Smith 2005; Lee 2005; Noland 2007.

the famine are likely to have influenced the extent of subsequent excess mortality and the main causes of death.[51]

Given that annual food production in North Korea today
is about five million tons, the potential importance of food
aid—a total of 3.6 million metric tons from the United States,
Japan, and other WFP donors between 1996 and 2004,
plus substantial donations from China and South Korea—in
saving lives is evident. There are signs in the late 2000s
that better harvests and a modicum of economic reform,
including freer food markets, have been having some impact. Aggregate agricultural production is still far below the
levels achieved in the 1980s and early 1990s, even though
the number of mouths to feed has increased by about 2.5
million. Output had recovered from the dismal levels of the
mid-1990s by 2000–2001, but growth has been sluggish
since then.

The picture is brighter insofar as nutrition is concerned.
In 1998 a joint European Union–United Nations International Children's Emergency Fund–WFP survey found
15.6 percent of North Korean children "wasted" (i.e., low
weight-for-height), 62.3 percent "stunted" (low height-for-
age), and 60.6 percent underweight (low weight-for-age).
The United Nation's *Fifth Report on the World Nutrition
Situation* (2004) revealed a significant improvement in
nutritional status. The proportions of young children
wasted, stunted, and underweight had fallen to 10.4, 45.2,
and 27.9 percent, respectively—an outcome more consistent with chronic than acute malnutrition, and if genuine,

[51] Http://www.unescap.org/stat/data/apif/dpr_korea_apif2004.pdf. According to Central Intelligence Agency data, life expectancy in North Korea
in 2007 was 69.2 years for males and 74.8 years for females.

indicating that by 2004 conditions in North Korea were no worse than they were throughout much of the developing world. In India, for example, using the same definitions, 15.7 percent of young children were wasted, 44.9 percent stunted, and 46.7 percent underweight.[52] World Health Organization 1980–92 data on child nutrition offer added perspective, indicating that 9.2 per cent of *all* children aged less than five years in the developing world were wasted, 42.7 percent stunted, and 35.8 percent underweight. Moreover, in 2007 the Central Intelligence Agency reckoned life expectancy at birth in North Korea to be 71.9 years, which is still lower than in the early 1990s, but ahead of India (68.6 years), Indonesia (70.2 years), or the Philippines (70.5 years). These trends suggest that humanitarian aid to North Korea has been reaching its intended targets in recent years.

[52] The data are reported in table 5 of the report, available at http://www.unsystem.org/scn/publications/AnnualMeeting/SCN31/SCN5Report.pdf.

CHAPTER IX

An End to Famine?

Famine goes, but the stains remain.

—*Kashmiri proverb*

No happiness . . . can compensate perpetual hunger, and all the
evils in its train, for one year, much less can it compensate
for the dreadful suffering of starvation.

—*David Ricardo, letter, 1822*

I BEGAN WITH ECONOMIST MALTHUS, who regarded famine as
"the last and most dreadful mode by which nature represses
a redundant population": a tragic but necessary corrective
that repeatedly throughout history, reduced population to a
sustainable level "with one mighty blow." To what extent
does the historical record support Malthus's account? And
what of the future? Is Malthus now finally history, and is an
end to famine in sight?

Mortality in the past was certainly sensitive to fluctuations in harvest size, food prices, and real wages. That is as
Malthus would have expected—and as statistician Louis
Messance had shown for France in his *Recherches sur la
population . . . avec des réflexions sur la valeur du bled* (1766).
Messance found that years of high prices were the most lethal
and unhealthy in different parts of France. Such evidence,
widely replicated elsewhere, supports the Malthusian case
for famine as a positive check on population. Famine also

caused birthrates to fall, typically with about a year's lag. But those responses were already much weaker in the England of Malthus's day than they had been two or three centuries earlier, and they disappeared from Europe during the nineteenth century and from across most of the globe by the end of the twentieth.

Whether famine ever quite fulfilled the "leveling" or equilibrating role envisaged by Malthus is still disputed (as already noted in chapter 4). Slow population growth in past centuries is at least consistent with a high death rate due in part to barely adequate food supplies. This in turn might be linked to a vulnerability to famine. But in the past the demographic impact of famines tended to be relatively short-lived, so whether they ever effectively succeeded in maintaining a balance between population and "the food of the world" remains doubtful. That they do not do so in the few remaining famine-prone countries is not in question. The rapid growth of population in places such as Niger and Ethiopia confirms the marginal role of famine nowadays as the ultimate positive check.

As for predictions about the future of famine, it is worth noting that the prognostications of past students of hunger and famine have rarely got it right. Stanford University biologist Paul Ehrlich's doomsday forecast in the late 1960s is a notorious case in point. His prediction of global famine in the 1970s—"hundreds of millions of people . . . going to starve to death in spite of any crash programs embarked upon now"[1]—got it almost exactly wrong. Geographer William Dando fared no better; in 1980, he delineated "a globe-girdling Future Famine Zone" encompassing forty countries, all of which would have "very serious food problems and,

---

[1] Ehrlich 1968, 1.

possibly, famines by 1985 or 1990." Dando further predicted that future famines would be long lasting and cover broad areas. They would "undoubtedly be man-made," and "of a transportation, cultural, political or overpopulation type."[2]

The Ethiopian famine of 1974 forced Wallace Aykroyd, another famine scholar, to add an epilogue to his *The Conquest of Famine*, in which he tempered optimism with the hope that the knowledge and experience gained in Ethiopia would prove useful in relieving famines elsewhere in future. In the following decade, the fear of global overpopulation prompted hard-line (and high-profile) Malthusian writers to predict the "Great Die-Off" in which some four billion people would perish, or to counsel against food aid to nations at continued risk from population pressure and famine, on the grounds that it would only exacerbate their problems or postpone a solution to them. David Arnold wrote his classic *Famine: Social Crisis and Historical Change* (1988) at a time when famine seemed to be stalking the third world much like it had Europe in an earlier age.[3] Much has changed for the better since the 1980s, however, and a different perspective on famine seems warranted today.

Several changes in the nature of famine described in earlier parts of this book justify tempered optimism about the immediate future. First, we have seen how the frequency of famines has been declining over time, and how, despite a series of catastrophic famines between the 1920s and 1960s, famine mortality has also been falling. The famines that have struck since the 1960s have been small by historical standards. These trends are plausibly linked to global economic growth—world GDP per head has trebled since 1950 and

[2] Dando 1980, 90–91.

[3] Aykroyd 1974; Arnold 1988: 1, 140–42. Ehrlich predicted the Great Die-Off, and ecologist Garrett Hardin argued against famine relief.

quintupled since 1900—and the accompanying globalization
of disaster relief. Second, we have seen how Stalin, Hitler,
and Mao, three totalitarian despots linked to some of the
greatest famines of all time, have left no important heirs. The
scope for human agency to produce cataclysmic famine even
in peacetime has thereby been reduced. Third, we have seen
how improvements in medical technology, by reducing the
incidence of infectious disease in poorer countries, also reduce its power to kill when famine strikes. And fourth, we
have seen how modern information and communication
technologies enable today's policymakers and relief agencies
to anticipate the risk of famine and react more quickly to its
appearance than in the past. Such changes support de Waal's
opening declaration in *Famine Crimes* that "famine is con-
querable" and Sen's repeated claims that famines are easily
preventable, given the political will.[4]

In this final chapter, I further examine some trends and
shifts likely to impact on the probability of famine in the
coming decade or two. I first discuss trends in current and
likely future agricultural output and productivity, both globally and in the poorest economies, and the challenges posed
by climate change and desertification. Then, I focus again
on the last redoubts of famine, and finally, discuss the role
of institutions, local and foreign, in causing, preventing, or
mitigating future famines.

AGRICULTURAL TRENDS

The link between the aggregate food supply and famine is
looser nowadays than in Malthus's time. Still, most major

[4] De Waal 1997, 1; Sen 1995.

famines on record have involved reductions in a precarious food supply, so trends in global food output are of interest. At the global level, food output per head has risen by about one-third since the early 1960s. It is particularly reassuring to find agricultural output outstripping population in former famine-prone countries such as China and India (figure 9.1). Chinese food output per head is now three times what it was four decades ago, and Indian output per head is about one-third higher. Moreover, although numbers employed on the land have risen globally, the *share* of the labor force mainly dependent on agriculture has been declining almost everywhere. In 1950, only one-fifth of the labor force in today's developing countries was employed outside of agriculture; today the proportion is nearly one-half. The nonagricultural share has risen in India from 25 to 46 percent, in China from 12 to 33 percent, and in Africa from 18 to 44 percent.

Only in sub-Saharan Africa has the food output failed to keep pace with the population. FAO data imply that food production per head in that vast region is probably less today than it was in the 1960s. The significant decline in output per head in the 1970s and early 1980s, associated with years of drought and poor harvests, has been stemmed but not entirely reversed: since the early 1960s the decline has been about 10 percent (figure 9.1). As a consequence, the reliance on imported food has grown.

Figures 9.2a–9.2c, all based on FAO data, compare the race between population (represented by the smoother curves) and food production since the 1960s in Niger and sub-Saharan Africa, on the one hand, and China (where the race is no longer a contest), on the other. In those parts of Africa least affected by HIV/AIDS, such as Niger and the

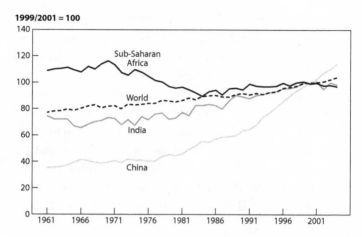

1999/2001 = 100

FIG. 9.1.   Food production per capita, 1961–2004.
Source: FAO 2004.

Sahel generally, the continued rise in population has been the product of high fertility and an increasing life expectancy. In Niger, the rise in farm output has occurred mainly through the extension of the area under cultivation: crop yields per hectare are lower now than in the early 1960s, although they have recovered somewhat in recent years. The huge increase in Niger's cropped area since the 1970s puts claims of rampant desertification in the Sahel region (discussed in more detail below) in perspective. Yet its extreme poverty means that despite relative political stability, the resources to provide public services and improve infrastructure are virtually nonexistent. Is it too much to hope that backward economies such as Niger can in due course diversify away from subsistence agriculture, and instead import foodstuffs from economies with a comparative advantage in their production?

1999/2001 = 100

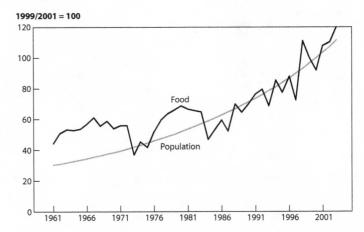

FIG. 9.2a.   Niger, 1961–2003.
Source: FAO 2004.

1999/2001 = 100

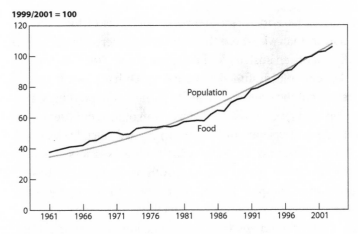

FIG. 9.2b.   Sub-Saharan Africa, 1961–2003.
Source: FAO 2004.

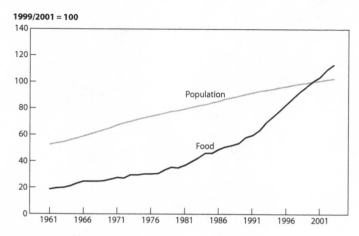

FIG. 9.2c.   China, 1961–2004.
Source: FAO 2004.

Elsewhere in Africa, the recent histories of food production in Malawi, where the progress registered in the 1990s
has not been sustained in the 2000s, and Zimbabwe, where
despotic and dysfunctional governance has more than canceled out the economic benefits of the human fertility transition, also give pause. Zimbabwe, 78th of 130 countries on the
Human Development Index in 1990, had fallen back to 151th
of 177 by 2006. In Malawi the decline was less dramatic,
from 116th of 130 in 1990 to 166th of 177 in 2006. In both
countries, despite limited diversification into vegetables,
grasses, and fruit, millet remains the dominant crop.

Today the omens for food production in another vulnerable area, the People's Republic of North Korea, are mildly
encouraging. Better harvests and a modicum of economic reform, including freer food markets, have helped. By 2000–
2001 agricultural output had recovered from the dismal,

famine-inducing levels of the mid-1990s; since then it has grown sluggishly, and with interruptions in years of flooding such as 2007. Imports have played an important role in controlling malnutrition; the latest available statistics on child nutrition (see the details in chapter 8 above) offer reassuring evidence that humanitarian aid has been reaching those who needed it. Meanwhile, the North Korean authorities have been seeking to stem the inflow of food, citing better harvests and the risk of endemic dependence on foreign aid. North Korea's low total fertility rate—which the Central Intelligence Agency reckoned at 2.05 children born per woman in 2007—reduces the pressure on its agricultural resources.[5]

In Bangladesh (with a population of over 150 million in 2007 and Asia's poorest economy apart from Afghanistan), food production has barely kept up with population. Output per agricultural worker has been rising, however, particularly in the last decade or so, and the proportion of the population dependent on the land for a living has dropped from over 80 percent in the 1960s to about half today. Although the food balance remains rather precarious, the downward trends in under-five mortality (149 per thousand in 1990, and 77 per thousand in 2004), the proportion of children underweight (66.6 percent in 1990, and 48 percent in 1996–2004), and the total fertility rate (6.3 in 1975, and 3.1 today) offer some grounds for optimism.

Such data support the note of "tempered hope" sounded by demographer Tim Dyson's 1996 survey of global prospects

---

[5] A population's total fertility rate is a synthetic demographic measure. It is the average number of children who would be born to a woman over her lifetime if she were to experience the age-specific fertility rates obtaining in her country.

for the period to 2020. Dyson predicted that food production per head in 2020 would be about the same as in 1990, but that this would be compatible with a rise in food consumption per head across most of the globe. Dyson's more benign scenario was contingent on the increased application of nitrogenous fertilizers, irrigation, water pricing, and new varieties of high-yielding crops.[6]

Although the likelihood of future famines is linked to food supply, much also hinges on population growth and the speed of the fertility transition. Today (2009) the world's population is about 6.5 billion, and increasing by around 76 million annually. In 2006, the United Nations revised its forecast of population in 2050 upward to 9.1 billion (compared to 8.9 billion according to the 1998 and 2002 revisions). Life expectancy has been rising in most of the handful of countries still at risk from textbook Malthusian famine, but they lag behind in terms of fertility decline.

A key issue is how the fertility transition, scarcely yet under way, unfolds in such vulnerable economies. A hopeful historical lesson for the last remaining pretransition nations is that the transition, once in motion, has been much more rapid in late-coming than in pioneering societies. Meanwhile, Africa's laggard fertility transition, itself a function of economic underdevelopment, has increased its share of the global population from only 8.8 percent in 1950 to 14 percent today; it is set to reach 21.7 percent by 2050. Even though a drop in the annual growth rate in Africa as a whole is implied (from 2.5 percent during the past half century to 1.4 percent the next), the latest United Nations' projections predict a tripling of population by mid-century in

[6] Dyson 1996.

impoverished countries such as Niger, Uganda, and Mali. Given that most of the growth will be in massive, densely settled cities, these projections must imply—and allow for—increasing vulnerability to pandemics, if not famines.

Such concerns were amplified by the striking and largely unexpected rise in food prices in 2007–08, and the fear that a combination of demand and supply factors would continue to drive them upward. All of a sudden, rising incomes in countries such India and China were seen to be fueling demand, just as lagging crop yields, poor harvests, and the diversion of farmland to ethanol production were beginning to limit supply. For some months, as price rises led to widespread food riots, the outlook seemed particularly bleak. By mid-2008, however, prices had peaked and the Food and Agriculture Organization was predicting an improvement in global cereal supplies in 2008/09.[7]

CLIMATE AND DESERTIFICATION

Since the turn of the new millennium, optimism about the future has been tempered by increasing concern at the implications of climate change, and in particular the prospect of massive increases in CO_2 emissions leading to accelerated global warming. By 2005, new scientific information had prompted Dyson to discard his earlier optimism for a much bleaker prognosis that castigated world leaders for ignoring an emerging scientific consensus on this issue. In the absence of corrective action, rising income and population

[7] "Global Cereal Supply and Demand Brief." Available at http://www.fao.org/docrep/010/ai465e/ai465e04.htm (accessed June 16, 2008).

along with increased urbanization would lead to "food price rises, large scale migration and possibly significant socio-political disruption."[8] The latest global population forecasts do indeed highlight the difficulties of keeping CO_2 levels constant. Unless remedial action is taken in time, the prospect of cropland losses, rising food prices, and ensuing political instability in the medium term are real.

Before the modern industrial age, the CO_2 level in the atmosphere hovered around 280 parts per million for centuries. Today it exceeds 380 parts per million, and the Intergovernmental Panel on Climate Change (which shared the Nobel Peace Prize in 2007) has projected a rise to between 650 and 970 parts per million by the end of the present century, if greenhouse gas emissions continue at or above current rates. Such an increase would raise the average global temperatures by between 1.4 and 5.8 degrees Celsius. These are global predictions; the implications for arid, famine-prone zones are bleaker, although for some regions, higher temperatures and increased rainfall could result in higher crop yields. Shifting comparative advantage might then dictate significant changes in the global geography of food production and human settlement. Be that as it may, the constraints posed by action taken in the coming years to control climate change loom larger than they did a decade ago.

One link that causes particular concern is that between population pressure and soil exhaustion. Again, the link is not new. Over half a century ago, archaeologist Adolf Reifenberg described the history of agriculture in the Levant as one of "struggle between the desert and the sown." In the

---

[8] Dyson 2005.

same vein and around the same time, historian Michael Postan claimed that in medieval England, too, population pressure had reduced the productivity of the soil. Pressure on the land had led to deforestation and overgrazing, shortened fallow periods, and consequent soil exhaustion and reductions in productivity. Such accounts of soil depletion have been contested or rebutted, but they have a particular resonance for the modern history of the Sahel, the famine-prone arid zone straddling a thinly populated area of 5.5 million square kilometers at the southern edge of the Sahara. So is desertification increasing the risk of famine?

Since the 1970s the Sahel, which stretches from Senegal to Somalia, has been notorious for desertification, a process whereby the soil loses its capacity to maintain necessary moisture. The United Nations has been hosting discussions about desertification since 1977, yet in 2002 one of its environment programs claimed that nearly half of Africa was in the grip of desertification, with the Sahel region being worst affected. Desertification and the attendant famine risk were blamed on a combination of declining rainfall and destructive farming methods. The latter included the introduction of new breeds of cattle, the destruction of wooded areas for firewood, and in some areas, a shift from corn or wheat to rice as the staple crop.[9]

Desertification is commonly described as an irreversible process. Yet the record in the Sahel suggests a more complex picture. The fate of two of its greatest lakes is instructive here. Lake Chad is a source of water to millions of people in the four countries that surround it (Chad, Cameroon, Niger, and Nigeria). Through a combination of natural and

[9] Eckholm and Brown 1997.

human-induced factors, the lake has shrunk from ten thousand to twenty-six thousand square kilometers (with the size
depending on the season and the year) in the 1960s to about
thirty-five hundred square kilometers today. Lower rainfall
has been mainly responsible, but an increased reliance on
lake water for irrigation purposes has also been a factor. Lake
Faguibine in Mali, West Africa's largest lake (eight hundred
square kilometers), is also at serious risk. Drought in 1973
and the following years turned it into a virtual desert; by 1985
most of its lakeside inhabitants had left—their boats "a mere
memory in the minds of the former fishermen."[10]

After drying out completely for a time in 1984, water levels in Lake Chad have recovered slightly since the early
1990s, but the risks to the remaining water basin from
human action are pressing.[11] In the meantime, to the extent
that the shrinkage has led to significant land reclamation in
the lake's hinterland, and as long as further shrinkage can
be controlled, it may seem a fair price to pay. Lake Faguibine also dried out completely for a few years; today, thanks
to a higher annual rainfall than in the 1970s and 1980s, it
has reverted to a slightly healthier, but still precarious state.

Severe droughts in the 1970s also turned part of northern Burkina Faso into a desert for a time, but that process
has been largely reversed. Increased precipitation since the
mid-1980s has been mainly responsible (see figure 9.3),
although NGOs stress the part played by soil and water
conservation, particularly through the prevention of soil

[10] Salgado 2004, 12, 125.

[11] Global International Waters Assessment, *Lake Chad Basin: Regional
Assessment 43* (Kalmar, Sweden: University of Kalmar, on behalf of United
Nations Environment Programme, 2004). Available at http://www.giwa
.net/areas/reports/r43/assessment_giwa_r43.pdf.

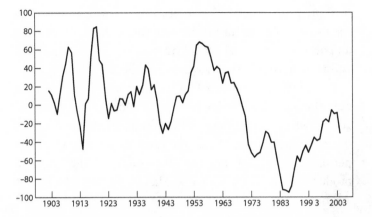

Fig. 9.3.   Sahel rainfall index, 1903–2004 (June–September moving average).
Source: Http://jisao.washington.edu/data_sets/sahel/.

leaching. Fieldworkers in eastern Burkina Faso point to the combined impact of careful husbandry, the use of livestock manure, the intensive weeding and thinning of crops, and the (limited) application of nitrogenous fertilizer. Such microevidence squares with the economic presumption that land being the scarce resource, farmers will use great ingenuity in conserving and reclaiming it. The case for relentless desertification underestimates "the abilities of local farmers" to operate within the constraints they face.[12]

In other parts of the Sahel, desertification never became prevalent, and there has been a significant increase in vegetation over the past fifteen years or so in the area as a whole, with recent satellite images revealing the greening of a band of desert stretching all the way from Mauritania in the west

[12] Mazzucato and Neimeijer 2000.

to Eritrea in the east. The reversal has also been linked to the reduction in sulfur dioxide emissions in North America and Europe produced by "clean air" legislation since the 1980s, resulting in the increased rainfall.[13]

FAO data also indicate that both cropped area and food output in the Sahel region have risen considerably since the 1980s, which would have been difficult in the presence of major desertification. (True, the same data imply a variable performance: significant increases in both land use and productivity in Burkina Faso, Mauritania, and Mali, but stagnant productivity in Niger.)

WHERE BACKWARDNESS PERSISTS

History shows, as already noted in chapter 8, that the correlation between underdevelopment and famine, although strong, is by no means perfect. When famine struck the Soviet Union in 1921–22 and 1931–33, its productive capacity was twice that of, say, Niger today. The lack of major "death-dealing" famines in England since the 1720s is hardly surprising, but the severity of the Irish famine of the 1840s, in a region of what was by then "the workshop of the world." is as noteworthy as is the absence of major famines in India since the 1940s. China, on the other hand, was only marginally richer in the late 1950s than it had been in the 1870s, when another famine killed proportionately more people than in

[13] Australian meteorologist Leon Rotstayn has linked the dramatic decline in annual precipitation in the Sahel after 1970 to air pollution, and the recovery since the mid-1980s to improved air quality (see Rotstayn and Lohmann 2002).

1959–61. While the Great Leap Forward famine was in part the product of Mao's reckless effort to fast-track Chinese modernization, economic backwardness was also a factor.

Moreover, as noted in chapters 1 and 8, wars exacerbate economic backwardness and vulnerability to famine. It is hardly surprising, then, that in the eighteen economies most subject to chronic food emergencies since the mid-1980s, the FAO reckons that current or past conflict has been a major factor in fourteen cases, weather (principally drought) in eight cases, and what the FAO dubs "economic problems" in five cases. One economy, Haiti, has been subject to all three; the most vulnerable, Angola, has been subject mainly to the first. Civil strife and political instability have been endemic throughout much of Africa over the past half century; the claim that the continent has suffered 186 coups and 26 major wars in that period is frequently recycled. While most countries included in the FAO list ranked low on the United Nations' Human Development Index rankings, they included several placed little more than halfway down the table (Armenia, Georgia, and Iraq).

Nonetheless, the link between living standards and vulnerability to famine is patent. Over two centuries ago, Malthus deemed wages in the United States so high that "a famine seems to be almost impossible." Happily his prediction that future population growth in the United States would eventually lead to labor being "much less liberally rewarded" was not borne out, at least in the long run.[14] Since the Industrial Revolution, increases in living standards have reduced the threat of famine everywhere. Most of the globe today has reached or overtaken the standard already attained

---

[14] Malthus 1872, 260.

by the United States in Malthus's time, and by most of Europe (apart from in wartime) half a century later. India has been spared major famine in peacetime for over a century, apart from the drought-induced famine that resulted in an excess mortality of about 130,000 in the western state of Maharashtra in 1972–73. Bangladesh, with only half of India's GDP per head, has been spared famine since 1974–75. The Chinese GDP per head today is more than three times and India's GDP almost double that of the United States in 1820, making the likelihood nowadays of a major famine in those countries remote. Apart from the high-profile exceptions of North Korea and, possibly, parts of Afghanistan, the threat of famine has virtually disappeared from Asia. At present only the poorest regions of Africa remain at risk, and *prolonged* famine anywhere is conceivable only in contexts of endemic warfare or blockade.

Consider again Niger, where the GDP per head is only about half that of Ireland on the eve of the Great Irish Famine of the 1840s, and illiteracy rates and child mortality rates are higher, and which is among the poorest economies in the world today. In 2006 Niger ranked last of 177 countries on the Human Development Index, some distance behind Sierra Leone, Mali, and Burkina Faso. Since the 1960s its agricultural output has more than trebled, barely keeping pace with a population growth rate averaging 3 percent, and showing no signs of deceleration. That means that for food output to match population, productivity gains stemming from capital accumulation and efficiency gains had to rise by an annual average of nearly 2 percent—a high rate by historical standards. As in much of sub-Saharan Africa, agriculture in Niger has been running in order to stand still.

Today, Niger's total fertility rate—about 7.4 children born per woman—is the highest in the world, and its median age at marriage (15.3 years for females in 1998) probably is the lowest in the world.[15] It remains one of the few countries in the world where the demographic transition to later marriage and smaller families has not yet begun. Meanwhile, life expectancy has risen from 38.4 years in 1970–75 to about 44 years today. Even though the proportions of underweight and moderately or severely stunted children have also been on the rise—from 36 and 32 percent, respectively, in the early 1990s, to 40 and 40 percent now—the survival chances of infants and young children have been rising. Probably nowhere else at present is population pressing harder on the margins of subsistence than in Niger.

When the drought-induced crisis in Niger attracted global media attention in 2005, NGOs repeatedly highlighted Niger's ranking as the second-poorest economy in the world. Two other African countries hit by famine or near famine in the new millennium, Ethiopia and Malawi, are also among the poorest in the world. Their GDPs per capita today are less than half in real terms that of the United States two centuries ago. Several of Africa's poorest countries have experienced declining GDP per capita in recent decades; although real GDP per head has risen across most of the continent since the 1960s, in Niger it is reckoned to have fallen by over two-fifths and in war-ravaged Angola by over one-third.

By FAO definitions, the world still contains about eight hundred million malnourished people. As the absolute numbers rise, the proportions fall: the percentage of malnourished people in the less developed world has fallen from 29

[15] Schoumaker 2004.

percent in 1979–81 to 20 percent in 1990–92 and 17 percent today. Progress has been fastest in the Far East and South Asia, two traditionally famine-prone regions, but in sub-Saharan Africa, famine's remaining redoubt, the proportion malnourished today remains about one-third. The link between malnutrition and famine remains. Still, mass hunger and the eradication of HIV/AIDS present far greater challenges now to the global community than famine. It is an uncomfortable truth—all too familiar to NGOs—that soliciting sympathy and funding for once-off disaster relief is much easier than obtaining relief for endemic malnutrition or disease. Sadly, while life expectancy at birth in Niger, Mali, and Ethiopia—three famine-prone countries—rose by several years between 1970 and 2003, in Botswana and Zimbabwe—less threatened by famine, but ravaged by HIV/AIDS—it fell by twelve to thirteen years over the same interval.[16] And looking ahead, a pessimist might well warn that nowadays we have more to fear from some new pandemic (such as a human variant of avian flu) than from famines.

A STITCH IN TIME

In principle, preempting small-scale famines such as those in the Sudan in 1998 and Niger in 2005 should be "easier" in the future. Not only is there ample food worldwide but the transmission of information is, or can be, instantaneous, and transport is relatively cheap and quick. The United States Agency for International Development–funded Famine Early Warning System (FEWS) and other agencies have been studying and reporting on food security throughout

---

[16] Ó Gráda 2007, table 5. See also de Waal and Whiteside 2003.

Africa since the 1980s. Their reports, which monitor harvests scientifically, and track prices and the sociopolitical
landscape, offer usually reliable guides to the risk of a food
supply shortfall. Media depictions of famine prompt up-
surges of compassion for the third world, and hundreds of
NGOs worldwide vie for the funds that ensue. The "tuning
in" to famine, however fleeting, through events such as
George Harrison's Concert for Bangladesh, Live Aid, and
their myriad local replicas offer powerful evidence of a globalized concern that cannot be ignored.

Yet problems remain, even in relieving a relatively mild
crisis. The case of Niger in 2005 again highlights these.
Reports of the likely impact of drought and locust attacks
on the harvest had been circulating from October 2004; before the year's end, FEWS had already listed Niger as "re-
quiring urgent attention" and the Niger authorities had a
"national emergency plan" in place. The WFP drew attention to the unfolding crisis in March 2005, but failed to attract donors. In April Médecins sans frontières was the first
NGO to warn of the crisis, which FEWS upgraded to an
"emergency" in June.[17] Media coverage in July produced a
stampede of NGOs toward Niger; by August, food and medical supplies began to reach the affected regions in volume.

Niger confirmed once again that stories of everyday
malnutrition and destitution are less newsworthy than the
famines to which they sometimes give rise. None of the
publicity surrounding the Live 8 pop concerts of early July
2005 focused on Niger, but NGOs were quick to capitalize
on the publicity generated by media reports a week or two

---

[17] "Niger Food Crisis: Early Diagnosis, Slow and Misguided Aid," June
23, 2005. Available at http://www.doctorswithoutborders.org/news/2005/
06-23-2005.cfm (accessed May 29, 2008).

later of a crisis, which—so it was repeatedly claimed—was threatening 4 million people, with "800,000 children at risk." For a few months Niger headlined the NGO's fundraising campaigns. By late 2005 millet prices had fallen by almost half from their summer peak, and the ratio of livestock to cereal prices had risen significantly. A crisis that had been described in midsummer as one of gargantuan proportions—"874,000 people are in danger of starving to death," according to the director of the Irish charity GOAL[18]—had virtually evaporated. By early 2006 the focus had shifted to the "catastrophe" about to engulf much of East Africa, unless urgent donations were forthcoming.[19]

The propensity to follow rather than preempt disasters has been an abiding weakness of NGOs. The scheme proposed in late 2004 by the WFP, whereby nations at risk (funded by donor countries and private investors) purchased insurance against famine-inducing drought or floods, reflects an attempt to deal with this weakness. In good years investors in the scheme would receive interest on their "catastrophe bonds," but in bad years they would lose some of the cash value of their bonds, which the WFP would spend on famine relief. The details of the scheme, which is not yet (as of 2009) operational, have still to be fully fleshed out. One difficult sticking point is that bad years would have to be defined by some agreed triggering signal (e.g., rainfall levels or the number of rainless days).[20]

[18] John O'Shea, "Let Down by the World," *Irish Examiner*, August 11, 2005. Available at http://www.goal-uk.org/newsroom/letdown0805.shtml (accessed May 29, 2008).

[19] "WFP Warns of Catastrophe in Horn of Africa," WFP press release, January 13, 2006.

[20] The scheme is described in detail at http://www.wfp.org/eb/docs/2005/wfp077056~3.pdf (accessed June 3, 2008).

The recent history of famine is not easily squared with the WFP's claim that "food emergencies" are twice as numerous today as they were in the 1980s, a decade in which famine mortality was much higher. NGOs also tend to paint a bleak and depressing picture of emergencies without end. The evidence suggests otherwise, though: probably for the first time in history, only pockets of the globe, such as parts of Africa, Afghanistan, and North Korea, now remain truly vulnerable to the threat of major famine.[21] Endemic malnutrition is a distinct and more intractable issue.

Another hopeful sign is the progress of democracy and relative political stability in Africa, where their absence often led to famines in the past. Widely used measures of good governance such as the "Freedom Index" and the "Polity Index" imply modest progress in this respect across most of Africa over the past decade or so. On the other hand, although the quality of economic policymaking has improved in the recent past—for instance, in most of sub-Saharan Africa governments no longer rely on inflation as a source of revenue—more democracy has not led to less corruption.[22] As much as anything else, the slow, onward march of accountable government will rid the world's last vulnerable

[21] Seaman 1993; Iliffe 1987, 255–57.

[22] Between 2000 and 2005, the values of the widely used Freedom Index rose in twenty-eight out of forty African countries. The average Polity 2 Index, another measure of good governance, for thirty-seven African nations rose from -4.5 in 1980 to 0.7 in 2003. On the other hand, between 1997 and 2005 the mean value of Transparency International's "Corruption Perception Index" (which ranged in 2005 from 1.7 for Chad to 9.7 for Iceland) fell in the thirteen sub-Saharan countries for which data are available. Estimated from data downloadable at the following Web sites: http://www.heritage.org/; http://www.transparency.org/; and http://www.cidcm.umd.edu/inscr/polity/.

regions of the scourge of famine. Yet any optimism about "making famine history" must be qualified by the realization that the threat of wars between and within nations is never far away. In today's heavily urbanized world, even a limited nuclear war could lead to a new age of famine. The prospect of a famine-free world hinges on improved governance and peace. It is as simple—or difficult—as that.

References

Adamets, Serguie. 2002. "Famine in Nineteenth- and Twentieth-century Russia: Mortality by Age, Cause, and Gender." In *Famine Demography: Perspectives from the Past and the Present*, ed. Tim Dyson and Cormac Ó Gráda, 157–80. Oxford: Oxford University Press.

———. 2003. *Guerre civile et famine en Russie: le pouvoir bolchevique et la population face à la catastrophe démographique*. Paris: Institut d'études slaves.

Aftalion, Florin. 1990. *The French Revolution: An Economic Interpretation*. Cambridge: Cambridge University Press.

Agence France-Presse. 2003. "Ethiopian Famine Strains Women, Children," August 21. Available at http://www.reliefweb.int/rw/rwb.nsf/AllDocsByUNID/c931e26f457 8336dc1256d8900490901 (accessed June 1, 2008).

Ahuja, Ravi. 2002. "State Formation and 'Famine Policy' in Early Colonial South India." *Indian Economic and Social History Review* 39 (4): 351–80.

Alamgir, Mohiuddin. 1977. *Famine 1974: Political Economy of Mass Starvation in Bangladesh: A Statistical Annex*. Dacca: Bangladesh Institute of Development Studies.

Allen, Robert C. 2003. *Farm to Factory: A Reinterpretation of the Soviet Industrial Revolution*. Princeton, NJ: Princeton University Press.

Almond, Douglas, Lena Edlund, Hongbin Li, and Junsen Zhang. 2007. "Long-term Effects of the 1959–1961 China Famine: Mainland China and Hong Kong." National Bureau of Economic Research working paper, no. 13384.

Ambirajan, Srinivasa. 1976. "Malthusian Population Policy and Indian Famine Policy in the Nineteenth Century." *Population Studies* 30:5–14.

American Red Cross. 1929. *The Report of the American Red Cross Commission to China.* Washington, DC: American National Red Cross.

Amery, Leonard S. 1988. *The Empire at Bay: The Leo Amery Diaries, 1929–1945.* Ed. John Barnes and David Nicholson. Vol. 2. London: Hutchinson.

Antonov, A. N. 1947. "Children Born during the Siege of Leningrad in 1942." *Journal of Pediatrics* 30:250–59.

Appleby, Andrew B. 1978. *Famine in Tudor and Stuart England.* Liverpool: Liverpool University Press.

———. 1980. "Epidemics and Famine in the Little Ice Age." *Journal of Interdisciplinary History* 10 (4): 643–63.

Arnold, David. 1988. *Famine: Social Crisis and Historical Change.* Oxford: Blackwell.

Ashton, Basil, Kenneth Hill, Alan Piazza, and Robin Zeitz. 1984. "Famine in China, 1958–61." *Population and Development Review* 10 (4): 613–45.

Aykroyd, Wallace R. 1974. *The Conquest of Famine.* London: Chatto and Windus.

Azeze, Fekade. 1998. *Unheard Voices: Drought, Famine, and God in Ethiopian Oral Poetry.* Addis Ababa, Ethiopia: Addis Ababa University Press.

Ballard, Charles. 1986. "Drought and Economic Distress: South Africa in the 1800s." *Journal of Interdisciplinary History* 17 (2): 359–78.

Banister, Judith. 1987. *China's Changing Population.* Stanford, CA: Stanford University Press.

Barber, John, and Andrei Dzeniskevich, eds. 2005. *Life and Death in Leningrad, 1941–44.* London: Palgrave Macmillan.

Barker, David J. P., ed. 1992. *Fetal and Infant Origins of Adult Disease.* London: BMJ Publishing Group.

Basu, Dipak R. 1984. "Food Policy and the Analysis of Famine." *Indian Journal of Economics* 64 (254): 289–301.

Batabyal, Rakesh. 2005. *Communalism in Bengal: From Famine to Noakhali.* New Delhi: Sage.

Becker, Jasper. 1996. *Hungry Ghosts: Mao's Secret Famine.* New York: Holt.

———. 2006. "Dictators: The Depths of Evil." *New Statesman,* September 4, 32.

Belozerov, Boris. 2005. "Crime during Siege." In *Famine and Death in Besieged Leningrad,* ed. John Barber and Andrei Dzeniskevich, 213–28. London: Palgrave Macmillan.

Bengtsson, Tommy, Cameron Campbell, and James Lee, eds. 2004. *Life under Pressure: Mortality and Living Standards in Europe and Asia, 1700–1900.* Cambridge, MA: MIT Press.

Bernstein, Thomas P. 1983. "Starving to Death in China." *New York Review of Books* 30, no. 10 (June 16): 36–38.

———. 1984. "Stalinism, Famine, and Chinese Peasants: Grain Procurements during the Great Leap Forward." *Theory and Society* 13 (3): 339–77.

———. 2006. "Mao Zedong and the Famine of 1959–1960: A Study in Wilfulness." *China Quarterly,* no. 186:421–45.

Bhatia, B. M. 1967. *Famines in India 1860–1965: A Study in Some Aspects of the Economic History of India.* 2nd ed. Bombay: Asia Publishing House.

Biswas, Atreyi. 2000. *Famines in Ancient India.* New Delhi: Gyan.

Blunt, Edward. 1937. *The I.C.S.: The Indian Civil Service.* London: Faber and Faber.

Bongaarts, John, and Mead Cain. 1982. "Demographic Responses to Famine." In *Famine,* ed. Kevin M. Cahill, 44–62. New York: Maryknoll.

Bourke, Austin. 1993. *The Visitation of God: The Potato and the Great Irish Famine*. Dublin: Lilliput Press.

Bourke, Austin, and Hubert Lamb. 1993. *The Spread of the Potato Blight in Europe in 1845–46 and the Accompanying Wind and Weather Patterns*. Dublin: Meteorological Service.

Bowbrick, Peter. 1986. "The Causes of Famines: A Refutation of Prof. Sen's Theory." *Food Policy* 11 (2): 105–24.

Boyle, Phelim P., and Cormac Ó Gráda. 1986. "Fertility Trends, Excess Mortality, and the Great Irish Famine." *Demography* 23:546–65.

Brading, David A., and Celia Liu. 1973. "Population Growth and Crisis: León, 1720–1860." *Journal of Latin American Studies* 5 (1): 1–36.

Braudel, Fernand. 1992. *The Structures of Everyday Life: Civilization and Capitalism, 15th–18th Century*. Vol. 1. Berkeley: University of California Press.

Braun, Rudolf. 1978. "Protoindustrialization and Demographic Changes in the Canton of Zurich." In *Historical Studies of Changing Fertility*, ed. Charles Tilly, 289–334. Princeton, NJ: Princeton University Press.

Braund, Henry B. 1944. "Famine in Bengal." Unpublished typescript. June 30 (deposited in British Library, Oriental and India Office Library, Mss. Eur. D792/2).

Brennan, Lance. 1984. "The Development of the India Famine Codes: Personalities, Policies, and Politics." In *Famine as a Geographical Phenomenon*, ed. B. Currey and G. Hugo, 91–111. Dordrecht: Reidel.

———. 1988. "Government Famine Relief in Bengal, 1943." *Journal of Asian Studies* 47 (3): 542–67.

Brojek, Joseph, Samuel Wells, and Ancel Keys. 1946. "Medical Aspects of Semistarvation in Leningrad." *American Review of Soviet Medicine*, no. 4:70–86.

Brooks, Francis J. 1993. "Revising the Conquest of Mexico: Smallpox, Sources, and Populations." *Journal of Interdisciplinary History* 24 (1): 1–29.

Brun, Thierry. 1980. "Comment on Dirks." *Current Anthropology* 21 (1): 34–35.

Bryceson, Anthony D. M. 1977. "Rehydration in Cholera and Other Diarrhoeal Diseases." In *Technologies for Rural Health*, ed. Royal Society, 109–14. London: Royal Society.

Buck, John L. 1937. *Land Utilization in China*. Chicago: University of Chicago Press.

Buck, Pearl. [1931] 1980. *The Good Earth*. New York: Monarch Press.

Bullard, Melissa M. 1982. "Grain Supply and Urban Unrest in Renaissance Rome: The Crisis of 1533–34." In *Rome and the Renaissance: The City and the Myth*, ed. P. A. Ramsey, 279–92. Binghamton, NY: Medieval and Renaissance Texts and Studies.

Burke, Edmund. [1795] 1960. 'Thoughts and Details on Scarcity'. In *Select Works of Edmund Burke*, Vol. 4, Francis Canavan, ed. Durham: Duke University Press.

Cai, Yong, and Wang Feng. 2005. "Famine, Social Disruption, and Miscarriage: Evidence from Chinese Survey Data." *Demography* 42 (2): 301–22.

Caldwell, John C. 1998. "Malthus and the Less Developed World: The Pivotal Role of India." *Population and Development Review* 24 (4): 675–96.

Campbell, Bruce M. S. 2008. "Four Famines and a Pestilence: Harvest, Price, and Wage Variations in England, 13th to 19th Centuries." Forthcoming.

Campbell, Gwynn. 2005. *An Economic History of Imperial Madagascar, 1750–1895: The Rise and Fall of an Island Empire*. Cambridge: Cambridge University Press.

Cantillon, Richard. [1755] 1931. *Essai sur la nature du commerce en général*. Henry Higgs, ed. London: Frank Cass.

Carefoot, G. L., and E. R. Sprott. 1969. *Famine on the Wind: Plant Diseases and Human History*. London: Angus and Robinson.

Carleton, William. [1847] 1972. *The Black Prophet*. Shannon, Ireland: Irish University Press.

Chakrabarti, Malabika. 2004. *The Famine of 1896–1897 in Bengal: Availability or Entitlement Crisis?* New Delhi: Orient Longman.

Chakraborty, Ratan L. 1997. *Rural Indebtedness in Bengal*. Calcutta: Progressive Publishers.

Chambers, David, and Brian Pullan. 2001. *Venice: A Documentary History, 1450–1630*. Toronto: University of Toronto Press.

Chang, Jung. 1991. *Wild Swans: Three Daughters of China*. New York: Simon and Schuster.

Chatterji, Joya. 1994. *Bengal Divided: Hindu Communalism and Partition, 1932–1947*. Cambridge: Cambridge University Press.

Chen, Ta. 1946. *Population in Modern China*. Chicago: University of Chicago Press.

Chen, Yuyu, and Li-an Zhou. 2007. "The Long-term Health and Economic Consequences of the 1959–61 Famine in China." *Journal of Health Economics* 26 (4): 659–81.

Cherepenina, Nadezhda. 2005. "Assessing the Scale of Famine and Death in the Besieged City." In *Life and Death in Leningrad, 1941–44*, ed. John Barber and Andrei Dzeniskevich, 28–70. London: Palgrave Macmillan.

Chi, Wen-Shun. 1965. "Water Conservancy in Communist China." *China Quarterly* 23:37–54.

Christensen, Erleen J. 2005. *In War and Famine: Missionaries in China's Honan Province in the 1940s*. Montreal: McGill-Queen's University Press.

Cicero, Marcus Tullius. 1913. *De Officiis*. Translated by Walter Miller. Cambridge, MA: Harvard University Press.

Cissoko, Sekene-Mody. 1968. "Famine et épidémies à Tombouctou et dans la Boucle du Niger du XVIe au XVIIIe siècle." *Bulletin de l'institut français d'Afrique noire*, no. 30:806–21.

Clark, Gregory. 2004. "The Price History of British Agriculture, 1209–1914." *Research in Economic History*, no. **22**:41–124.

Cobbing, Julian. 1994. Review of *The Dead Will Arise, Nongqawuse, and the Great Xhosa Cattle-Killing Movement of 1856–57*," by Jeffrey B. Peires. *Journal of South African Studies* 20 (2): 339–41.

Cohen, Mark Nathan. 1990. "Prehistoric Patterns of Hunger." In *Hunger in History: Food Shortage, Poverty, and Deprivation*, ed. Lucile F. Newman, 56–97. London: Blackwell.

Connell, Kenneth H. 1968. *Irish Peasant Society*. Oxford: Oxford University Press.

Courtois, Stéphane, ed. 1997. *Le Livre Noir du Communisme: Crimes, Terreur, Répression*. Paris: Fixot.

Cullen, Karen J., Christopher A. Whatley, and Mary Young. 2006. "William's Ill Years: New Evidence on the Impact of Scarcity and Harvest Failure during the Crisis of the 1690s on Tayside." *Scottish Historical Review* 85 (2): 250–76.

Cullen, Louis M. 1999. "The Food Crises of the Early 1740s: The Economic Conjoncture." In *Au contact des lumières: mélanges offers à Philippe Loupès*, ed. Anne-Marie Cocula and Josette Pontet, 283–306. Bordeaux: Presse Universitaires de Bordeaux.

Dando, William. 1980. *The Geography of Famine.* New York: Winston.

Dalrymple, Dana. 1964. "The Soviet Famine of 1932–34." *Soviet Studies* 15 (1): 250–84.

Das, Tarakchandra. 1949. *Bengal Famine (1943) as Revealed in a Survey of the Destitutes in Calcutta.* Calcutta: University of Calcutta Press.

Davies, Robert W., Mark Harrison, and Stephen G. Wheatcroft. 1994. *The Transformation of the Soviet Union, 1913–1945.* Cambridge: Cambridge University Press.

Davies, Robert W., and Stephen G. Wheatcroft. 2004. *The Years of Hunger: Soviet Agriculture, 1931–33.* London: Palgrave Macmillan.

Davies, Robert W., Oleg Khlevniuk, E. A. Rees, Liudmila P. Kosheleva, and Larisa A. Rogovaya, eds. 2003. *The Stalin-Kaganovich Correspondence 1931–36.* New Haven, CT: Yale University Press.

Davis, Mike. 2001. *Late Victorian Holocausts: El Niño Famines and the Making of the Third World.* London: Verso.

Devereux, Stephen. 1988. "Entitlements, Availability, and Famine: A Revisionist View of Wollo, 1972–74." *Food Policy* 13 (3): 270–82.

———. 2000. "Famine in the Twentieth Century." Institute of Development Studies, University of Sussex, working paper 105.

———. 2002. "The Malawi Famine of 2002." *Institute of Development Studies Bulletin* 33 (4): 70–78.

———. 2007. *The New Famines: Why Famines Persist in an Era of Globalization.* London: Routledge.

de Waal, Alex. 1989. *Famine That Kills: Darfur, Sudan, 1984–1985.* Oxford: Oxford University Press.

———. 1991. *Evil Days: Thirty Years of War and Famine in Ethiopia*. New York: Human Rights Watch.

———. 1997. *Famine Crimes: Politics and the Disaster Relief Industry in Africa*. London: Africa Rights.

———. 2007. "Deaths in Darfur: Keeping Ourselves Honest." Available at http://www.ssrc.org/blog/2007/08/16/deaths-in-darfur-keeping-ourselves-honest/ (accessed October 22, 2007).

de Waal, Alex, and Alan Whiteside. 2003. "'New Variant Famine': AIDS and Food Crisis in Southern Africa." *Lancet*, 362 (October 11): 1234–37.

Diamond, Jared M. 2000. "Archaeology: Talk of Cannibalism." *Nature*, no. 407:25.

Dias, Jill. 1981. "Famine and Disease in the History of Angola, c. 1830–1930." *Journal of African History*, no. 22: 349–78.

Dickson, David. 1997. *Arctic Ireland: The Extraordinary Story of the Great Frost and Forgotten Famine of 1740–41*. Belfast: White Row Press.

Digby, William. 1878. *The Famine Campaign in Southern India (Madras and Bombay Presidencies and Province of Mysore), 1876–1878*. 2 vols. London: Longmans, Green.

Dirks, Robert. 1980. "Social Responses during Severe Food Shortages and Famine." *Current Anthropology* 21 (1): 21–32.

Downs, Jennifer Eileen. 1995. "Famine Policy and Discourses on Famine in Ming China, 1368–1644." PhD diss., University of Minnesota.

Drèze, Jean, and Amartya Sen. 1989. *Hunger and Public Action*. Oxford: Oxford University Press.

Dunstan, Helen. 2006. *State or Merchant? Political Economy and Political Process in 1740s China*. Cambridge, MA: Harvard University Press.

Dwyer, Denis J. 1974. *China Now: An Introductory Survey with Readings*. London: Longman.

Dyson, Tim. 1991. "On the Demography of South Asian Famines, Parts 1 and 2." *Population Studies*. 45 (1): 5–25; 45 (2): 279–97.

———. 1996. *Population and Food: Global Trends and Future Prospects*. London: Routledge.

———. 2005. "On Development, Demography, and Climate Change: The End of the World as We Know It?" Lecture given at the twenty-fifth Conference of the International Union for the Scientific Study of Population, Tours, France, July 18.

Eckholm, Eric, and Lester R. Brown. 1997. *Spreading Deserts: The Hand of Man*. Washington, DC: Worldwatch Institute.

Edgar, William C. 1893. *The Russian Famine of 1891 and 1892*. Minneapolis: Millers and Manufacturers Insurance Co.

Edgerton-Tarpley, Kathryn. 2004. "Family and Gender in Famine: Cultural Responses to Disaster in North China, 1876–1879." *Journal of Women's History* 16 (4): 119–47.

———. 2008. *Tears from Iron: Cultural Responses to Famine in Nineteenth-century China*. Berkeley: University of California Press.

Ehrlich, Paul. 1968. *The Population Bomb*. New York: Ballantine Books.

Eiríksson, Andrés. 1996a. *Ennistymon Union and Workhouse during the Great Famine*. Dublin: National Famine Research Project.

———. 1996b. *Parsonstown Union and Workhouse during the Great Famine*. Dublin: National Famine Research Project.

———. 1997. "Food Supply and Food Riots." In *Famine 150: Commemorative Lecture Series*, ed. Cormac Ó Gráda, 67–93. Dublin: Teagasc.

Eldredge, Elizabeth A. 1987. "Drought, Famine, and Disease in Nineteenth-century Lesotho." *African Economic History*, no. 16: 61–93.

Elias, Sjoerd, G. Petra, H. Peeters, M. Diederick, E. Grobbee, and A. H. Paulus van Noord. 2004. "Breast Cancer Risk after Caloric Restriction during the 1944–1945 Dutch Famine." *Journal of the National Cancer Institute* 96 (April 7): 539–53.

Ellmann, Michael J. 2000. "The 1947 Soviet Famine and the Entitlement Approach to Famines." *Cambridge Journal of Economics* 24 (5): 603–30.

———. 2002. "Soviet Repression Statistics: Some Comments." *Europe-Asia Studies* 54 (7): 1151–72.

———. 2007. "Stalin and the Soviet Famine of 1932–33 Revisited." *Europe-Asia Studies* 59 (4): 663–93.

Engerman, David. 2000. "Modernization from the Other Shore: American Observers and the Costs of Soviet Economic Development." *American Historical Review* 105 (2): 383–416.

Ezra, Markos. 1997. "Demographic Responses to Ecological Degradation and Food Insecurity: Drought Prone Areas in Northern Ethiopia." PhD diss., University of Groningen.

Famine Inquiry Commission. 1945. *Report on Bengal*. New Delhi: Government of India Press.

FAO. 2004. *The State of Food Insecurity in the World 2004*. Rome: FAO.

Farr, William. 1846. "The Influence of Scarcities and of the High Prices of Wheat on the Mortality of the People of England." *Journal of the Royal Statistical Society* 9 (2): 158–74.

Farris, William. W. 2006. *Japan's Medieval Population: Famine, Fertility, and Warfare in a Transformative Age*. Honolulu: University of Hawai'i Press.

Fitzpatrick, Sheila. 1994. *Stalin's Peasants: Resistance and Survival in the Russian Village after Collectivization*. Oxford: Oxford University Press.

Fogel, Robert W. 2004. *The Escape from Hunger and Premature Death*. Cambridge: Cambridge University Press.

Freedman, Bob. 2008. "Famine Foods." Available at http://www.hort.purdue.edu/newcrop/faminefoods/ff_home.html (accessed June 1, 2008).

Fuglestad, Finn. 1974. "La grande famine de 1931 dans l'ouest nigérien: réflexions autour d'une catastrophe naturelle." *Revue française d'histoire d'outre-mer* 61 (222): 18–33.

Garenne, Michel, Dominique Waltisperger, Pierre Cantrelle, and Osée Ralijaona. 2002. "The Demographic Impact of a Mild Famine in an African City: The Case of Antananarivo, 1985–87." In *Famine Demography: Perspectives from the Past and the Present*, ed. Tim Dyson and Cormac Ó Gráda, 204–17. Oxford: Oxford University Press.

Garnsey, Peter. 1988. *Famine and Food Supply in the Graeco-Roman World: Responses to Risk and Crisis*. Cambridge: Cambridge University Press.

Ghosh, Tushar Kanti. 1944. *The Bengal Tragedy*. Lahore: Hero Publications.

Giblin, James. 1986. "Famine and Social Change during the Transition to Colonial Rule in Northeastern Tanzania, 1880–1896." *African Economic History*, no. 15:85–105.

Gorky, Maxim. 1968. *Untimely Thoughts: Essays on Revolution, Culture, and the Bolsheviks*. London: Garnstone Press.

Goswami, Omkar. 1990. "The Bengal Famine of 1943: Reexamining the Data." *Indian Economic and Social History Review* 27 (4): 445–63.

Gray, Peter. 1997. "Famine Relief Policy in Comparative Perspective: Ireland, Scotland, and North Western Europe, 1845–49." *Eire-Ireland* 32 (1): 86–108.

Greenough, Paul. 1982. *Prosperity and Misery in Modern Bengal.* Oxford: Oxford University Press.

Greil, Holle. 1998. "Age- and Sex-specificity of the Secular Trend in Height in East Germany." In *The Biological Standard of Living in Comparative Perspective,* ed. John Komlos and Joerg Baten, 467–83. Stuttgart: Franz Steiner Verlag.

Guinnane, Timothy W., and Cormac Ó Gráda. 2002. "The Workhouses and Irish Famine Mortality." In *Famine Demography: Perspectives from the Past and the Present,* ed. Tim Dyson and Cormac Ó Gráda, 44–64. Oxford: Oxford University Press.

Gupta, Partha Sarathi, ed. 1997. *Towards Freedom: Documents on the Movement for Independence in India, 1943–1944.* 3 vols. Delhi: Oxford University Press.

Häkkinen, Antti, ed. 1992. *Just a Sack of Potatoes? Crisis Experiences in European Societies, Past and Present.* Helsinki: Societas Historica Finlandiae.

Hall-Matthews, David. 1998. "The Historical Roots of Famine Relief Paradigms." In *A World without Famine?* ed. Helen O'Neill and John Toye, 107–28. London: Macmillan.

———. 2005. *Peasants, Famine, and the State in Colonial West India.* London: Palgrave Macmillan.

———. 2008. "Inaccurate Conceptions: Disputed Measures of Nutritional Needs and Famine Deaths in Colonial India." *Modern Asian Studies* 42 (1): 1–24.

Han, Dongping. 2003. "The Great Leap Famine, the Cultural Revolution, and Post Mao Rural Reform: The Lessons of Rural Development in Contemporary China." Available at http://www.chinastudygroup.org/article/26/ (accessed April 1, 2003).

Hartmann, Betsy, and James Boyce. 1983. *Needless Hunger: Voices from a Bangladesh Village*. San Francisco: International Food Development Program.

Hassig, Ron. 1981. "The Famine of One Rabbit: Ecological Causes and Social Consequences of a Pre-Columbian Calamity." *Journal of Anthropological Research*, no. 37:172–82.

Heiden, David. 1992. *Dust to Dust: A Doctor's View of Famine in Africa*. Philadelphia: Temple University Press.

Henderson, William O. 1984 [orig. pub. 1939]. *The Zollverein*. London: Frank Cass.

Hickey, Patrick. 2002. *Famine in West Cork: The Mizen Peninsula Land and People, 1800–1852*. Cork, Ireland: Mercier.

Hill, Allan G. 1989. "Demographic Responses to Food Shortages in the Sahel." *Population and Development Review* 15 (supplement): 168–92.

Hionidou, Violetta. 2006. *Famine and Death in Occupied Greece, 1914–1944*. Cambridge: Cambridge University Press.

Hodges, Sarah. 2005. "'Looting' the Lock Hospital in Colonial Madras during the Famine Years of the 1870s." *Social History of Medicine* 18 (3): 379–98.

Holman, Susan R. 2001. *The Hungry Are Dying: Beggars and Bishops in Roman Cappadocia*. Oxford: Oxford University Press.

Houser, Daniel, Barbara Sands, and Erte Xiao. 2008. "Three Parts Natural, Seven Parts Man-made: Bayesian Analysis of China's Great Leap Forward Demographic Disaster." *Journal of Economic Behavior and Organization*.

Howe, Paul, and Stephen Devereux. 2004. "Famine Intensity and Magnitude Scales: A Proposal for an Instrumental Definition of Famine." *Disasters* 28 (4): 353–72.

Hughes, Malcolm K., X. D. Wu, X. M. Shao, and Gregg M. Garfin. 1994. "A Preliminary Reconstruction of Rainfall in North-central China since A.D. 1600 from Tree-ring Density and Width." *Quaternary Research*, no. 42:88–99.

Iliffe, John. 1979. *A Modern History of Tanganika*. Cambridge: Cambridge University Press.

———. 1987. *The African Poor*. Cambridge: Cambridge University Press.

———. 1990. *Famine in Zimbabwe, 1890–1960*. Zimbabwe: Mambo Press.

———. 1995. *Africans: The History of a Continent*. Cambridge: Cambridge University Press.

Iriye, A. 2002. *Global Community: The Role of International Organizations in the Making of the Contemporary World*. Berkeley: University of California Press.

Jones, Eric. 1981. *The European Miracle*. Cambridge: Cambridge University Press.

Jordan, William. 1996. *The Great Famine: Northern Europe in the Early Fourteenth Century*. Princeton, NJ: Princeton University Press.

Jutikkala, Eino. 1955. "The Great Finnish Famine in 1696–97." *Scandinavian Economic History Review* 3:48–63.

Kannisto, Väinö, Kaare Christensen, and James W. Vaupel. 1997. "No Increased Mortality in Later Life for Cohorts Born during Famine." *American Journal of Epidemiology*, no. 145:987–94.

Kaplan, Stephen L. 1976. *Bread, Politics, and Political Economy in the Reign of Louis XV*. The Hague: Nijhoff.

———. 2008. "Mauvais pain, mauvais gouvernement." *Le Monde*, May 11.

Kaufman, Jeffrey C. 2000. "Forget the Numbers: The Case of a Madagascar Famine." *History in Africa*, no. 27:143–57.

Kaw, Mushtaq A. 1996. "Famines in Kashmir, 1586–1819: The Policy of the Mughal and Afghan Rulers." *Indian Economic and Social History Review* 33 (1): 59–71.

Keller, Wolfgang, and Carol Shiue. 2007. "Markets in China and Europe on the Eve of the Industrial Revolution." *American Economic Review* 97 (4): 1189–1216.

Kennedy, Liam. 1999. "Bastardy and the Great Irish Famine." *Continuity and Change* 14 (3): 429–52.

Kerr, Donal. 1994. *A Nation of Beggars? Priests, People, and Politics in Famine Ireland, 1846–1852*. Oxford: Oxford University Press.

Keys, Ancel, Josef Boržek, Austin Henschel, Olaf Mickelsen, and Henry Longstreet Taylor. 1950. *The Biology of Human Starvation*. Minneapolis: University of Minnesota Press.

Khlevniuk, Oleg V. 2004. *The History of the Gulag: From Collectivization to the Great Terror*. New Haven, CT: Yale University Press.

Khoroshinina, Lidiya. 2005. "Long-term Effects of Lengthy Starvation in Childhood among Survivors of the Siege." In *Life and Death in Leningrad, 1941–44*, ed. John Barber and Andrei Dzeniskevich, 197–212. London: Palgrave Macmillan.

Kirschenbaum, Lisa A. 2006. *The Legacy of the Siege of Leningrad, 1941–1995: Myths, Memories, and Monuments*. Cambridge: Cambridge University Press.

Kirton, Walter. 1907. *A Silent War or the Great Famine in Kiangpeh*. Shanghai: North China Daily News and Herald.

Klein, Ira. 1984. "When the Rains Failed: Famine Relief and Mortality in British India." *Indian Economic and Social History Review*, no. 21:185–214.

Kochina, Elena. 1990. *Blockade Diary*. Ann Arbor, MI: Ardis.

Koponen, Juhari. 1988. "War, Famine, and Pestilence in Pre-colonial Tanzania: A Case for a Heightened Mortality." *International Journal of African Studies* 21 (4): 637–76.

Kozlov, Igor, and Alla Samsonova. 2005. "The Impact of the Siege on the Physical Development of Children." In *Life and Death in Leningrad, 1941–44*, ed. John Barber and Andrei Dzeniskevich, 174–96. London: Palgrave Macmillan.

Kreike, Emmanuel. 2004. *Re-creating Eden: Land Use, Environment, and Society in Southern Angola and Northern Namibia*. Portsmouth, NH: Heinemann.

Krypton, Constantine. 1954. "The Siege of Leningrad." *Russia Review* 13 (4): 255–65.

Kueh, Y. Y. 1984. "A Weather Index for Analyzing Grain Yield Instability in China, 1952–81." *China Quarterly* 97:68–83.

———. 1995. *Agricultural Instability in China, 1931–1990: Weather, Technology, and Institutions*. Oxford: Oxford University Press.

Kumar, B. Gopalkrishna. 1990. "Ethiopian Famines, 1973–1985: A Case Study." In *The Political Economy of Hunger*, ed. Jean Drèze and Amartya Sen. Vol. 2. Oxford: Oxford University Press.

Lachiver, Marcel. 1991. *Les années de misère: la famine au temps du Grand Roi*. Paris: Fayard.

Lamb, Hubert H. 1970. "Volcanic Dust in the Atmosphere; with a Chronology and Assessment of Its Meteorological Significance." *Philosophical Transactions of the Royal Society of London. Series A, Mathematical and Physical Sciences* 266 (1178): 425–533.

Lardy, Nicholas. 1987. "Economic Recovery and the First Five Year Plan." In *The Cambridge History of China*, ed.

Roderick MacFarquhar and John K. Fairbank, 14:144–84. Cambridge: Cambridge University Press.

Lee, Suk. 2005. *The DPRK Famine of 1994–2000: Existence and Impact*. Seoul: Korea Institute of National Unification.

Leonard, Pamela. 1994. "The Political Landscape of a Sichuan Village." Chapter 5 of PhD diss., Cambridge University. Available at: http://xiakou.uncc.edu/chapters/history/famine.htm (accessed September 6, 2007).

Le Roy Ladurie, Emmanuel. 1974. *The Peasants of Languedoc*. Urbana: University of Illinois Press.

Li, Lillian. 1991. "Life and Death in a Chinese Famine: Infanticide as a Demographic Consequence of the 1935 Yellow River Flood." *Comparative Studies in Society and History* 33 (3): 466–510.

———. 2007. *Fighting Famine in North China: State, Market, and Environmental Decline, 1690s–1990s*. Stanford, CA: Stanford University Press.

Li, Wei, and Dennis Tao Yang. 2005. "The Great Leap Forward: Anatomy of a Central Planning Disaster." *Journal of Political Economy* 103 (4): 840–77.

Lin, Justin Yifu. 1990. "Collectivization and China's Agricultural Crisis in 1959–61." *Journal of Political Economy* 98 (6): 1228–52.

Lin, Justin Yifu, and Dennis Tao Yang. 2000. "Food Availability, Entitlements, and the Chinese Famine of 1959–61." *Economic Journal* 110 (1): 136–58.

Livi-Bacci, Massimo. 1991. *Population and Nutrition: An Essay on European Demographic History*. Cambridge: Cambridge University Press.

Livius, Titus. 1912. *The History of Rome, Vol. 1*. Ernest Rhys, ed. London: J.M. Dent. Available at http://etext.virginia

.edu/toc/modeng/public/LivIHis.html (accessed November 5, 2008).

Loveday, Alexander. 1914. *The History and Economics of Indian Famines*. Repr., New Delhi: Usha Publications, 1985.

Lucas, Henry S. 1930. "The Great European Famine of 1315, 1316, and 1317." *Speculum* 5 (4): 343–77.

Lumey, Lambert H. 1998. "Reproductive Outcomes in Women Prenatally Exposed to Undernutrition from the Dutch Famine Birth Cohort." *Proceedings of the Nutrition Society*, no. 57:129–35.

Luo, Sheng. 1988. "Reconstruction of Life Tables and Age Distributions for the Population of China, by Year, from 1953 to 1982." PhD diss., University of Pennsylvania.

McCormick, Michael. 2001. *Origins of the European Economy: Communications and Commerce AD 300–900*. Cambridge: Cambridge University Press.

MacFarquhar, Roderick. 1983. *The Origins of the Cultural Revolution, Vol. 2: The Great Leap Forward, 1958–1960*. Oxford: Oxford University Press.

———. 1997. *The Origins of the Cultural Revolution, Vol. 3: The Coming of the Cataclysm, 1961–1966*. Oxford: Oxford University Press.

Macintyre, Kate. 2002. "Famine and the Female Mortality Advantage." In *Famine Demography: Perspectives from the Past and the Present*, ed. Tim Dyson and Cormac Ó Gráda, 240–60. Oxford: Oxford University Press.

Maddox, Gregory. 1990. "*Mtunya*: Famine in Central Tanzania, 1917–1920." *Journal of African History*, no. 31:181–97.

Mahalanobis, Prasanta C., Ramkrishna Mukherjea, and Ambica Ghose. 1946. *Famine and Rehabilitation in Bengal.*

Part I: A Sample Survey of After Effects of the Bengal Famine of 1943. Calcutta: Statistical Publishing Society.

Maharatna, Arup. 1996. *The Demography of Famines.* Delhi: Oxford University Press.

Majd, Mohammad Gholi. 2003. *The Great Famine and Genocide in Persia, 1917–1919.* Lanham, MD: University Press of America.

Malanima, Paolo. n.d. "Wheat Prices in Tuscany, 1260–1660." Available at http://www.iisg.nl/hpw/malanima .php (accessed November 5, 2008).

Mallory, Walter H. 1926. *China: Land of Famine.* New York: American Geographical Society.

Malthus, Thomas Robert. 1798. *An Essay on the Principle of Population.* 1st ed. London: Murray.

———. [1800] 1970. *An Investigation of the Cause of the Present High Price of Provisions.* In *The Pamphlets of Thomas Robert Malthus,* 5–26. Repr., New York: Kelley.

———. 1872. *An Essay on the Principle of Population.* 7th ed. London: Reeves and Turner.

———. 1963. *Occasional Papers of T.R. Malthus on Ireland, Population, and Political Economy.* New York: Burt Franklin.

Mansergh, Nicholas. 1973. *The Transfer of Power, Vol. IV: The Bengal Famine and the New Viceroyalty, 15 June 1943–31 August 1944.* London: HMSO.

Manzoni, Alessandro. 1972. *The Betrothed.* Harmondsworth, UK: Penguin Books.

Marlar, Richard A., Banks L. Leonard, Brian R. Billman, Patricia M. Lambert, and Jennifer E. Marlar. 2000. "Biochemical Evidence of Cannibalism at a Prehistoric Puebloan Site in Southwestern Colorado." *Nature,* no. 407:74–78.

Marx, Karl. 1967. *Capital, Vol. 1. A Critical Analysis of Capitalist Production.* New York: International Publishers.

————. 1973. *Surveys from Exile. Political Writings, Vol. 2.* Harmondsworth, UK: Penguin Books.

Matossian, Mary Kilbourne. 1989. *Poisons of the Past: Molds, Epidemics, and History.* New Haven, CT: Yale University Press.

Mazzucato, Valentina, and David Neimeijer. 2000. "The Cultural Economy of Soil and Water Conservation: Market Principles and Social Networks in Eastern Burkina Faso." *Development and Change* 31 (4): 831–55.

McAlpin, Michelle B. 1983. *Subject to Famine: Food Crisis and Economic Change in Western India, 1860–1920.* Princeton, NJ: Princeton University Press.

Menken, Jane, and Susan C. Watkins. 1985. "A Quantitative Perspective on Famine and Population Growth." *Population and Development Review* 11 (4): 647–75.

Menon, Roshni. 2007. "Famine in Malawi: Causes and Consequences." United Nations Development Programme, Human Development Report Office, occasional paper 2007/35.

Merewether, F.H.S. 1898. *A Tour through the Famine Districts of India.* London: Innis.

Mill, John Stuart. 1857. *Principles of Political Economy.* Rev. ed. London: Parker.

Mitra, Ashok. 1989. "Famine of 1943 in Vikrampur, Dacca." *Economic and Political Weekly* 24 (5): 253–64.

Mokyr, Joel. 1980. "The Deadly Fungus: An Econometric Investigation into the Short-term Demographic Impact of the Irish Famine, 1846–51." *Research in Population Economics,* no. 2:237–77.

Mokyr, Joel, and Cormac Ó Gráda. 2002. "What Do People Die of during Famines? The Great Irish Famine in Comparative Perspective." *European Review of Economic History* 6 (3): 339–64.

Monahan, W. Gregory. 1993. *Year of Sorrows: The Great Famine of 1709 in Lyon.* Columbus: Ohio State University Press.

Moon, Penderl. 1973. *Wavell: Viceroy's Journal.* Oxford: Oxford University Press.

Moskoff, William. 1990. *The Bread of Affliction: The Food Supply of the USSR during WW II.* Cambridge: Cambridge University Press.

Mukerjee, Karunamoy. 1947. "The Famine of 1943 and the Nature of Land Transfer in a Village in Bengal." *Modern Review* (Calcutta), no. 80:309–12.

Mukerji, Karunamoy. 1965. *Agriculture, Famine, and Rehabilitation in South Asia: A Regional Approach.* Santiniketan, India: Visva-Bharati.

Murray, Christopher J. L., and Alan D. Lopez. 1994. "Global and Regional Cause-of-death Patterns in 1990." *Bulletin of the World Health Organization* 72 (3): 447–80.

Nathan, Andrew J. 1965. *A History of the China International Famine Relief Commission.* Cambridge, MA: Harvard East Asian Monographs.

National Bureau of Statistics. 1999. *Comprehensive Statistical Data and Materials on Fifty Years of New China.* Beijing: China Statistical Publishing House.

Neal, Frank. 1998. *Black '47: Great Britain and the Famine Irish.* London: Macmillan.

Noland, Marcus. 2007. "North Korea as a 'New' Famine." In *The New Famines: Why Famines Persist in an Era of Globalization,* ed. Stephen Devereux, 197–221. London: Routledge.

Notestein, Frank W. 1938. "A Demographic Study of 38,256 Rural Families in China." *Milbank Memorial Fund Quarterly* 16 (1): 57–79.

O'Flaherty, Liam. 1929. *House of Gold.* London: Jonathan Cape.

Ó Gráda, Cormac. 1993. *Ireland before and after the Famine: Explorations in Economic History.* 2nd ed. Manchester: Manchester University Press.

———. 1994. *Ireland: A New Economic History.* Oxford: Oxford University Press.

———. 1999. *Black '47 and Beyond: The Great Irish Famine in History, Economy, and Memory.* Princeton, NJ: Princeton University Press.

———. 2001. "Markets and Famines: Evidence from Nineteenth Century Finland." *Economic Development and Cultural Change* 49 (3): 575–90.

———. 2005. "Markets and Famines in Pre-industrial Europe." *Journal of Interdisciplinary History* 26 (2): 143–66.

———. 2006. *Ireland's Great Famine: Interdisciplinary Perspectives.* Dublin: University College Dublin Press.

———. 2007. "Making Famine History." *Journal of Economic Literature* 45 (1): 5–38.

———. 2008. "The Ripple That Drowns? Twentieth-century Famines as Economic History." *Economic History Review* 61 (S1): 5–37.

Ó Gráda, Cormac, and Jean-Michel Chevet. 2002. "Famine and Market in *ancien régime* France." *Journal of Economic History* 62 (3): 706–33.

Ó Gráda, Cormac, and Kevin H. O'Rourke. 1997. "Mass Migration as Disaster Relief: Lessons from the Great Irish Famine." *European Review of Economic History*, no. 1:3–25.

Ó Gráda, Cormac, Richard Paping, and Eric Vanhaute. 2007. *When the Potato Failed: Causes and Effects of the "Last" European Subsistence Crisis.* Turnhout, Belgium: Brepols.

Okamoto, Katsuo, Shuji Kamoto, and Hiroyuki Kawshima. 1998. "Estimation of Flood Damage to Rice Production in North Korea in 1995." *International Journal of Remote Sensing* 19 (2): 365–71.

Okazaki, Shoko. 1986. "The Great Persian Famine of 1870–71." *Bulletin of the School of Oriental and African Studies* 49 (1): 183–92.

Olcott, Martha Brill. 1981. "The Collectivization Drive in Kazakhstan." *Russian Review* 40 (2): 122–42.

Ó Murchadha, Ciarán. 1996. *Sable Wings over the Sand: Ennis, County Clare, and Its Wider Community during the Great Famine*. Ennis, Ireland: Clasp Press.

Osborne, S. Godolphin. 1850. *Gleanings from the West of Ireland*. London: Boone.

Oxfam 2005. *Food Aid or Dumping? Separating Wheat from Chaff*. Oxford: Oxfam.

Painter, Rebecca C., Tessa J. Roseboom, Patrick M. M. Bossuyt, Clive Osmond, David J. P. Barker, and O. P. Bleker. 2005. "Adult Mortality at Age 57 after Prenatal Exposure to the Dutch Famine." *European Journal of Epidemiology* 20 (8): 673–76.

Pankhurst, Richard K. 1986. *The History of Famine and Epidemics in Ethiopia Prior to the Twentieth Century*. Addis Ababa, Ethiopia: Relief and Rehabilitation Commission.

Paque, Claude. 1980. "Comment on Dirks." *Current Anthropology* 21 (1): 37.

Patenaude, Bruce M. 2002. *The Big Show in Bololand: The American Relief Expedition to Soviet Russia in the Famine of 1921*. Palo Alto, CA: Stanford University Press.

Patterson, K. David. 1988. "Epidemics, Famines, and Population in the Cape Verde Islands, 1580–1900." *International Journal of African Historical Studies*, no. 21:291–313.

Pavlov, Dimitri V. 1965. *Leningrad 1941: The Blockade.* Chicago: University of Chicago Press.

Peking United International Relief Committee. 1971. *The North China Famine of 1920–1922 with Special Reference to the West Chihli Area.* Peking. Repr., Taipei: Ch'eng Wen Publishing Company.

Perkins, Dwight H. 1969. *Agricultural Development in China 1368–1968.* Edinburgh: Edinburgh University Press.

Persson, Karl-Gunnar. 1999. *Grain Markets in Europe, 1500–1900: Integration and Deregulation.* Cambridge: Cambridge University Press.

Phoofolo, Pule. 2003. "Face to Face with Famine: The Basotho and the Rinderpest, 1897–1903." *Journal of South African Studies* 29 (2): 503–27.

Pinnell, Leonard G. 2002. *With the Sanction of Government: The Memoirs of L.G. Pinnell, C.I.E., I.C.S. (1896–1979).* Perth: M. C. Pinnell. (Copies in the Centre of South Asia Studies, Cambridge, and the British Library.)

Pitkänen, Kari. 1992. "The Road to Survival or Death?" In *Just a Sack of Potatoes? Crisis Experiences in European Societies, Past and Present,* ed. Antti Häkkinen, 87–118. Helsinki: Societas Historica Finlandiae.

———. 1993. *Deprivation and Disease: Mortality during the Great Finnish Famine of the 1860s.* Helsinki: Finnish Demographic Society.

Polanyi, Karl. [1944] 1957. *The Great Transformation.* Boston: Beacon Press.

Post, John D. 1977. *The Last Great Subsistence Crisis in the Western World.* Baltimore: Johns Hopkins University Press.

———. 1985. *Food Shortage, Climatic Variability, and Epidemic Disease in Preindustrial Europe: The Mortality Peak in the Early 1740s.* Ithaca, NY: Cornell University Press.

Poyer, Lynn. 2004. "Dimensions of Hunger in Wartime: Chuuk Lagoon, 1943–1945." *Food and Foodways* 12 (2–3): 137–64.

Pullan, Brian. 1963–64. "The Famine in Venice and the New Poor Law, 1527–1529." *Bollettino dell'Istituto di storia della società e dello stato veneziano,* no. 5–6:141–213.

Purcell, Deirdre, and Pat Langan. 1985. *Ethiopia: The Dark Hunger.* Dublin: Magill.

Rashid, Salim. 1980. "The Policy of Laissez-faire during Scarcities." *Economic Journal,* no. 90: 493–503.

Ravallion, Martin. 1987. *Markets and Famines.* Oxford: Oxford University Press.

———. 1997. "Famines and Economics." *Journal of Economic Literature* 35 (3): 1205–42.

Ravelli, G. P., Zena A. Stein, and Mervyn W. Susser. 1976. "Obesity in Young Men after Famine Exposure in Utero and Early Infancy." *New England Journal of Medicine,* no. 295:349–90.

Razzaque, Abdur. 1988. "Effect of Famine on Fertility in a Rural Area of Bangladesh." *Journal of Biosocial Science* 20 (3): 287–94.

———. 1989. "Sociodemographic Differentials in Mortality during the 1974–75 Famine in a Rural Area of Bangladesh." *Journal of Biosocial Science* 21 (1): 13–22.

Read, Piers Paul. 1974. *Alive: The Story of the Andes Survivors.* New York: Lippincott.

Reinhardt, Volker. 1991. *Überleben in der frühnuezeitlichen Stadt: Annona und Getreideversorgung in Rom, 1563–1797.* Tübingen: Neimeyer.

Ricardo, David. 1951–73. *The Works and Correspondence of David Ricardo.* Ed. Piero Sraffa. Vols. 1–11. Cambridge: Cambridge University Press.

Riskin, Carl. 1998. "Seven Lessons about the Chinese Famine of 1959–61." *China Economic Review* 9 (2): 111–24.

Roesle, Emil. 1925. The Mortality in Germany, 1913–1921: The Effects of War Casualties and Famine on Mortality." *Journal of the American Statistical Association* 20 (149): 163–78.

Rothschild, Emma. 2001. *Economic Sentiments: Adam Smith, Condorcet, and the Enlightenment.* Cambridge, MA: Harvard University Press.

Rotstayn, Leon D., and Ulrike Lohmann. 2002. "Tropical Rainfall Trends and the Indirect Aerosol Effect." *Journal of Climate*, no. 15:2103–16.

Sainath, P. 2005. "The Raj and the Famines of Good Governance." *Hindu*, August 16. Available at http://www.thehindu.com/2005/08/16/stories/2005081602880800.htm (accessed May 28, 2008).

Saito, Osamu. 2002. "The Frequency of Famines as Demographic Correctives in the Japanese Past." In *Famine Demography: Perspectives from the Past and the Present*, ed. Tim Dyson and Cormac Ó Gráda, 218–39. Oxford: Oxford University Press.

Salama, Peter, Fitsum Assefa, Leisel Talley, Paul Spiegel, Albertien van der Veen, and Carol A. Gotway. 2001. "Malnutrition, Measles, Mortality, and the Humanitarian Response during a Famine in Ethiopia." *Journal of American Medical Association* 286 (5): 563–71.

Salgado, Sebastião. 2004. *Sahel: The End of the Road.* Berkeley: University of California Press.

Salisbury, Harrison. [1969] 2000. *The 900 Days: The Siege of Leningrad.* London: Pan Books.

Sami, Leela. 2002. "Gender Differentials in Famine Mortality: Madras (1876–78) and Punjab (1896–97)." *Economic and Political Weekly*, June 29–July 5, 2593–2600.

Schellekens, Jona. 1996. "Irish Famines and English Mortality in the Eighteenth Century." *Journal of Interdisciplinary History* 27 (1): 29–42.

Schoumaker, Bruno. 2004. "Poverty and Fertility in Sub-Saharan Africa: Evidence from 25 Countries." Paper presented at the Population Association of America meeting, April 1–3. Available at http://paa2004.princeton.edu/download.asp?submissionId=40032 (accessed September 2005).

Seaman, John. 1993. "Famine Mortality in Africa." In "New Approaches to Famine," ed. Jeremy Swift. Special issue, *Institute of Development Studies Bulletin* 24 (4): 27–31.

Sen, Amartya. 1981. *Poverty and Famines: An Essay on Entitlement and Deprivation.* Oxford: Oxford University Press.

———. 1995. "Nobody Need Starve." *Granta*, no. 52:213–20.

———. 2001. *Development as Freedom.* Rev. ed. Oxford: Oxford University Press.

Sharma, Sanjay. 2001. *Famine, Philanthropy, and the Colonial State.* Delhi: Oxford University Press.

Shears Paul, Angela M. Berry, Roseanne Murphy, and Michael A. Nabil. 1987. "Epidemiological Assessment of the Health and Nutrition of Ethiopian Refugees in Emergency Camps in Sudan, 1985." *British Medical Journal* 295 (6593): 314–18.

Shiue, Carol H. 2004. "Local Granaries and Central Government Disaster Relief: Moral Hazard and Intergovernmental Finance in Eighteenth- and Nineteenth-century China." *Journal of Economic History* 64 (1): 100–124.

———. 2005. "The Political Economy of Famine Relief in China, 1740–1820." *Journal of Interdisciplinary History* 36 (1): 33–55.

Simmons, Cynthia, and Nina Perlina. 2002. *Writing the Siege of Leningrad: Women's Diaries, Memoirs, and Documentary Prose.* Pittsburgh: University of Pittsburgh Press.

Smith, Adam. [1776] 1976. *An Inquiry into the Nature and Causes of the Wealth of Nations.* Oxford: Oxford University Press.

Smith, Hazel. 2005. *Hungry for Peace: International Security, Humanitarian Assistance, and Social Change in North Korea.* Washington, DC: United States Institute for Peace Press.

Smith, Wilfred J. 1960. "Economic Growth of Communist China." Publication no. L60–168. Washington, DC: Industrial College of the Armed Forces.

Solar, P. M. 1989. "The Great Famine Was No Ordinary Subsistence Crisis." In *Famine: The Irish Experience*, ed. E. M. Crawford, 112–33. Edinburgh: Donald.

———. 1995. "Poor Relief and English Economic Development before the Industrial Revolution." *Economic History Review* 48 (1): 1–22.

———. 1996. "The Potato Famine in Europe." In *Famine 150: Commemorative Lecture Series*, ed. Cormac Ó Gráda, 113–27. Dublin: Teagasc.

———. 2007. "The Crisis of the Late 1840s: What Can Be Learned from Prices?" In *When the Potato Failed: Causes and Effects of the "Last" European Subsistence Crisis*, ed. Cormac Ó Gráda, Richard Paping, and Eric Vanhaute, 79–94. Turnhout, Belgium: Brepols.

Solow, Barbara L. 1971. *The Land Question and the Irish Economy, 1870–1903.* Cambridge, MA: Harvard University Press.

Sorokin, Pitirim A. [1922] 1975. *Hunger as a Factor in Human Affairs.* Gainesville: University of Florida Press.

Sparén, Pär, Denny Vågerö, Dmitri B. Shestov, Svetlana Plavinskaja, Nina Parfenova, Valeri Hoptiar, Dominique Paturot, and Maria R. Galanti. 2004. "Long Term Mortality after Severe Starvation during the Siege of Leningrad: Prospective Cohort Study." *British Medical Journal* 328, no. 7430 (January 3): 11.

Spencer, Edmund. 1970 [1596]. *A View of the Present State of Ireland.* Ed. W. L. Renwick. Oxford: Oxford University Press.

Stanner, Sara A., K. Bulmer, C. Andrès, O. E. Lantseva, V. Borodina, V. V. Poteen, and John S. Yudkin. 1997. "Does Malnutrition in Utero Determine Diabetes and Coronary Heart Disease in Adulthood? Results from the Leningrad Siege Study, a Cross Sectional Study." *British Medical Journal*, no. 315:1342–49.

Starling. Ernest H. 1920. "The Food Supply of Germany during the War." *Journal of the Royal Statistical Society* 83 (2): 225–54.

Stathakopoulos, Dionysios. 2004. *Famine and Pestilence in the Late Roman and Early Byzantine Empire: A Systematic Survey of Subsistence Crises and Epidemics.* Aldershot, UK: Ashgate.

St. Clair, David, Mingqing Xu, Peng Wang, Yakin Yu, Yourong Fang, Feng Zhang, Xiaoying Zheng, Niufan Gu, Guoyin Feng, Pak Sham, and Lin He. 2005. "Rates of Adult Schizophrenia following Prenatal Exposure to the Chinese Famine of 1959–1961." *Journal of the American Medical Association*, no. 294:557–62.

Tannahill, Reay. 1975. *Flesh and Blood: A History of the Cannibal Complex.* London: Hamish Hamilton.

Tauger, Mark. 1990. "The 1932 Harvest and the Famine of 1933." *Slavic Review* 50, no. 1 (Spring): 70–89.

———. 2001. "Natural Disaster and Human Action in the Soviet Famine of 1931–1933." Carl Beck Papers in Russian and East European Studies, no. 1506.

———. 2003. "Entitlement, Shortage, and the 1943 Bengal Famine: Another Look." *Journal of Peasant Studies* 31, no. 1 (October): 45–72.

———. 2006. "Arguing from Errors: On Certain Issues in Robert Davies' and Stephen Wheatcroft's Analysis of the Soviet Grain Harvest and the Great Soviet Famine of 1931–33." *Europe-Asia Studies* 58 (6): 973–84.

Tawney, Richard H. [1932] 1964. *Land and Labour in China.* New York: Octagon Books.

Thibon, Christian. 2002. "Famine Yesterday and Today in Burundi." In *Famine Demography: Perspectives from the Past and the Present,* ed. Tim Dyson and Cormac Ó Gráda, 142–57. Oxford: Oxford University Press.

Titow, Jan Z. 1960. "Evidence of Weather in the Accounts of the Bishopric of Winchester, 1209–1350." *Economic History Review* 12 (3): 360–407.

Toole, M. J., Phillip Nieburg, and Ronald J. Waldman. 1988. "The Association between Inadequate Rations, Undernutrition Prevalence, and Mortality in Refugee Camps: Case Studies of Refugee Populations in Eastern Thailand, 1979–80, and Eastern Sudan, 1984–85." *Journal of Tropical Pediatrics,* no. 34:218–24.

Tomasson, Richard F. 1977. "A Millennium of Misery: The Demography of the Icelanders." *Population Studies* 31 (3): 405–27.

Trienekens, Gerard. 2000. "The Food Supply in the Netherlands during the Second World War." In *Food, Science, Policy, and Regulation in the Twentieth Century,* ed. David F. Smith and Jim Phillips, 117–33. London: Routledge.

Tyson, Robert E. 1986. "Famine in Aberdeenshire, 1695–1699: Anatomy of a Crisis." In *From Lairds to Louns*, ed. D. Stevenson, 32–52. Aberdeen, SD: Aberdeen University Press.

Vallin, Jacques, France Meslé, Serguie Adamets, and Serhii Pyrozhkov. 2002. "A New Estimate of Ukrainian Population Losses during the Crises of the 1930s and 1940s." *Population Studies* 56 (3): 249–64.

Vandier, Jacques. 1936. *La famine dans l'égypte ancienne.* Cairo: Imprimerie de l'institut français d'archéologie orientale.

Vanhaute, Eric. 2007. "'So Worthy an Example to Ireland': The Subsistence and Industrial Crisis of 1845–1850 in Flanders." In *When the Potato Failed: Causes and Effects of the "Last" European Subsistence Crisis*, ed. Cormac Ó Gráda, Richard Paping, and Eric Vanhaute, 123–48. Turnhout, Belgium: Brepols.

Vaughan, Megan. 1989. *The Story of an African Famine: Hunger, Gender, and Politics in Malawi.* Cambridge: Cambridge University Press.

Vincent, Joan. 1982. *Teso in Transformation: The Political Economy of Peasant and Class in Eastern Africa.* Berkeley: University of California Press.

Vink, Markus. 2003. "The World's Oldest Trade: Dutch Slavery and Slave Trade in the Indian Ocean in the Seventeenth Century." *Journal of World History* 14 (2): 131–77.

Virlouvet, Catherine. 1985. *Famines et émeutes à Rome des origines de la république à la mort de Néron.* Rome: École française de Rome.

von Braun, Joachim, Tesfaye Teklu, and Patrick Webb. 1999. *Famine in Africa: Causes, Responses, and Prevention.* Baltimore: Johns Hopkins University Press.

Waldman, Ronald. 2001. "Public Health in Times of War and Famine: What Can Be Done? What Should Be Done?" *Journal of the American Medical Association* 286 (5): 588–90.

Walford, Cornelius. 1879. *The Famines of the World Past and Present*. London: Royal Statistical Society.

Walsh, Brendan. M. 1970. "Marriage Rates and Population Pressure: Ireland, 1871 and 1911." *Economic History Review* 23 (1): 148–62.

Walter, John. 1992. "Subsistence Strategies, Social Economy, and the Politics of Subsistence in Early Modern England." In *Just a Sack of Potatoes? Crisis Experiences in European Societies, Past and Present*, Antti Häkkinen, 53–85. Helsinki: Societas Historica Finlandiae.

Walter, John, and Keith Wrightson. 1976. "Dearth and the Social Order in Early Modern England." *Past and Present*, no. 71:22–42.

Watt, John. 1961. "The Effect of Transportation on Famine Prevention." *China Quarterly*, no. 6:76–80.

Watts, Michael. 1983. *Silent Violence: Food, Famine, and Peasantry in Northern Nigeria*. Berkeley: University of California Press.

Webb, Patrick. 2001. "Emergency Relief during Europe's Famine of 1817: Anticipated Crisis-Response Mechanisms of Today." *Journal of Nutrition* 132 (supplement 7): 2092–95.

Webb, Patrick, and Joachim von Braun. 1994. *Famine and Food Security in Ethiopia: Lessons for Africa*. New York: Wiley.

Weiss, Holger. 1998. "Dying Cattle: Some Remarks on the Impact of Cattle Epizootics in the Central Sudan during the Nineteenth Century." *African Economic History*, no. 26:173–99.

Wheatcroft, Stephen G. 1983. "Famine and Epidemic Crises in Russia, 1918–22: The Case of Saratov." *Annales de Démographie Historique*, 329–52.

———. 1993. "Famine and Food Consumption Records in Early Soviet History, 1917–25." In *Food, Diet, and Economic Change Past and Present*, ed. Catherine Geissler and Derek J. Oddy, 151–74. Leicester: Leicester University Press.

White, Theodore A. 1978. *In Search of History: A Personal Adventure*. New York: Harper.

Will, Pierre-Étienne. 1990. *Bureaucracy and Famine in Eighteenth-century China*. Stanford, CA: Stanford University Press.

Wolfe, Bertram D. 1967. *The Bridge and the Abyss: The Troubled Friendship of Maxim Gorky and V.I. Lenin*. London: Pall Mall Press.

Woodham-Smith, Cecil. 1962. *The Great Hunger*. London: Hamish Hamilton.

World Bank. 2001. *Social Protection Sector Strategy: From Safety Net to Springboard*. Washington, DC: World Bank.

Wright, William. 1882. *The Chronicle of Joshua the Stylite, Composed in Syriac, A.D. 507*. Cambridge: Cambridge University Press.

Wrigley, E. A., and R. Schofield. 1981. *The Population History of England, 1541–1871: A Reconstruction*. London: Edward Arnold.

Yang, Dali. 1996. *Calamity and Reform in China: State, Rural Society, and Institutional Change since the Great Leap Famine*. Stanford, CA: Stanford University Press.

Yao, Shujie. 1999. "A Note on the Causal Factors of China's Famine in 1959–1961." *Journal of Political Economy* 107 (6.1): 1365–69.

Yates, Robin D. S. 1990. "War, Food Shortages, and Relief Measures in Early China." In *Hunger in History: Food Shortage, Poverty, and Deprivation*, ed. Lucile F. Newman, 147–77. London: Blackwell.

Young, Arthur. 1800. *The Question of Scarcity Plainly Stated, and Remedies Considered*. London: Richardson.

Zuckerman, Yitzhak. 1993. *A Surplus of Meaning: Chronicle of the Warsaw Uprising*. Berkeley: University of California Press.

Index

CPSIA information can be obtained
at www.ICGtesting.com
Printed in the USA
JSHW030247181122
33413JS00001B/2